INTRODUCTION TO TURKISH LAW

Editors
Tuğrul ANSAY
and
Don WALLACE Jr.

Second edition

SOCIETY OF COMPARATIVE LAW, ANKARA, TURKEY
OCEANA PUBLICATIONS, INC., DOBBS FERRY, NEW YORK

ISBN 0-379-20332-4 Oceana

Distribution within Turkey:
Hukuk Fakültesi Kitap Satış Bürosu, Cebeci - Ankara

Printed in Turkey by Ajans - Türk Gazetecilik ve Matbaacılık Sanayii
Ankara - 1978

PREFACE

The Introduction to law course at Middle East Technical University at Ankara is a two semester course given in the English language for the first year students of the Faculty of Administrative Sciences. During the first semester general principles of law, such as justice, equity and sources of law are discussed. The second semester covers some of the fields of Turkish positive law administered by Turkish courts and other agencies.

The main purpose of this book is to serve as a text for the second semester of this course, although it does not in fact include all the subjects which are covered in the semester. However, it is also hoped that this book will be of some use to forein practicing lawyers and scholars as preliminary reference and key to the basic institutions, principles and rules of Turkish law. For this reason some details have been added in footnotes, bibliographies given at the end of Chapters and a selected bibliography of books and articles is annexed to the book.

The articles in this book were written by their authors in the English language and have been edited in varying degrees by Professors Ansay and Wallace, who have also attempted to make the articles consistent with each other. Professor Wallace has also to some extent resived the language of the articles. The editors, however, do not take any responsability for the contents of, or the ideas expressed in, the articles (except that Dr. Ansay of course accepts the responsibilities of an author for those articles written by himself).

In this second edition the Chapters on Constitutional Law, Administrative Law and Family Law are prepared by new authors. The other Chapters have been brought up to date by the authors who prepared these Chapters for the first edition. The editors are grateful to all authors who have contributed articles to this book. They would also like to express their thanks to George Spina, Bruce Seymour and Henry P. Williams, III for their most valuable aid in editing the new edition. Mr. Henry P. Williams, III has also undertaken the responsibility of preparing the Glossary.

Dr. Tuğrul ANSAY, M. C. L., LL. M. (Columbia). Professor of Law, University of Ankara, Director, Society of Comparative Law.

Don WALLACE Jr., LL. B. (Harvard). Professor of Law and Director, Institute for International and Foreign Trade Law, Georgetown University. Former Deputy Assistant General Counsel, Agency of International Development.

GENERAL OUTLINE

CHAPTER 1, SOURCES OF TURKISH LAW .... 1 — 22
   Professor Dr. *Adnan GÜRİZ*

CHAPTER 2, CONSTITUTIONAL LAW .... 23 — 52
   Professor Dr. *Ergun ÖZBUDUN*

CHAPTER 3, ADMINISTRATIVE LAW .... 53 — 84
   Associate Prof. Dr. *Rona AYBAY*

CHAPTER 4, LAW OF PERSONS .... 85 — 98
   Professor Dr. *Tuğrul ANSAY*

CHAPTER 5, LEGAL PERSONS, SOCIETIES AND ASSOCIATIONS .... 99 — 114
   Professor Dr. *Tuğrul ANSAY*

CHAPTER 6, FAMILY LAW .... 115 — 130
   Professor Dr. *Tuğrul ANSAY*

CHAPTER 7, LAW OF SUCCESSION .... 131 — 146
   Professor Dr. *Tuğrul ANSAY*

CHAPTER 8, LAW OF PROPERTY .... 147 — 158
   Professor Dr. *Tuğrul ANSAY*

CHAPTER 9, LAW OF OBLIGATIONS .... 159 — 172
   Professor Dr. *Tuğrul ANSAY*

CHAPTER 10, CRIMINAL LAW .... 173 — 188
   Professor Dr. *Feyyaz GÖLCÜKLÜ*

CHAPTER 11, LAW OF PROCEDURE (CIVIL AND CRIMINAL) .... 189 — 225
   Professor Dr. *Feyyaz GÖLCÜKLÜ*;
   Professor Dr. *Tuğrul ANSAY*

ANALYTICAL TABLE OF CONTENTS
CHAPTER 1
SOURCES OF TURKISH LAW

	Pages
I. Introduction	1
II. Customary law	1
A. Custom in civil law	1
B. The function of customary rules in other branches of the law	4
III. Legislation	5
A. In general	5
B. Legislation in the Turkish legal system	5
C. The main characteristics of legislation	6
D. The hierarchy of enacted or written law	6
E. Codes in Turkey	9
F. The problem of interpretation	11
G. Retroactivity of laws	13
H. Enforcement of statutes	14
I. Repeal of statutes	14
IV. Court decisions	15
A. General considerations	15
B. Precedents in Turkey	16
C. Court of Cassation	17
D. Council of State	17
E. The Military Court of Cassation	19
V. Doctrine	19

CHAPTER 2
CONSTITUTIONAL LAW

I. Historical background	23
II. The general characteristcs of the 1961 Constitution	28
1. National State	30
2. Democratic State	30
3. Secularism	32
4. Social State	33
5. The rule of law	34
III. The legislature	36
1. The structure of the legislature	37
2. Legislative process	39
3. Control over the executive	40
4. Budgetary powers	42
IV. The executive	42
1. The President of the Republic	42
2. The Council of Ministers	43
V. The judiciary	46
1. The independence of the judiciary	46
2. The Constitutional Court	48

CHAPTER 3
ADMINISTRATIVE LAW

	Pages
I. Introduction	53
A. Nature and subject matter of administrative law	53
B. General characteristics of Turkish administrative law	54
C. Development of administrative law	55
II. Some fundamental principles	56
A. The rule of law	56
B. Legality of public administration	57
C. Secularism	57
D. Indivisibility of administration and centralism	58
III. Administrative organization	59
A. Introduction	59
B. Central administration	59
C. Local administration	59
D. Functional autonomous corporations and organisations	68
E. Public personnel and functionaries	70
F. Public possessions	72
IV. Emergency powers of administration	73
V. Control of public administration	75
A. Political control	75
B. Administrative control	76
C. Financial control	76
D. Citizens complaints	77
E. Judicial review	77

CHAPTER 4
LAW OF PERSONS

I. General	85
II. Beginning and end of personality	85
III. Registry of personal status	86
IV. Persons as subjects of rights ; capacity	87
A. Persons as subjects of rights	87
B. Capacity to act	88
V. Domicile	92
A. In general	92
B. Domicile of choice	92
C. Domicile by operation of law	92
D. Rules	93
VI. Names	93
VII. Nationality	93
VIII. Protection of personality	94
A. In general	94
B. Protection of personality against others	94
C. Protection of personality against oneself	96

CHAPTER 5
LEGAL PERSONS, SOCIETIES AND ASSOCIATIONS

		Pages
I.	General	99
II.	Theories of personality	100
III.	Classification of legal personalities	101
	A. Associations of persons and dedication of a fund to a specified purpose	101
	B. Public, private and mixed legal persons	101
IV.	Ordinary partnership	102
V.	Societies	102
	A. General	102
	B. Formation	103
	C. Capacity of societies	104
	D. By-laws	104
	E. Organization	105
	F. Membership	107
VI.	Business associations	108
	A. General classification	108
	B. Persons versus capital	108
	C. Corporations	110
VII.	Foundations	112

CHAPTER 6
FAMILY LAW

I.	In general	115
II.	Engagement	116
	A. Agreement to marry	116
III.	Marriage	117
	A. General	117
	B. Conditions of a valid marriage	117
	C. Celebration of marriage	118
	D. Marital duties between spouses	119
IV.	Matrimonial property systems	120
V.	Divorce and judicial separation	121
	A. General	121
	B. Grounds for divorce	122
	C. The role of the judge in a divorce suit	123
	D. Judicial separation	123
	E. Legal consequences of divorce	123
VI.	Parent and child	124
	A. General	124
	B. Legitimate child	124
	C. Illegitimate child	125
	D. Adoption	126
	E. Parental authority	127

	Pages
VII. Guardianship, curatorship, statutory advisors	128
A. Guardianship	128
B. Curatorship	128
C. Statutory advisor	129

CHAPTER 7
LAW OF SUCCESSION

I. In general	131
II. Intestate succession	131
A. Parentels	131
B. Other persons who may inherit	134
III. Testate succession	135
A. Wills	135
B. Agreement of inheritance	139
IV. Reserved portion	139
A. General	139
B. Reduction of dispositions	140
C. Debarment from inheritance and loss of inheritance rights	141
V. Transfer of estate	141
A. General	141
B. Universal succession	141
C. Legal status of the heirs before partition of the estate	142
D. Determination of heirs	142
E. Debts of the estate	143
F. Disclaimer of inheritance	144
VI. Partition and distribution of the estate	144
A. Distribution by the heirs	144
B. Distribution by the court	144

CHAPTER 8
LAW OF PROPERTY

I. In general	147
II. Property	147
III. Ownership	148
A. The meaning of ownership	148
B. Ownership and possession	150
IV. Possession	150
A. Elements of possession	150
B. Acquisition of possession	151
C. Land registry	152
V. Extent of ownership	153
A. Ownership under and above the land	153
B. Component part or fixture	153
C. Accessories	154

	Pages
VI. Participation of several persons in ownership	155
A. Co - ownership	155
B. Joint ownership	155
VII. Acquisition of ownership	155
A. Acquisition of movable property	155
B. Acquisition of immovable property	156
VIII. Servitudes	157
A. Definition	157
B. Usufruct	157
C. Real servitude	157
D. Mortgage	158

CHAPTER 9
LAW OF OBLIGATIONS
PART 1
CONTRACTS

I. Definition and classification	159
A. Definition	159
B. Classification of contracts	160
II. A valid agreement	161
A. In general	161
B. The offer	161
C. The acceptance	161
III. Capacity	162
IV. Genuineness of assent	162
A. Mistake	162
B. Fraud	164
C. Duress	164
V. Legal cause	164
VI. Legality of the subject matter	164
A. Freedom of contract	164
B. Limitation of freedom of contract	165
VII. Form of contract	167
A. In general	167
B. Effects of the written form	167
VIII. Termination of contracts	168

PART 2
TORTS

I. In general	169
II. Conditions for torts	169

PART 3
UNJUST ENRICHMENT

I. General	171
II. Conditions	171

CHAPTER 10
CRIMINAL LAW

	Pages
I. Introduction	173
A. Purpose	173
B. Theories of punishment for crimes	173
II. Crime	174
A. Definition of the crime and its elements	174
B. General elements of crime	174
C. Participation in a crime	180
D. Multiplicity of crimes and punishments	180
III. Punishment ; prevention of crime	181
A. General	181
B. Application of punishments	183
C. Suspension of punishments	184
D. Dismissal of actions and setting aside of punishments	184
E. Restoration of rights	185

CHAPTER 11
LAW OF PROCEDURE

PART 1
INTRODUCTION

I. General	187
II. Court structure	187
III. Persons participating in the administration of justice	189
A. Judges	189
B. Court reporters or clerks	190
C. Public prosecutors	190
D. Practicing lawyers	191
E. Notary	191

PART 2
CIVIL PROCEDURE

I. Commencing an action	191
A. General	191
B. Ordinary procedure	192
II. Evidence	196
A. Burden of proof	196
B. Means of proof	197
C. Depositions	201
D. View	201
III. Rendition of judgement	201
A. Final decision	201
B. Form of judgement	202
C. Effect of judgement	203

		Pages
IV.	Appeal	203
	A. General	203
	B. Questions open on appeal	204
	C. Procedure	205
V.	Summary procedure	205
VI.	Execution and garnishment procedure	206

PART 3
CRIMINAL PROCEDURE

I.	Subject of criminal procedure	208
II.	Systems of criminal procedure	209
	A. Accusatorial system	209
	B. Inquisatorial system	209
	C. Mixed system	209
III.	The structure of the judicial system	210
	A. General principles	210
	B. Sources	210
	C. Judges and courts	210
	D. Criminal courts	211
IV.	Jurisdiction : «Natural» judge and court	212
V.	Parties to criminal proceedings	214
	A. Public prosecutor	214
	B. The defendant	215
VI.	Evidence ; burden of proof	218
VII.	Commencement and conduct of proceedings	219
	A. Preparatory investigation	219
	B. Preliminary investigation	220
	C. Final investigation	221
VIII.	Legal review	223
IX.	Special procedures	225
	Bibliography	227
	Glossary	235
	Alphabetical index	245

ABBREVIATIONS

Art.	Article
C. C.	Civil Code
C. C. Pr.	Code of Civil Procedure
C. Cr. Pr.	Code of Criminal Procedure
C. E. B.	Code of Execution and Bankruptcy
C. O.	Code of Obligations
Comm. C.	Commercial Code
Const.	Constitution
Cr. C.	Criminal Code
T. N. A.	Turkish Nationality Act

CHAPTER 1

SOURCES OF TURKISH LAW

Prof. Dr. Adnan GÜRİZ *

I. INTRODUCTION :

The law has evolved and continues to evolve from different sources or beginnings. These sources include historical and material sources such as religion, morality and old laws. The source of a current legal rule may be found in Roman law, or practices or moral laws applied in bygone ages. But «sources of law» also refers to the collection of contemporary legal rules, the positive law, on which a judge bases a decision. The line between the different sources is sometimes difficult to draw and the exact content of each source difficult to fix. After the triumph of the movement for codification in Europe in the beginning of the Nineteenth century many continental countries codified much of their law, both public and private. On the other hand, in the Anglo - Saxon countries the notion of uncodified law prevailed and is still predominant, and the majority of legal rules are derived from customary principles and judicial precedents. Turkey has followed the continental pattern and with the reception and codification of many European laws, legislation has become the most important source of law. To a lesser extent, customary law and case law or judicial precedent are sources; finally books of authority or doctrine, is a subsidiary source of Turkish law.

We will examine custom first; although not as important as legislation it may give us some insights into the development of law, as other rules have mainly developed from custom.

II. CUSTOMARY LAW (Örf ve Âdet Hukuku)

A. Custom in Civil Law :

In primitive communities customary observances supported by supernatural sanctions played an immensely important role in re-

---

* Faculty of Law, University of Ankara and the Hacettepe University.

gulating social life. Fishing, hunting, family relations, even the waging of war, were all regulated by customary rules sometimes down to the smallest detail. Custom constituted the generally and strictly observed course of conduct of the society.

With the evolution of primitive societies into modern societies and the development of legislatures, the importance of custom as a source of law has increasingly diminished [1].

In the modern world, the legislature may, by statute, deprive a customary rule of its legal status and custom has become a subordinate source of law [2]. This is especially true of Turkish law where legislation is consciously designed to change or restrain trends in the community's behaviour. In Turkey some laws are directly set against existing customs in order to develop and westernize the country according to European patterns.

For a custom to have legal validity in the Turkish system the following requirements must be satisfied:

1. Antiquity:

As a rule, a custom must have existed for a long time and no living person should know the beginning of it. This principle was stated in article 166 of the *Mecelle*, the collection of Islamic laws which was applied in Turkey between 1876 and 1925. However, it seems reasonable to make an exception for customs more recently established as a result of new inventions or patterns of trade. Thus for example, it may not be possible to meet the condition of antiquity for a custom related to transactions concerning air navigation.

2. Continuity:

A custom must be continuously observed. If it is abandoned or its practice is interrupted in favour of another custom, the requirement of continuity is not realized. Article 41 of the *Mecelle* clearly stated that there must be continuity for a custom to be valid. So too, a law of Süleyman the Magnificent asserted that in a certain district a custom with respect to cattle breeding which had been continuously observed should be considered binding and valid. Similarly, in laws passed during the XVth and XVIth centuries in Turkey customary principles were clearly stated to be enforceable

---

[1] W. D. Smith, *Handbook of Elementary Law*, p. 5 (St. Paul, Minn. 1939).
[2] H.L.A. Hart, *The Concept of Law*, p. 44 (Oxford 1961).

if continuously observed[3]. The condition of continuity is the material and objective factor applied to prove the validity of customary observance.

3. Popular Belief in the Rightness of a Custom:

Custom must consciously or unconsciously be considered right by the members of the society. Roman jurists called this spiritual and subjective condition *opinio necessitatis* or *opinio juris*.[4] There should be a belief among the members of society about the rightness and binding force of a custom. If a custom is maintained only by force, it cannot be considered as valid. Therefore, a certain mode of conduct which is not voluntarily observed by the members of society but forced upon them by an external or internal power is not to be deemed a custom.

4. State Sanction:

Until the courts apply customs, giving them the sanction of state authority, they are not law. A customary rule receives legal recognition when it is enforced by court order, unlike a statute which is law even before it is enforced by a court.

Current Turkish statutes clearly state when customary rules are to be used by the courts. If no clear reference is made by statutory law, judges refrain from resorting to customary rules. In the first article of the Turkish Civil Code the scope of the application of customary rules is stated:

> "The law must be applied in all cases which come within the letter or spirit of any of its provisions. Where no provisions are applicable the judge should decide according to existing customary law and in default thereof, according to the rules which he would lay down if he had himself to act as legislator. In this he must be guided by approved legal doctrine and case law."

Thus in cases under the Civil Code, and the Code of Obligations, judges are allowed to apply customary principles when the statutes are silent. Examples of this are found in article 621 of the Civil Code which states that the term «non-essential parts» of a

---

[3] In the Law of *Bozok*, articles 9 and 10 express the application of custom even in criminal matters. Ömer Lütfi Barkan, *XV ve XVI. Asırlarda Osmanlı İmparatorluğu'nda Ziraî Ekonominin Hukuki ve Mali Esasları* p. 125 (İstanbul 1943).

[4] N. Bilge, *Hukuk Başlangıcı Dersleri*, p. 43 (Ankara 1977).

property is to be understood according to the local customary practice, and in the second paragraph of article 270 of the Turkish Code of Obligations where it is provided that agricultural produce is to be divided between tenant and landlord according to local customs.

It should be noted that judges will usually consult experts to ascertain the content of customary rules.

5. *Agreement with Statuory Law :*

A custom contrary to statutory law will not be legally valid. It is axiomatic that statutory law is superior to custom and that judges are bound by statutes passed by the legislature, so long as they do not violate the constitution. This is true even though the statute is not properly or regularly applied by the courts. Thus when polygamy was abolished by law in Turkey the religious custom justifying polygamy became null and void, although it may still have been followed by some at the time. Customs opposed to written law can never be considered as legally valid though some continue to be observed in the society.

B. The Function of Customary Rules in other Branches of the Law :

1. *Criminal Law :*

The principle of «*nullum crimen nulla poena sine lege*» (there is neither crime nor punishment without law) is stated both in the Turkish Constitution (Art. 33) and the Turkish Criminal Code (Art. 1). Crimes and punishments cannot be established by customary law. The principle of written law for crimes and punishments is respected in Turkey as in other democratic countries as a safeguard of personal liberties. It is only in the field of criminal law that judges are not allowed to apply customary principles even when there is no provision in the code applicable to the case. This is done to guaranty personal freedom against arbitrary action by the judiciary and executive.

2. *Commercial Law :*

Customs and usages relating to commerce are considered superior to the non-commercial provisions of the Turkish Civil Code and the Code of Obligations which might otherwise be applicable in the absence of an express provision in the Commercial Code (Commercial Code, Art. 1 II). A commercial custom, however, cannot alter the obligatory rules of the Commercial Code.

To be applied, a commercial custom or usage must be proven to be «notorious», that is to say widely known. This is essential, so that it can be reasonably believed that both parties contracted in the light of the usage. A clearly and notoriously established commercial custom may be accepted as law even though it is not very old.

A custom will not be enforced if it tends to nullify or vary the express terms of a contract.[5]

3. *International Law:*

Custom plays a more considerable role in public international law than in other branches of law. However it is difficult to determine whether an international custom is or will actually be accepted as law or merely considered as part of the *«comitas gentium».* The question as to which customs are law in the sphere of public international law may be decided by decisions of international courts and by international treaties.

III. LEGISLATION

A. **In General:**

In order to regulate the life of a society, general and legal rules are set down in written form by the highest legislative authority of a country. The constitution designates such highest legislative authority, and possibly authorities subordinate to the highest authority which may also lay down subordinate written rules.

Acts of legislation are generally called a code, law or statute and are enacted to give a satisfactory answer, by means of general rule to the needs and requirements of society.

B. **Legislation in the Turkish Legal System**[6]:

The Turkish Constitution provides that the Grand National Assembly has sole authority to enact laws for application throughout Turkey. The 5th article of the Turkish Constitution states that

---

[5] Under article 2 of the Commercial Code usages may be used to interpret the intentions of the parties to a contract only where the contract is not explicit on a point. Commercial usages prevail over non-commercial usages. Local usages have priority over general usages. Usages are collected by the Chambers of Commerce and Industry.

[6] For details see Chapter 2, III.

«legislative power is vested in the Turkish Grand National Assembly. This power shall not be delegated». The Grand National Assembly can only delegate under certain terms the power of legislation to the Council of Ministers.

C. The Main Characteristics of Legislation :

Legislation permits both making new laws and abrogating old ones and is an essential instrument for the regulation of modern social life and the carrying out of reforms. It should be remembered that the reforms of *Atatürk* were introduced and realized through legislation. Ideally, legislation is passed only after extensive consideration, examination by experts and long parliamentary debate and therefore should be superior in quality to unwritten customary rules.

Legislation usually consists of rules of general application to many situations and cases and may be easily referred to. Being explicit and general, legislation can in theory be more easily understood than customary law even by laymen, justifying the proper enforcement of the principle that «ignorance of law is no excuse» (*Kanunu bilmemek mazeret sayılmaz*, «*ignorantia legis neminem excusat*», Art. 44 of the Turkish Criminal Code).

D. The Hierarchy of Enacted or Written Laws :

Written laws or rules may be classified into six categories of descending authority and importance. These categories, and some of their characteristics, are as follows :

1. *The Constitution* (Anayasa) [7] :

In the hierarchy of enacted laws the constitution occupies the first place. The constitution is a kind of code defining the form and ideology of the state, the principal organs of government, the rights and duties of the individual and of the state to the individual citizen and of the legal relationship between the individual and the state. It contains the most general and abstract legal rules of the country. As it is the supreme law of the country, no law can be contrary to it.

The supremacy of the constitution is expressed clearly in the 8th article of the Turkish Constitution which states that «laws shall not be in conflict with the constitution. The provisions of the

---

[7] See Chapter 2 on the Constitutional Law.

constitution shall be fundamental legal principles binding the legislative executive and judicial organs, administrative authorities and individuals». The new Turkish Constitution of 1961 has introduced the judicial control of legislative acts under the Constitution and a special Constitutional Court has been created to perform this function.

2. *Codes and Statutes* (Kanunlar):

Different codes and statutes, many of which are the subject of extensive discussion in this book, have different scopes and applications. The Civil Code and the Criminal Code are applied in all parts of Turkey and all Turkish citizens and residents are subject to them. On the other hand, the Labor Law is drafted to regulate the economic relations of only certain classes of people, namely employers and employees. In a rare case, a law may apply only to a certain citizen. The surname *Atatürk* was given to the first president of Turkey by a special act of Parliament. Similarly, laws passed after an earthquake or other disaster to relieve the stricken population are exceptional, as they do not exhibit the main characteristics of written laws, namely generality and abstractness.

A law is applied until it is abrogated or changed by a new law. But there are some laws which are applied only for a certain period of time. For example, budget laws are valid only for one year.

3. *International Treaties* (Milletlerarası Andlaşmalar):

International treaties to which Turkey is a party are approved by the Turkish Grand National Assembly by enactment of a law. Technically, therefore, treaties are statutes, which like all other statutes become enforceable after their publication in the Official Gazette. However, the constitutionality of treaties, unlike other statutes, may not be challenged. This is so that the other parties to the treaties may rely on their validity once they are passed into law.

Some treaties become binding without the official approval of the Turkish Parliament. According to article 65 of the Turkish Constitution «treaties which regulate economic, commercial, and technical relations and which are not effective for a period longer than one year, may be put into effect through promulgation in the Official Gazette provided they do not entail a financial commitment on the state and provided they do not infringe upon the status of individuals or upon the right of ownership of Turkish citizens in foreign lands». But such treaties are to be brought to the attention of the Turkish Parliament within two months following their promulgation. Similarly, economic, commercial and technical treaties concluded pursuant to the authority of parliamentary acts are not subect to the approval of the Grand National Assembly. However, such commercial and economic treaties or treaties affecting the rights of individuals shall not be put into effect unless promulgated.

4. *Statutory Decrees* (Kanun Hükmünde Kararnameler):

The Turkish Grand National Assembly can authorize the Council of Ministers, by special statute, to issue statutory decrees (decrees having the effect of law) on certain topics. In these special statutes the scope, principles, and duration of the power to issue statutory decrees are clearly stated. Statutory decrees become enforceable on the day of their publication in the Official Gazette, and they are submitted for the review and approval of the Grand National Assembly on the day of their publication.[8] The Council of Ministers cannot issue statutory decrees concerning the fundamental liberties and political rights of indivuduals. The Constitutional Court is empowered to exercise judicial control over the constitutionality of statutory decrees, just as it is authorized to consider the constitutionality of the other statutes.[9]

5. *Regulations* (Tüzükler = Nizamnameler) [10]:

Regulations governing the mode of enforcement of statutes, provided that they do not conflict with existing legislation, may be issued by the Council of Ministers. According to the Turkish Constitution, such regulations must have been examined by the Council of State,[11] signed by the President of the Republic, and promulgated in the same manner as statutes.[12]

Every valid regulation is dependent upon a statute. Since they are issued to govern the enforcement and application of statutes, they can only be issued if there is a clear reference in the statute to the promulgation of regulations.

---

[8] Law No. 1488, dated Sept. 22, 1971 (Const. 64).
[9] Ibid.
[10] See Chapter 3 on the Administrative Law.
[11] See The Law of the Council of State, No. 521, dated Dec. 31, 1964, Arts. 48 and 53.
[12] Published in the Official Gazette (Cons. Art. 107). See also Chapter 3 on the Administrative Law.

Regulations cannot contain provisions contrary to statutes. In the hierarchy of laws, therefore regulations come after statutes and contain more concrete and specific rules than statutes.[13]

Regulations containing provisions contrary to statutes will not be enforced by the courts. A suit of annulment against such regulations may be brought before the Council of State.[14] If the meaning of a regulation or one of its articles is not clear, it is to be interpreted by the courts or administrative authorities.

6. *By-Laws* (Yönetmelikler = Talimatnameler) :

Article 113 of the Turkish Constitution provides that «the ministries and public corporate bodies may issue by-laws with the purpose of ensuring the enforcement of statutes and regulations related to their particular fields of operation and in conformity with such statutes and regulations. By-laws shall be published in the Official Gazette».

Ministries and other public organizations such as universities and municipalities may issue by-laws, in conformity with statutes and regulations, in order to regulate their internal business or their relations with individuals. However, if it is provided for in statute concerned, a by-law may be issued by the Council of Ministers.[15] By-laws may not contain provisions contrary to statutes or regulations. To become enforceable they are to be published in the Official Gazette.

The Council of State is empowered to declare a by-law or any of its provisions null and void if it is contrary to a statute or regulation. It is generally agreed by Turkish jurists that other courts are also authorized to exercise a legal control over by-laws and to consider them invalid if they are contrary to statutes and regulations.[16]

E. Codes in Turkey :

After the proclamation of the Edict of Reorganization of 1839 *(Tanzimat Fermanı)*, Ottoman rulers aimed at renewing the social and the political structure of Turkey along western lines, and some

---

[13] Some examples of Regulations : Commercial Registry Regulation *(Ticaret Sicili Nizamnamesi)*, Land Registry Regulation *(Tapu Sicili Nizamnamesi)*.
[14] See the Law of the Council of State, note 11, Art. 44.
[15] The Law of State Personnel, No. 657, dated, July 23, 1965, Temporary Art. 19.
[16] Some examples of by-laws : By-laws of State Hospitals *(Hastahaneler Yönetmeliği)*, By-laws on Trade Marks *(Markalar Kanunu'nun Uygulama Şeklini Gösterir Yönetmelik)*.

European codes of law were adopted. In 1856 another Edict confirmed the principles of the Edict of 1839. The reforms introduced after 1839 were not radical in nature and old institutions were preserved while new ones were introduced. In the period between 1839 and 1923, though some modern western statutes were adopted from Europe, the old Islamic laws and institutions were also maintained.[17]

After the proclamation of the Republic in 1923, radical reforms were introduced in legal matters as in other spheres of social life. The adoption of the Swiss Civil Code and Code of Obligations which contain the law of persons, family law, succession, property, contracts, torts and unjust enrichment, both of which were adopted in 1926 with some minor alterations, represented a profound change in the social life of Turkey. The Swiss lawyer and scholar Sauser-Hall, referring to the adoption of the Swiss Civil Code by Turkey says that «such a radical and rapid change is unknown to history».[18]

The Turkish Code of Execution and Bankruptcy was adopted in 1929, based on the Swiss Federal Code of 1889. It was replaced in 1965 by a new Code to satisfy the changing requirements of Turkish economic and commercial life.[19]

Not only in the field of private law but also in the sphere of public law western codes were received. The Criminal Code which is an important one, was adopted in 1926,[20] based on the Italian Criminal Code of 1889. Though it has been modified several times to adapt it to the conditions of the country its essence has been preserved. Codes of administrative law were mainly adopted from France as a result of the strong French influence on the administrative system of Turkey which began just after the reform of 1839.[21]

---

[17] For the history of this period see Okandan, *Amme Hukukumuzun Ana Hatları*, Kitap 1 (İstanbul 1957) and Chapter 2. I on the Constitutional Law.

[18] In Bilge, *Hukuk Başlangıcı Dersleri*, p. 121, (Ankara, 1977).

[19] May 4, 1929, Law No. 1424, Subsequently Law of June 9, 1932, Law No. 2004 as amended in March 6, 1965. The Code of Civil Procedure of October 5, 1927 is taken from the law of the Swiss Canton Neuchatel (See below Ch. 11, Part 2 on the Law of Procedure). The Commercial Code of January 1st. 1957 contains many provisions which are taken mainly from German and Swiss laws.

[20] Law of March 9, 1926 (See Chapter 10 on the Criminal Law). The Turkish Code of Criminal Procedure of April 4, 1929 is taken from German law (See below. Chapter 11, Part 2 on the Law of Procedure).

[21] See below Chapter 3 on the Administrative Law.

F. The Problem of Interpretation:

1. In General:

Statutes are usually framed in more or less general terms and in order to apply these general terms to particular cases interpretation becomes necessary. Not only the famous Byzantine Emperor Justinian, but also the framers of the Prussian and Napoleonic Codes attempted to take away this power of interpretation from the judiciary. But these efforts and similar ones all failed because interpretation is unavoidable whenever a written formula has to be applied to a particular case.

When interpreting the meaning of a legal rule the judge has first to discover the true facts of the case before him and secondly he has to find out what the legislator intended him to do under the existing circumstances.

Before we examine the methods of interpretation it should be noted that interpretation of laws by the legislature is forbidden by the new Turkish Constitution of 1961. The retroactive interpretation of laws by the Parliament was practiced and sometimes abused between 1924 and 1961. Today only judicial and administrative organs are allowed to interpret laws.

2. Methods of Interpretation:

a) **Grammatical Interpretation:** In this method of interpretation the judge is bound by the very words of the provisions which he interprets. In interpreting any provision, if the grammatical meaning of the words is clear, the judge is bound to give effect to them and he cannot look further. Whether the provision is ethically unsound or unreasonable is immaterial; he has to construe and apply it word by word. This method gives expression to the formula «the statute speaks for itself».

b) **Logical Interpretation:** In this kind of interpretation the judge goes a step further in interpreting the law. In construing a statute obvious grammatical and verbal errors are to be corrected. Similarly, if a provision of the law is incomplete the gap is to be filled by way of logical interpretation. Moreover, the judge has to take into consideration the spirit of the code when interpreting the meaning of a particular article.

If grammatical interpretation points to ambiguous language, the statute will be evaluated by the method of logical interpretation.

If there is an inconsistency between two articles of a code, both applicable to the same case, the judge will again determine which provision is to be applied to the case by the method of logical interpretation.

In some cases there may not be any provision of customary rule directly applicable to the question in hand. In this case the judge will decide by using the methods of *analogy* and *argument a contrario* based on the logic of the legal system. However both *analogy* and *argument a contrario* are to be used only in exceptional situations. As a matter of principle both in criminal law and tax law logical interpretation is permissible only when favourable to the accused or tax payer.

c) Historical Interpretation : This method of interpretation essentially seeks to discover the intention of the legislator when the words of the statute do not reveal it by the methods discussed in (a) and (b) above. The judge takes into consideration all the circumstances surrounding the passing of a statute. Drafts of the code, work of parliamentary commissions, parliamentary debates, covering memorandums, are all examined to discover the real intention of the law-maker. This method of interpretation gives a high value to the conscious intentions of the law-makers. However laws are usually passed by a crowded parliament. Therefore it is often quite difficult to understand what the real intention of the law-maker was. Moreover, it should be born in mind that parliamentary documents and proceedings concerning a code relate to the past and indicate circumstances prevailing in the past. But as law is made for the future, and its innumerable and unknowable cases, the knowledge gained from the past may be misleading. For construing recent legislation the historical method of intrepretation may prove useful. However, as time passes, it becomes less useful to apply the statute in the light of the intent of the original legislator without reference to new needs and conditions.

d) Teleological Interpretation : This method of interpretation aims at extending the application of statutes to situations beyond the scope of legislative intention. This method is the opposite of the historical interpretation. In historical interpretation a statute is construed according to its original purpose. Teleological interpretation on the other hand, implies the construing of a statute only in view of its present purpose. When the judge applies this method, he considers the realities of social life and interpretation becomes a creative activity. Of course the judge may benefit from the notions of justice, social justice and social utility in this difficult task. The French Civil Code dated 1804, which is still applied, owes its vitality to the unending efforts of the French judges who have mainly preferred the method of teleological interpretation.

G. Retroactivity of Laws (Kanunların makable şümulü):

In the Turkish legal system, as in other legal systems, the non-retroactivity of laws is accepted as a general principle. If a statute can change rules applicable to past events, the confidence of the citizen in the law can be shaken, as no one can know the content of laws which will be passed in the future. The principle of non-retroactivity is a safeguard of democracy and personal freedom against the arbitrary interference of the state. In the past, *ex post facto* laws were condemned both by the Greeks and Romans. The *Corpus Juris Civilis* strongly rejected the retroactive application of laws. Later, retroactive legislation was forbidden by the Declaration of Human Rights and constitutions put into force in the XVIII th century.

In the Turkish Constitution the non-retroactivity of criminal codes is clearly expressed. Article 33 says that «no person shall be punishable for an act which is not considered an offence under the law in force at the time the act was committed». The same principle is also stated in the second article of the Turkish Criminal Code.[22] Moreover in the Statute Regulating the Application of the Turkish Civil Code the non-retroactivity of the Civil Code is also stressed. (A similar provision was introduced in the first article of the Statute Concerning the Application of the Turkish Commercial Code of 1957).

However, the non-retroactivity of the laws is not an absolute principle applicable to all cases. Certain types of retroactive laws are favoured, or at least tolerated, by the Turkish system of law. Thus, the principal of non-retroactivity is usually not applied to laws of a procedural character, whether civil or criminal, in the belief that the subsequent procedural rules will govern the case better than the previous rules.

---

[22] «If the provisions of the law in force at the time of the commission of a felony or misdemeanor differ from the provisions of a law enacted after its commission, the law in favour of the accused shall be applied and executed».

H. Enforcement of Statutes :

Statutes are published in the Official Gazette [23] after their promulgation by the President of the Republic. Usually the effective date of a statute is specified in the statute itself, by some such phrase as «this statute becomes effective on the date of its publication in the Official Gazette», or «this statute becomes effective six months after its publication date». A special law has been passed to solve problems concerning the publication and effectiveness of statutes where the statute in question is not clear. According to this law,[24] if there is no provision in the statute itself governing the date of validity, it becomes effective 45 days after its publication in the Official Gazette.

Generally, Turkish statutes are applied within the frontiers of Turkey to every individual, Turk or foreigner. This principle is not absolute; in some cases, foreign laws may be applied to foreigners living in Turkey. For example, in an action of divorce between a German wife and German husband living in Turkey, German law will be applied to them if they accept the jurisdiction of Turkish courts.[24a] Cases concerning personality and family law are regulated by foreign laws provided that these laws do not contain provisions contrary to Turkish public order and morals. Similarly foreigners living in Turkey are not allowed to vote in political elections in Turkey. On the other hand, Turkish statutes may be applied to some cases which take place in foreign lands. Certain crimes are tried and punished in Turkey even if they are committed in foreign lands and might be tried by the foreign courts. Many of these problems are the subject of that branch of the law called private international law, or the rules of conflicts of law, which is beyond the scope of this book.

I. Repeal of Statutes :

It is not always easy to determine when a statute is annulled. Generally a new law contains an article nullifying the previous law

---

[23] The Official Gazette *(Resmi Gazete)* which is puslished in Ankara daily, except holidays, includes not only the statutes, but also regulations, by-laws, decrees, some decisions of the courts and official announcements. The official texts of statutes may also be found in a publication called *Düstur*, published by the Prime Ministry, which is issued annually. The *Düsturs* issued since the new Constitution of 1961 are the «Fifth Series». Laws carry numbers.
[24] Law No. 1322, dated May 28, 1928.
[24a] The nationality problem is regulated in the Nationality Act of 1964 (See below Chapter 4 on the Law of Persons ; T. Ansay, *American - Turkish Private, International Law* (New York, 1966).

on the subject. For example in the Statute Concerning the Application of the Civil Code, article 43 clearly states that the «*Mecelle* has been repealed». In this case one law has explicitly been annulled by another law. But in some cases such a clear reference to a previous law may not be found. Instead, a general provision may state that «articles of other statutes contrary to this statute are repealed». In this case the judge has to decide which articles of the previous statutes are annulled by the new statute. In some cases no article can be found in the new statute nullifying a previous statute.

In relating different statutes inconsistencies should be settled by the judge according to certain general principles of law. Thus, if there is a contradiction between the articles of two laws of equal rank (e.g. both statutes) the later will prevail over the earlier. In some cases there may be a conflict between the provisions of a general code and a particular code. In that case, the judge will assume that an earlier general rule is replaced by the more recent particular rule. If there is a conflict between a prior particular rule and a later general rule the conflict is to be resolved by the judge according to the «assumed intention of the legislature».

IV. COURT DECISIONS

A. General Considerations :

In most countries the decisions of superior courts are treated with respect by inferior courts which will follow them when they are called upon to decide similar cases. The question arises whether such decisions can be considered precedents, that is «a judgment or decision of a court of law cited as authority for deciding a similar set of facts».[25]

Judges in determining uncertain points of law will necessarily tend to decide in accordance with the pattern of previously decided cases. The reasons for this development are several. From the **psychological** point of view any one who is going to decide a dispute likes to justify his decision by referring to a past decision. Moreover it is highly desirable that court decisions should be uniform. If there is no uniformity among court decisions, the principal aim of justice **to promote security in society** may not be realized. Contrarily, if **the decisions of courts in similar cases are similar, the faith of the people in the system of justice is maintained.**

---

[25] **James S. Philip**, *Introduction to English Law, p. 10* (London 1955).

Contrary to Anglo-American legal systems,[26] in continental countries judicial precedents are not in theory regarded as a source of law, due to the view that the legislature is the sole source of new law, and the only law maker as such. According to this prevailing point of view, although prior decisions may assist a judge in arriving at a conclusion, they are not binding upon him and he must decide a case as he himself thinks right. Notwithstanding this theory, in practice it is generally accepted on the Continent that to secure certainty and uniformity, as suggested above, among court decisions the previous decisions of superior courts, especially of a country's supreme court, are to be as binding as statutory law.

B. Precedents in Turkey :

Turkish courts are bound to make their decisions in conformity with the statutory law, the function of the judiciary being to interpret and apply the law.

Where no statutory rule fits a civil law case before him, a Turkish judge is also authorized to decide according to customary law as discussed above. If there is no applicable customary rule, then the Turkish judge should act as a law-maker and lay down a new rule within the framework of the general principles of law, benefiting from precedent and doctrine i. e. books of authority. By authorizing the judge to act as law-maker in these exceptional cases the first article of the Turkish Civil Code has set up an important and revolutionary principle.

In Turkey certain precedents are followed. Thus inferior civil and criminal courts are bound by some decisions of the Court of Cassation and the Court of Cassation in turn is bound by some of its own decisions. Similarly in administrative cases the decisions of the Council of State are also authoritative and binding for inferior administrative courts, including the Court of Accounts. Binding and authoritative decisions of the higher courts, i. e. the Court of Cassation, the Council of State and the Military Court of Cassation [27] are as binding and authoritative on the courts and agencies within their jurisdictions as the rules of a statute.

---

[26] The role of judicial decisions and precedents in Anglo-American law is discussed in the following works : Dias and Hughes, *Jurisprudence*, pp. 52 ff. (London 1957); A. Ross, *On Law and Justice*, pp. 84 ff. (London 1958); W. D. Smith, *Handbook of Elementary Law*, pp. 87 ff. (St. Paul, Minn. 1939).

[27] See D, E and F below. On Constitutional Court see Chapter 2, V, 2 on the Constitutional Law. The decisions of the Constitutional Court are also binding and they are officially published (Const., Art. 152).

Therefore, by interpreting and applying the law, superior courts enjoy the privilege of laying down rules as effective as the rules of a statute.

C. Court of Cassation (Yargıtay, Temyiz Mahkemesi) :[28]

Not all decisions of the Court of Cassation enjoy the prestige and authority of precedent. Only the decisions of the General Assembly of all Chambers of the Court of Cassation are binding. If there is a contradiction between the decisions of a chamber of the Court of Cassation or between two chambers or if it is necessary to alter established precedent the General Assembly on the Unification of Judgments makes a unifying decision (*İçtihadı Birleştirme Kurulu Kararı*) which binds all other courts and the Court of Cassation itself after they are published in the Official Gazette.[29] The other decisions of the Court of Cassation, including the decisions made by the Assembly of Civil or Criminal Chambers are not made legally binding upon the inferior courts and they are not published in the Official Gazette. However, though these decisions are not considered legally binding, inferior courts generally pay attention to them. This is partly due to the fact that judges of inferior courts respect decisions made by the Court of Cassation. Besides, the decisions of the judges of the inferior courts are evaluated by the Court of Cassation in considering their professional advancement. The other decisions of the Court of Cassation are irregularly published in the Journal of this Court (*Yargıtay Kararları Dergisi*) and in some other periodicals.

In conclusion, it should be born in mind that, notwithstanding all these practical developments, in Turkey there has never been an important body of judge made law as exists in the Anglo - American countries.

D. The Council of State (Danıştay, Devlet Şurası) :[30]

The Council of State settles administrative conflicts, expresses opinions on draft laws submitted by the Council of Ministers, exam-

---

[28] On the structure of the Court of Cassation see below Chapter 11, Part 2, IV on the Law of Procedure.
[29] Law No. 1221, dated Apr. 14, 1928. Art. 8.
[30] Law of Council of State, No. 521. dated Dec. 31, 1964. See Chapter 3 on the Administrative Law.

ines draft regulations and concession contracts and discharges other duties prescribed by the law.

Its members are elected by the permanent and alternate members of the Constitutional Court after two candidates for each vacancy are proposed by the Council of Ministers and the General Assembly of the Council of State.

The Council of State is composed of twelve chambers, nine of which function as judicial chambers and three of which function as administrative chambers. The duties of the administrative chambers are to express opinions on draft laws, to examine draft regulations and concession contracts, and to give opinions on other matters referred to it by the office of the Prime Minister.

The judicial function of the Council of State is extremely important both as a safeguard of the individual against the interference of the state and as an arbiter between the state and the individual. Thus Article 114 of the Constitution states that, no act or procedure of the administration shall be immune from the review of law enforcing courts. However, judicial power cannot be used to limit the exercise of administrative (executive) power in accordance with laws. No judicial decision can replace an administrative act or procedure. In court actions instituted as a result of administrative acts, statute of limitations shall start from the date of written notification. The administration is liable for the damages resulting from its acts and operations.

Unifying decisions made by the General Assembly on the Unification of Judgements bind all inferior administrative courts and the Council of State itself and are published in the Official Gazette. When there is a conflict between the decisions of different judicial chambers or different decisions of the General Assembly of Judicial Chambers, the first President of the Council of State, chairmen of the concerned judicial chambers, and the Chief Prosecutor of the Council of State may require the General Assembly on the Unification of Judgements to make a unifying decision.[31]

The High Military Administrative Court, *(Askeri Yüksek İdare Mahkemesi)* established in 1972 is authorized to exercise judicial control over the acts and procedures of the administartion related to military personnel. A special law has been passed by the Grand National Assembly establishing the composition and the rights and duties of this Court. It is the final decision making body

---

[31] Law of Council of State, above note 30, Arts. 45 and 46.

in administrative cases concerning military personnel and its decisions cannot be examined or reversed by either the Council of State or the Military Court of Cassation.

Other decisions of the Council of State which do not bind the inferior administrative courts are published in the Journal of Decisions of the Council of State *(Danıştay Kararlar Dergisi)* and in other legal periodicals.[32]

E. The Military Court of Cassation (Askerî Yargıtay):

The Military Court of Cassation (Const. Art. 141) is the court of last instance in military cases. It is composed of three chambers; each has a chairman and seven members. In addition to the three chambers there is a first President, a second President and a Military Chief Public Prosecutor. The members are selected by the President of the Republic from among candidates nominated by the General Assembly of the Military Court of Cassation.

Unlike the Civil Court of Cassation, all decisions made by the General Assembly on the Unification of Judgements and the General Assembly of the Chambers bind all inferior military courts and the Military Court of Cassation itself. The Chamber of Unifying Decisions consists of the first President, second President, Chief Military Public Prosecutor, the Chairmen of all the Chambers and at least five members from each chamber; while the General Assembly of the Chambers is presided over by the second President and comprises only sixteen members.

V. DOCTRINE (Books of Authority):

The task of the legal writer, or jurist, is to discover by logical analysis the several possible interpretations of laws and to indicate their practical consequences. However it should be remembered that the function of the jurist is not only to construe the existing positive law, but also to make recommendations about changes in and

---

[32] The Court of Accounts *(Sayıştay, Divanı Muhasebat,* Art. 127 of the Constitution) is in charge of auditing on behalf of the Turkish Grand National Assembly the revenues, expenditures and property of the government and its agencies, deriving from general and annexed budgets. The Court of Accounts also makes decisions regarding the accounts and operations of responsible government officials. There are four chambers of the Court of Accounts. The decisions of the court consist of decisions of a chamber, decisions of the General Assembly of the Chambers and Unifying Decisions of the General Assembly of the Chambers (See the Law of the Court of Accounts, No. 2514, dated June 25, 1934, Art. 58). Decisions of the Court of Accounts touching on administrative matters may be reviewed by the Council of State acting as a court of appeal.

additions to the existing law which ought to be enacted in the future. Along with the dynamic evolution of the community its ideological basis changes. This development exercises a strong influence upon the legal system of the community. Jurists not only guide the authorities administering the law, that is judges and administrators, but also the legislator.

In accordance with the Roman law tradition on the Continent the writings of legal authors form a source of law. The writings may not be obligatory on judges, but they are often highly persuasive.

Juristic works are not an independent «source of law», although in some cases juristic opinion leads to the formation of law. Especially where the positive law is silent, juristic opinion may be resorted to. Though the views of academicians are rarely quoted by the Turkish courts, nevertheless, it may confidently be stated that professional opinion is going to play an increasingly important role in the Turkish legal system.[33]

SELECTED BIBLIOGRAPHY

Akipek, J.: **Türk Medeni Hukuku**, I. Cilt, **Başlangıç Hükümleri, Şahsın Hukuku**, Birinci Cüz, **Medeni Kanun Başlangıç Hükümleri** (Ankara, 1973).

Ansay, S. Ş.: **Hukuk Bilimine Başlangıç** (Ankara, 1958).

Bilge, N.: **Hukuk Başlangıcı Dersleri** (Ankara, 1977).

Gözübüyük, A. Şeref: **Hukuka Giriş ve Hukukun Temel Kavramları** (Ankara, 1973).

Velidedeoğlu, H. V.: **Türk Medeni Hukukunun Umumi Esasları** (İstanbul, 1959).

Yörük, A. K.: **Hukuk Başlangıcı** (İstanbul, 1956).

Allen, C. K.: **Law in the Making** (Oxford, 1961).

Bodenheimer, E.: **Jurisprudence, the Philosophy and Method of Law** (Harvard University Press, 1962).

Dias, R. W. M. and Hughes G. B. J.: **Jurisprudence** (London, 1957).

Friedmann, W.: **Legal Theory** (New York, 1967).

Geldart, W.: **Elements of English Law** (Oxford University Press, 1953).

Hart, H. L. A.: **The Concept of Law** (Oxford, 1961).

Holland, T. E.: **The Elements of Jurisprudence** (Oxford, 1924).

---

[33] The recent decisions of the Court of Cassation make references to books of authority.

James, P. S.: **Introduction to English Law** (London, 1972).
Kantorowicz, H.: **The Definition of Law** (Cambridge, 1958).
Karlen, D. and Arsel, I.: **Civil Litigation in Turkey** (Ankara, 1957).
Maine, H.: **Ancient Law** (London, 1960).
Patterson, E. W.: **Jurisprudence, Men and Ideas of the Law** (Brooklyn, 1953).
Ross, A.: **On Law and Justice** (London, 1958).
Smith, W. D.: **Handbook of Elementary Law** (St. Paul, Minn, 1939).
Salmond, J.: **Jurisprudence** (London, 1937).
Stone, J.: **The Province and Function of Law** (Sydney, 1950).

CHAPTER 2

CONSTITUTIONAL LAW

Prof. Dr. Ergun ÖZBUDUN *

I. HISTORICAL BACKGROUND

Turkey has a prominent place among today's developing countries by the length of its experience, albeit an interrupted one, with constitutional government. By «constitutional government,» I mean a system in which political power is shared and reciprocal controls are legally established among different branches of government, in other words, a system of «checks and balances.» In this sense, constitutional government is not necessarily identical with «constitutional democracy,» since the latter must, by definiton, be based on effective and widespread political participation by the people.

Historically speaking, constitutional government preceded constitutional democracy both in Turkey and in the West. Of all non-Western nations, the Ottoman Empire made one of the earliest efforts to establish a constitutional government. The various rescripts *(ferman)* of the Reform period (notably, the Rescript of *Tanzimat* of 1839, and that of *Islahat* of 1856) are usually considered the beginnings of the constitutionalist movement in the Empire. Legally, these documents were no more than a unilateral declaration and recognition by the Sultan of certain basic human rights for his subjects, including security of life, honor, and property, the abolition of tax farming *(iltizam)*, fair and public trial of persons accused of crimes, and the equality of all Ottoman subjects irrespective of religion. No effective legal mechanism was set up to ensure the enforcement of such provisions, which remained only morally binding upon the Sultan. Yet, one should not minimize the significance of the Reform rescripts in the constitutional development of the Ottoman Empire. They signified the first important break with the autocratic and absolutist political traditions of the Empire, and they paved the way for a still more important step, the promulgation of the first Ottoman Constitution in 1876.

* Faculty of Law, University of Ankara.

The Ottoman Constitution of 1876, promulgated by Sultan Abdülhamid II acting under the pressure of a small group of reformist bureaucrats, provided, for the first time, some constitutional mechanisms to check the absolute powers of the Sultan. The most important novelty of the Constitution was the creation of a legislative assembly at least partially elected by the people. The Ottoman legislature, called the «General Assembly» *(Meclis-i Umumî)*, was composed of two chambers: the Senate *(Heyet-i Âyan)*, and the Chamber of Deputies *(Heyet-i Mebusan)*. The members of the Senate were to be appointed for life by the Sultan, while the deputies were to be elected by the people through indirect elections and a system of limited suffrage in which only property owners were allowed to vote.[1] The General Assembly was granted certain powers to enact laws and to exercise control over the executive. On both accounts, however, the ultimate authority rested with the Sultan, who thus remained the cornerstone of the constitutional system.

The 1876 Constitution was far from having established a «parliamentary monarchy,» in which the substance of political power rests with the parliament and the monarch's role is restricted to ceremonial and symbolic matters. Nevertheless, even this limited experiment in constitutional government proved too much for Abdülhamid II, who dissolved the Chamber of Deputies in 1878 and returned to absolute rule. However, the influence of Western liberalism continued and expanded under his authoritarian rule. Increasing numbers of students, intellectuals, bureaucrats, and army officers joined the opposition. Eventually, the Sultan was forced to restore the Constitution in 1908.

This period is called the «Second Constitutionalist period» *(İkinci Meşrutiyet)* in Ottoman history. The restored Constitution of 1876 was substantially amended in 1909 to increase the powers of the legislature and to restrict those of the Sultan. Thus, a constitutional system finally came into being, more or less similar to the parliamentary monarchies of Western Europe. This liberal era did not last long, however, and it was quickly transformed into the dictatorship of the dominant party, the Union and Progress *(İttihat ve Terakki)*. With the defeat of the Ottoman Empire in World War I,

---

[1] Indirect elections mean that the representatives are chosen not directly by the whole electorate but by a much smaller group of «second electors» who are elected by the «first electors» (i.e., the entire electorate). It was not until 1946 that «direct» elections were introduced in Turkey. The system of limited suffrage was the prevalent European practice at the time of the 1876 Constitution.

the Ottoman government collapsed in fact, if not in theory; while the Istanbul government maintained a shaky existence during the Armistice years (1918 - 1922) under the control of the occupying armies of the Allies, a new governmental structure was developed in Anatolia by the nationalists resisting the occupation.

This era of «National Liberation» is a most interesting period in Turkey's constitutional history and is full of constitutional innovations. Following the arrest and deportation by the Allied occupation forces of many deputies with nationalist sympathies and the consequent prorogation of the Chamber of Deputies in Istanbul on March 18, 1920, Mustafa Kemal called for the election of a new assembly «with extraordinary powers» to convene in Ankara. This body, called the Turkish Grand National Assembly, was different from the Ottoman Parliament in that it held both legislative and executive powers. It was, in a real sense, a constituent and revolutionary assembly, not bound by the Ottoman Constitution.

The Grand National Assembly enacted a Constitution in 1921. This was a short (it contained only 23 articles) but very important document. For the first time, it proclaimed the principle of «national sovereignty,» calling itself the «only and true representative of the nation.» Legislative and executive powers were vested in the Assembly, as they had been since the opening of the Assembly on April 23, 1920. This was, undoubtedly, a republican form of government, since neither the principle of national sovereignty nor an all-powerful Assembly could, in fact, be reconciled with a monarchical system. However, for tactical political reasons, the Assembly did not officially abolish the sultanate until after the final victory over the invading Greek armies was won. The sultanate was abolished on October 30, 1922, and the Republic was officially proclaimed about a year later, on October 29, 1923.

The Turkish Republic clearly needed a new Constitution. The Constitution of 1921 was not meant to be a constitution in the full sense of the word; rather, it was a document dealing only with the most urgent constitutional problems of the moment. The new Constitution adopted by the Grand National Assembly in 1924 retained most of the basic principles of the 1921 Constitution, notably the principle of national sovereignty. The Grand National Assembly was considered, as it was in the 1921 Constitution, «the sole representative of the nation, on whose behalf it exercises the rights of sovereignty» (Art. 4). Theoretically, both legislative and executive powers were concentrated in the Assembly (Art. 5), but the Assembly was to exercise its executive authority through the President of the Republic elected by it and a Council of Ministers appointed by the President (Art. 7). The Assembly could at any time control the Council of Ministers and dismiss it, while the Council had no power to dissolve the Assembly to hold new elections.

In classical constitutional theory, this was an «assembly government» based on the unity or concentration of the legislative and executive powers, rather than a parliamentary government where such powers are, to some extent, separated from each other. In practice, however, the theoretical supremacy of the Assembly is often transformed into the domination of the executive, since normally the executive is composed of party or faction leaders, while the legislature includes a numerically larger, but politically much weaker, group of back-benchers. This was also the case in Turkey. Both in the single-party (1924-1946) and the multi-party (1946-) years, the authoritarian leadership of the chief executives and strong party discipline reduced the Assembly to a secondary role.

The Constitution of 1924 was undoubtedly a democratic constitution in spirit. But this was a «majoritarian» or «Rousseauist» concept of democracy, rather than a «liberal» democracy, based on an intricate system of checks and balances. The majoritarian concept of democracy holds that sovereignty is the «general will» of the nation (which, in practice, has to be interpreted as and majority's will), and it is, as such, absolute, indivisible, and infallible. Within a representative system, this means that the legislature represents the true will of the nation. Hence, limiting the powers of the legislature would be tantamount to restricting the national will, which would, in turn, limit the sovereignty of the nation. Furthermore, such limitations would be neither necessary nor useful, since, under the Rousseauist concept of democracy, the general will is always right.

Needless to say, modern democratic theory no longer depends on such metahpysical concepts as the general will. Nevertheless, Rousseauist ideas made a lasting impact on the French democratic thought, through which they influenced the thinking of the Turkish revolutionaries. Nor should one lose sight of the fact that the Constitution of 1924 was the culmination of a long struggle against the sultans. It is not surprising, therefore, that the only perceived threat to national interests was that which could come from the sultans; once this threat was removed, the revolutionaries thought, there would be no need to protect the nation against its own true representatives. Evidently, the framers of the 1924 Constitution were not sufficiently aware that the tyranny of a majority was just as possible, and as dangerous, as a personal tyranny.

This rather simplistic view of democracy was present in many aspects of the 1924 Constitution : its creation of an all-powerful Assembly; its sometimes emotional and unnecessary distrust of the executive; its insufficient safeguards for the independence of the judiciary; its failure to institute formal restraints on the legislative power, notably the lack of a judicial mechanism for reviewing the constitutionality of laws. Although the Constitution declared and enumerated the basic rights of Turkish citizens, it often stated that such rights would be enjoyed only «within the limits stipulated by law.» Hence, the Assembly would be constitutionally free to restrict basic rights almost at will.

Lack of constitutional checks and balances did not pose a major problem during the single-party years, since a single-party system itself implies a heavy concentration of governmental authority. Furthermore, it can reasonably be argued that the modernizing reforms of the Kemalist era could hardly have been carried out by a political system where such authority was divided and dispersed. But, with the transition to a multi-party system in 1946, the weaknesses of the Constitution became obvious. The unrestrained nature of the legislative power, coupled with an electoral system which produced lopsided majorities in the legislature, made it tempting for the leaders of the majority party to use their vast powers to suppress, or at least harrass, the opposition. Thus, in the late 1950's, tension increased greatly between the governing Democrats and the opposing Republicans. Some overly authoritarian measures taken by the government in the spring of 1960 created widespread unrest in the country. Finally, on May 27, 1960, units of the Turkish armed forces overthrew the Menderes government.

In the interim period between the military takeover and the ratification of the 1961 Constitution, the country was ruled by the National Unity Committee *(Millî Birlik Komitesi)* composed of the 38 revolutionary officers. Under a Provisional Constitution adopted by the Committee, many provisions of the 1924 Constitution were amended or abrogated, and the Committee was vested with legislative and executive powers. However, most members of the National Unity Committee, as well as most of the armed forces generally, were intent on returning power to civilians once a new and democratic constitution was adopted. At first, the Committee charged a group of university professors with the preparation of a new constitution. When it was perceived that such a group would not be sufficiently representative of public opinion, the Committee decided, on January 6, 1961, to establish a Constituent Assembly *(Kurucu Meclis)* for the task.

The Constituent Assembly was composed of two chambers: the National Unity Committee and the House of Representatives. Some members of the latter were elected by the people through indirect elections, while others were chosen by various institutions, such as the Head of State, the National Unity Committee, the existing political parties (CHP and CKMP), the judiciary, universities, bar associations, labor unions, chambers of trade and industry, farmers' associations, the press, etc. The Constitution of 1961 was prepared and adopted by this Assembly and finally came into force after being ratified by popular vote on July 9, 1961.[2]

II. THE GENERAL CHARACTERISTICS OF THE 1961 CONSTITUTION

In many respects, the Constitution of 1961 represents a reaction to the severe problems observed in the functioning of the 1924 Constitution. Clearly, the new Constitution was inspired by a pluralistic, rather than a majoritarian, concept of democracy. Instead of a constitutional structure based on an omnipotent legislative assembly, a system of checks and balances was introduced and powerful guarantees for minority rights were provided. It was thought that the public good would be better served by allowing for the free interplay of opposing forces than by concentrating all legitimate authority in a single branch of government.

The divergent philosophies of the two constitutions can best be illustrated by comparing the different roles each assigned to the legislature. Under the Constitution of 1924, the Assembly was the sole representative of the national will; it exercised the rights

---
[2] Substantially amended in 1971 and 1973.

of sovereignty on behalf of the nation, and, as such, it was subject to no effective constitutional limitations. On the other hand, the Constitution of 1961 states that «the nation shall exercise its sovereignty through the authorized agencies in accordance with the principles laid down in the Constitution» (Art. 4). This formula clearly suggests that the legislature no longer has a monopoly on legitimate authority, in the exercise of which other branches and agencies of government also have a rightful share. It further suggests that the new Constitution subscribes to the philosophy of limited government, which holds that the exercise of authority is legitimate only so long as it remains within the limits prescribed by law. This is fundamentally different from the idea of a legislature solely representing the will of the nation, defined as absolute, indivisible, and infallible.

Another good vantage point from which to compare the underlying philosophies of the two constitutions is their different approaches to civil liberties. As mentioned above, the Constitution of 1924, while enumerating most of the classical civil liberties, gave the Assembly the exclusive right to define their limits. Since the limitations would be determined by law and there were few constitutional rules to restrict the powers of the Assembly, it was not impossible for the legislators to pass laws which would render civil liberties practically meaningless. In contrast, the Constitution of 1961 contains a much more detailed Bill of Rights. Its provisions effectively limit the scope of legislative action with respect to civil liberties. For example, no law can impose press censorship, subject the publication of newspapers and periodicals to the requirements of prior permission or to the payment of a deposit, empower the administrative authorities to close newspapers and periodicals, or provide for the seizure or confiscation of printing shops and printing equipment, etc. (Arts. 22-25). Furthermore, the Constitution stipulates that the law cannot infringe upon the essence of any right or liberty (Art. 11). This is construed by the Constitutional Court as prohibiting any infringement which would make the exercise of a right or liberty impossible or particularly difficult.

Such concepts as limited government and liberal democracy would have had no effective legal safeguards had the judicial review of the constitutionality of laws not also been introduced by the new Constitution. We shall dwell upon judicial review at greater length below. It suffices to note here that this is perhaps the most important innovation of the 1961 Constitution. Without such review, the supremacy of the Constitution would lose much of its practical significance, since the legislature could pass unconstitutional laws without obtaining the special quorum stipulated by the Constitution for constitutional amendments.[3]

The principal characteristics of the Turkish Republic have been stated in Article 2 of the Constitution : «The Turkish Republic is a national, democratic, secular, and social state based on human rights, the rule of law, and the basic principles laid down in the Preamble.» A few words are in order on each of these characteristics.

1. National State :

«National State» indicates that the human component of the Republic is the Turkish nation. Article 3 confirms this by stating that the Turkish State is an indivisible whole with its nation and territory, and that its official language is Turkish. In the same vein, Article 4 vests sovereignty unconditionally in the nation and prohibits its delegation to any one person, group, or class. As such, the idea of national state is not compatible with either total integration with a supra-national entity, or with a theocratic state where the human element is a religious community, not a nation. A rather long definition of Turkish nationalism is given in the Preamble, according to which it is a doctrine «which unites all individuals, be it in fate, pride or distress, as an indivisible whole around national consciousness and ideals, and aims at exalting our nation in the spirit of national unity as a respected and equal member of the world family of nations.» This is clearly a confirmation of the Kemalist notion of nationalism which rejects racism, chauvinism, and irredentism.

2. Democratic State :

The democratic character of the Republic is stated not only in Article 2 but throughout the Constitution. Two essential features of a democratic system, specifically dealt with by the Constitution are worth mentioning here. One is the principle of free and competitive elections based on universal suffrage. The Constitution (Art. 55) provides that elections will be conducted on the basis of

---

[3] Proposals for the amendment of the Constitution may be submitted in writing by at least one - third of the full membership of the Turkish Grand National Assembly. An amendment proposal shall be adopted by a minimum of two - thirds majority of the full membership of each House separately (Art. 155).

free, equal, secret, direct, and universal suffrage and that the counting and sorting of the ballots shall be carried out in public.

A system of judicial control of the electoral process has also been established by the Constitution (Art. 75). A Supreme Board of Election *(Yüksek Seçim Kurulu)* was empowered to take all necessary measures to ensure the fair and orderly conduct of elections, to review and decide upon all complaints of illegal practices regarding electoral matters, and to ratify the election credentials of the elected members of Parliament. The Board is composed of seven regular members and four alternates. Six of the members are elected by the plenary session of the Court of Cassation *(Yargıtay)* and five by the plenary session of the Council of State *(Danıştay)* from among their own members. There are also electoral boards with similar, but more limited, powers in all provincial *(il)* and county *(ilçe)* seats. The provincial electoral boards are composed of, and the county boards are presided over by, the local judges.

While the Constitution thus lays down the basic principles governing the electoral process, it does not subscribe to any particular electoral system. Under the present electoral laws, elections to both Houses are held in accordance with the «d'Hondt» version of proportional representation. Every province constitutes an electoral district. The number of deputies or senators to be elected by each province varies in proportion to its population. The law sets the voting age as 21.

Another essential feature of a democratic system of government is the existence of more than one freely organized political party. Modern democracy is party democracy. Parties structure the vote and make political representation possible by aggregating the infinite variety of interests existing in modern societies into a few discernible policy alternatives. Yet, reference to political parties in constitutions is a relatively recent phenomenon. The Turkish Constitution of 1961 follows the example of the post-World War II European constitutions by recognizing the right to organize political parties and by explicitly stating that political parties, whether in power or in opposition, are indispensable elements of democratic political life. Parties can be founded without prior permission and operate freely within the limits prescribed by the Constitution (Art. 56).

Freedom of political organization and activity is not without limits under the Constitution. Political parties have to conform to the principles of a democratic and secular republic based on human rights and liberties and to the principle of the national and territorial integrity of the State. Parties which fail to conform to these rules are to be permanently disbanded by the Constitutional Court (Art. 57). Under this provision, political parties aiming at the overthrow of the democratic system, as well as theocratic and separatist parties do not enjoy constitutional protection. All political parties are also accountable to the Constitutional Court with respect to their finances.

It can be concluded from this analysis that the democratic theory underlying the Turkish Constitution is that of a liberal, pluralistic democracy, based on human rights, checks and balances, limited government, multiplicity of political parties, and free interparty competition. It is not compatible with strictly majoritarian notions of democracy. Nor is it compatible with such contemporary distortions of the democratic theory as authoritarian democracy, guided democracy, tutelary democracy, or people's democracy.

3. *Secularism:*

Secularism has been one of the pillars of the Atatürk reforms.[4] In the West, secularism has meant complete separation of religion and the State. The Kemalist conception of secularism, however, has allowed for some measure of State control over religion. It was feared that total non-interference between religion and the State would, in fact, result in the interference of religion in governmental affairs, since Islam is not only a system of faith but also a system of law, a social and political ideology, and a total way of life. If religious affairs were left entirely in the hands of community organizations without any governmental supervision, it would be inevitable that Islam would retain its hold over the society, over its laws, politics, and economics. The Constitution of 1961 maintained this peculiar conception of secularism; while it clearly recognized the freedom of religion (which comprises the freedom of faith and the freedom of worship), it kept the Directorate of Religious Affairs *(Diyanet İşleri Başkanlığı)* as part of the administrative apparatus (Art. 154). The Constitution (Art. 153) also accorded special protection to the eight principal Reform Laws *(Devrim Kanunları)* passed during the Atatürk era and embodied

---

[4] The Constitution of 1924 was amended in 1928 to delete the provision declaring Islam as the State religion. In the 1937 amendment to the Constitution, secularism was introduced as one of the six basic principles of the Republic.

the principles of Kemalist secularism. These are the laws establishing secular education and civil marriage, adopting the Turkish alphabet and the international numerals, introducing the hat, closing the dervish convents, abolishing certain titles, and prohibiting the wearing of certain garments. Under Article 153 of the Constitution, no provision of the Constitution shall be construed as rendering unconstitutional the enumerated Reform Laws which aim at safeguarding the secular character of the Republic. In other words, such laws cannot be found unconstitutional by the Constitutional Court.

Another constitutional provision protecting the secular character of the State is the ban on the use of religion for political purposes. The Constitution prohibits the exploitation of religion or religious feelings for the purpose of political or personal benefit, and forbids even partial establishment of the fundamental social, economic, political, and legal order of the State upon religious principles. Persons who violate this provision shall be punishable under the pertinent laws, and political parties in violation of this provision shall be permanently disbanded by the Constitutional Court (Art. 19). Finally, Article 21 of the Constitution allows for governmental supervision of religious instruction by stating that «no educational institutions shall be set up that are incompatible with the principles of contemporary science and education.»

4. *Social State:*

One of the main differences between the Constitutions of 1924 and 1961 is the latter's emphasis on social and economic rights. The framers of the 1961 Constitution were rightly aware that a political democracy would not be healthy unless it were supplemented by economic and social democracy. The term «social state» is used by the Constitution to denote what is more commonly known as «welfare state» in the West, a term which comprises social rights, social security, and social justice.

Among the principal social rights introduced by the Constitution may be cited the right to unionize, the right to strike, the right of collective bargaining, the right to vacation with pay, the right to social security, the right to medical care and the right to education. The State is charged with the responsibility for establishing social security and social welfare organizations for all citizens (Arts. 42 - 53).

Social justice implies measures reducing inequalities in wealth and income. One group of such measures is progressive taxation on income and various taxes on wealth. Another more specific one is land reform explicitly stated in the Constitution (Art. 38). In the case of expropriations *(kamulaştırma)* carried out with the purpose of distributing land to landless peasants, payment for expropriated lands can be made in equal installments over a period not exceeding twenty years. This was one of the most intensely debated articles of the Constitution in the Constituent Assembly, and ultimately the maximum period of payment was set as ten years. In the 1971 amendment of the Constitution, this period was extended to twenty years. Another measure that can be used for redistributing wealth and income is the nationalization of private enterprises under Article 39 of the Constitution. If a nationalization act provides for payment in installments, the repayment period may not exceed ten years.

A social welfare state requires a much greater degree of government intervention in social and economic affairs than is required under a liberal economy. Such intervention, in turn, makes planning an imperative. The Constitution of 1961 provides for economic and social planning and establishes a State Planning Organization charged with the responsibility of preparing long-term development plans (Arts. 41 and 129).

5. *The Rule of Law:*

The rule of law *(hukuk devleti),* or the supremacy of law, signifies a system where the governmental agencies must operate within the framework of law and their actions are subject to review by independent judicial authorities.[5] To put it differently, it is a system where the legal security of the individual is assured. Implicit in this definition are three elements absolutely essential to the rule of law: (a) judicial control of the legality of administrative acts; (b) judicial control of the constitutionality of laws; and (c) the independence of the judiciary.

In Turkey, as in most Continental European countries, the judicial control of the legality of administrative acts is performed not by the general courts but by administrative courts, at the apex of which is found the Council of State. As long as the administrative courts are accorded the same degree of independence as are the

---

[5] See also, Ch. 3, below.

general courts, such a dual judicial structure does not, in any way, impair the principle of the rule of law. One of the fundamental safeguards for the rule of law is embodied in Article 114 of the Turkish Constitution, which states that «all acts and actions of the administration are subject to judicial review.» In other words, access to the courts on account of administrative acts or actions cannot be barred by law, as was sometimes done before the adoption of the Constitution of 1961. This article also instructs the administrative courts not to refuse to deal with cases involving administrative acts or actions. Prior to 1961, the Turkish Council of State did refuse to intervene on certain occasions, stating that the acts involved were of a highly political nature and, therefore, beyond the scope of judicial review. Under the present Constitution, the administrative courts are not allowed to engage in such self-limitation by creating a category of «acts of state» or «political questions» *(hükûmet tasarrufları)* immune to judicial review.

While judicial review of administrative acts is necessary to the rule of law, if judicial review of the constitutionality of laws is not also established, the legislature would be legally free to restrict the basic rights and liberties of the individual at will.

As long as such restrictions are imposed by law, administrative courts can provide no protection for the individual. It would even be possible, as mentioned above, for the legislature to pass laws excluding certain administrative acts from judicial review and thus further destroy the basis of the rule of law. There is no reason to limit the meaning of the rule of law to the legality of administrative acts. On the contrary, it implies that *all* branches and agencies of government have to conform to law in their respective fields of activity. Just as the administrative agencies are bound by legislative acts, so the legislature is bound by the constitution. Consequently, judicial review of the constitutionality of laws is just as natural, and as indispensable, an ingredient of the rule of law as judicial review of the legality of administrative acts. Judicial review of the constitutionality of laws will be treated in greater detail below.

Another indispensable element of the rule of law is the independence of the judiciary. If judges remained under the influence of political departments (i.e., the legislative and the executive branches), judicial review, of either legislative or administrative acts, would lose much of its significance. This too, will be discussed in greater detail below.

The Constitution of 1961 provides further safeguards for the rule of law. One is the non-retroactivity of criminal laws. Article 33 states that «no person shall be punishable for an act not considered an offense under the law in force at the time the act was committed.» Similarly, «no person shall be punishable with a heavier penalty than that provided in the law for that offense at the time the offense was committed.» Another safeguard is the principle of «legal (or natural) judicial process» *(kanunî yargı yolu)* laid down in Article 32, according to which no one can be put to trial before a court other than the one previously determined by law. No extraordinary judicial bodies can be established which would lead to the violation of this principle. Finally, «denial of justice» is specifically prohibited by the Constitution. Under Article 31, no court of law shall refuse to deal with a case within its jurisdiction. All these constitutional safeguards are essential to the maintenance of the legal security of the individual, the underlying principle of the rule of law.

III. THE LEGISLATURE

The Constitution of 1961 vests the legislative authority in the Turkish Grand National Assembly. Such authority cannot be delegated to any other branch of government (Art. 5). The Turkish Grand National Assembly is composed of two chambers: the National Assembly and the Senate of the Republic. Thus, the Constitution of 1961 departed from the unicameralism of the 1924 Constitution by creating a bicameral legislature. Although there was, among the makers of the 1961 Constitution, considerable consensus on the desirability of a second chamber, its method of election as well as its powers vis-à-vis the National Assembly were the subject of much heated discussion. The «Onar (or Istanbul) Committee,» composed of university professors charged with the task of preparing a draft constitution prior to the establishment of the Constituent Assembly, had proposed a second chamber only partially based on popular vote. Under this scheme, one-third of the Senators would be elected by electors who must have completed at least secondary education, and the rest would be chosen by various institutions. The Constituent Assembly rejected this proposal as incompatible with democratic principles, and opted for a second chamber that better reflected the popular will. It also kept the powers of the second chamber much more limited than what had been proposed by the Onar Committee.

1. The Structure of the Legislature:

The National Assembly is composed of 450 deputies, all elected by direct, universal suffrage (Art. 67). To be eligible, one must be a Turkish national 30 years of age or over and literate in Turkish. In addition, those who have been sentenced for offenses enumerated in the Constitution are not eligible (Art. 68). The term of the Assembly is four years. However, the Assembly may decide to hold new elections any time before the termination of its regular four-year term (Art. 69). On the other hand, if new elections cannot be held in time due to a state of war, they may be postponed for one year by law (Art. 74). Under certain circumstances to be discussed below, the President of the Republic may also call new elections for the National Assembly (Art. 108).

The Senate of the Republic, in contrast, comprises three categories of members: 150 Senators are elected by universal suffrage; 15 Senators are appointed by the President of the Republic from among people distinguished for their service to the nation in various fields (at least ten of such members are to be appointed from among political independents); finally, the third category is that of *ex-officio* or life-time members *(tabiî üyeler)*. The latter are the former Presidents of the Republic and the members of the National Unity Committee (Art. 70). Thus, while the National Assembly is based entirely on popular vote, the Senate of the Republic includes non-elected members, even though the latter constitute a comparatively small minority. This explains why the Constitution granted more limited powers to the Senate than to the Assembly.

The Senate of the Republic differs also from the National Assembly in its term of office and its eligibility rules. The term of office for the Senators is six years, except, of course, the life-time members. One-third of the elected and appointed members of the Senate is renewed every two years. Consequently, the Senate of the Republic, in contrast to the National Assembly, is a body with a continuous life. It can neither call new elections, nor can it be dissolved by the President of the Republic. In order to be eligible, members have to have completed their fortieth year of age and have received university-level education. Members appointed by the President of the Republic are exempt from the education requirement (Arts. 72, 73).

As a rule, the two chambers convene and work separately. Only in special instances enumerated in the Constitution do they meet in joint session. These are the declaration of war (Art. 66), the election of the President of the Republic (Art. 95) and his impeachment (Art. 99), the initiation of a parliamentary inquiry into the conduct of the ministers and their impeachment (Art. 90), the approval of the declaration of martial law (Art. 124), the approval of the decision by the Council of Ministers to take over the administration of the universities (Art. 120), and certain special cases in the making of laws. (Art. 92, last para.).

Members of both chambers enjoy the classical parliamentary privileges, such as freedom of speech and freedom from arrest (Art. 79). Freedom of speech *(yasama sorumsuzluğu)* means that members of the Grand National Assembly shall not be held responsible for the votes cast, speeches made, and opinions expressed in the course of legislative activities or for repeating and disclosing those activities outside the legislature. Freedom from arrest *(yasama dokunulmazlığı)*, on the other hand, protects the legislators from what may be arbitrary or politically - motivated detentions or arrests. The Constitution (Art. 79) states that no member of the Grand National Assembly can be detained, questioned, arrested, or tried without a prior decision by the chamber of which he is a member. If the chamber decides to remove the member's freedom from arrest, the member concerned or any other member may request the Constitutional Court to review such decision. The Constitutional Court may invalidate it if it is found inconsistent with the Constitution or the Standing Orders *(İçtüzük)* of the chamber (Art. 81).

All legislative proceedings in joint sessions are to be conducted in accordance with the Rules or the Standing Orders made by the Turkish Grand National Assembly, and each chamber establishes rules for its own proceedings. Standing Orders must assure the participation of each parliamentary party group in all legislative activities in proportion to its size. A parliamentary party group consists of at least ten members (Art. 85). The principle of proportional representation also applies to the composition of the «chairmanship council» *(başkanlık divanı)* of each chamber. The

Constitution has taken further measures to assure the **impartiality** of the Speakers *(Başkan)* of both chambers (Art. 84).

2. *The Legislative Process:*

As indicated above, the Constitution has accorded the National Assembly much greater influence in the legislative process than the Senate of the Republic. Bills can be introduced either by the Council of Ministers or by members of both chambers (Art. 91). However, all bills are first debated in the National Assembly. Bills passed, amended, or rejected by the National Assembly are then referred to the Senate of the Republic. If the text passed by the National Assembly is also passed by the Senate without any amendments, it becomes a law. If the Senate makes amendments, such bill goes back to the National Assembly. If the Assembly agrees with the amendments made by the Senate, the bill again becomes a law. If it does not concur, a joint committee *(karma komisyon)*, composed of an equal number of members from both chambers, is set up to reconcile the conflicting texts passed by each chamber. The draft prepared by the joint committee is then referred to the National Assembly, which has the right to choose among the three texts before it (the ones previously passed by each chamber and the one worked out by the joint committee). Thus, the final decision rests with the National Assembly. However, if the Senate amendments are made by an absolute majority of its full membership, the Assembly can choose its own text only by a vote of an equivalent majority.

If a bill rejected by the National Assembly is also rejected by the Senate of the Republic, it fails to become a law. If a bill rejected by the Assembly is passed by the Senate, with or without amendments, the matter is again reviewed by the National Assembly. If the National Assembly concurs with the text passed by the Senate, it becomes a law. If it rejects it again, the bill fails. If the National Assembly amends the text passed by the Senate, the matter is referred to joint committee which operates in accordance with the rules described above.

In case the Senate totally rejects a bill by an absolute (or two-thirds) majority of its full membership, the National Assembly can override the Senate's opposition only by passing it by a vote of an equivalent majority.

Bills dealing with elections to the legislative bodies and local governments, or with political parties are subject to a slightly different procedure. If the need for a joint committee arises in connection with such bills, the draft prepared by the joint committee is debated and passed not by the National Assembly but by the joint session of the Turkish Grand National Assembly (art. 92). Thus, for bills of a highly political nature, the Constitution has somewhat enhanced the role of the Senate in comparison with its role on other measures. However, there is no doubt that the Senate's role in the legislative process remains, on the whole, secondary compared to that of the National Assembly.

3. *Control over the Executive:*

As in the enactment of laws, the final authority with respect to the legislative control over the executive rests with the National Assembly. The Turkish Constitution has adopted a «parliamentary» system of government, where the cabinet, or the Council of Ministers, can stay in office only so longs as it enjoys the confidence of the legislature. In other words, the legislature can force the cabinet to resign by withholding such confidence. This is called the «political responsibility» of the cabinet. In Turkey, however, the cabinet is politically responsible only to the National Assembly. While the Senate of the Republic may exercise a certain amount of control over the cabinet, it has no power to vote it out of office.

The means of parliamentary control at the disposal of both chambers independently from each other are questions *(soru)*, oral questions with debate *(genel görüşme)*, and parliamentary investigations *(meclis araştırması)*. Parliamentary inquiries *(meclis soruşturması)* can be conducted jointly by both chambers. Finally, interpellations *(gensoru)* are within the power of the National Assembly only (Arts. 88 - 90).

Quetions can be put to the Prime Minister or to other ministers by any member of either chamber. Depending upon the type of answer expected of the ministers, questions can be oral or written. However, even oral questions do not generate a debate in the chamber, since only the questioner can speak after the answer of the minister concerned.

Oral question with debate is a new and somewhat more effective means of control introduced by the Constitution of 1961. In contrast to questions, here the minister's answer is followed by a general debate. At the end of the debate, however, no vote is taken involving the question of confidence in the minister or the cabinet. This method of control, therefore, does not endanger the life of a cabinet or the stay in office of an individual minister.

Parliamentary investigations can be initiated by each chamber to secure information on or to expose certain aspects of the conduct of the cabinet. But they do not directly involve the political responsibility of the cabinet or of individual ministers, since no vote of confidence is taken at the end of such investigations. Parliamentary investigations may also aim at gathering information necessary for drafting new legislation.

Among all means of legislative control of the executive, interpellation is the most powerful. It is the only one through which the legislature can vote a cabinet or a minister out of office. Consequently, it is regulated in great detail by the Constitution. Motions for interpellation may be put by the political party groups in the National Assembly, or by at least ten deputies. Whether the motion is to be debated is determined at the end of a preliminary debate in which one of the deputies who put the motion, the Prime Minister or a minister, and a representative of each parliamentary party group can speak. If the Assembly decides to debate the interpellation, it also determines the date on which the debate will take place. At the end of the debate, members may put forward motions of censure or of no-confidence (*güvensizlik önergesi*). Such motions are voted upon after the lapse of one full day, called the «cooling-off period.» An absolute majority of the full membership of the National Assembly is required for a vote of censure. This last provision aims at increasing the stability of government by preventing votes of censure by very small and accidental majorities.

Finally, parliamentary inquiries may be initiated by a decision of the Turkish Grand National Assembly to ascertain criminal responsibility of the Prime Minister or individual ministers in matters connected with their office. The inquiry is carried out by a joint committee composed of an equal number of members from each chamber. At the end of the inquiry, the Turkish Grand National Assembly decides, in joint session, whether or not to impeach the minister concerned. In case of impeachment, the minister is tried by the Constitutional Court (Art. 90).

4. Budgetary Powers:

Consenting to new taxes is one of the oldest prerogatives of representative assemblies, dating back to the Middle Ages. In the present times, this has taken the form of approving the budget. The budget bill is submitted to the Grand National Assembly by the Council of Ministers at least three months before the beginning of the new fiscal year. The budget bill is first reviewed by a joint committee composed of 35 deputies and 15 senators. The text approved by the joint committee is debated first in the Senate of the Republic and then in the National Assembly. As in the making of laws and the control over the executive, the National Assembly has the final word upon the budget. A rejection of the budget bill by the National Assembly is considered an indirect vote of censure for the Council of Ministers (Art. 94).

IV. THE EXECUTIVE

In Turkey, as in all other parliamentary systems, the executive branch has a dual structure. It is composed of a politically active and responsible Council of Ministers, and a largely ceremonial and apolitical President of the Republic.

1. The President of the Republic:

In contrast to the 1924 Constitution, the Constitution of 1961 has taken care to ensure the political neutrality and impartiality of the President of the Republic. The President is elected by the joint session of the Turkish Grand National Assembly for a term of seven years from among its own members. To be eligible, he must be at least 40 years of age and have received university - level education. A vote by the two - thirds majority of the full membership of the Grand National Assembly is required for election. If this majority cannot be obtained on the first two ballots, an absolute majority of the full membership will suffice. The President is not eligible for re-election for a consecutive second term. The President-elect must resign from his political party, and his membership in the Grand National Assembly is terminated upon his election (Art. 95).

As indicated above, the role of the President in the Turkish constitutional system is largely a ceremonial one, symbolizing the continuity of the State and the unity of the nation. Although the President shares in the exercise of the executive function (Art. 6), he is not authorized to act alone in executive matters. All presidential decrees must be counter-signed by the Prime Minister and the ministers concerned, who will bear political responsibility for such decrees (Art. 98). The President is not politically responsible for his actions connected with his office. Since it is one of the fundamental principles of public law that authority and responsibility must follow each other, the absence of responsibility of the President and the requirement of counter-signature in all presidential decrees imply that the executive function is, in reality, exercised by the politically responsible component of the executive branch, i.e., the Council of Ministers.

The President's freedom from responsibility is also extended to criminal matters connected with his office. Here, too, the responsibility is assumed by the Prime Minister and the ministers concerned. The President can be held criminally responsible only for high treason *(vatan hainliği)*, in which case he may be impeached by a vote of a two-thirds majority of the full membership of the Turkish Grand National Assembly and is tried by the Constitutional Court (Art. 99).

The President of the Republic, in addition to his participation in the exercise of the executive function, is constitutionally empowered, as the head of the State, to appoint the diplomatic representatives of the Turkish Republic and to receive the diplomatic representatives of foreign states, to ratify and promulgate international treaties, to promulgate laws, to pardon or commute criminal sentences on account of illness or old age, and to act as commander-in-chief of the nation's armed forces (Arts. 93, 97, 110). The Constitution has also accorded him certain powers which, being unrelated to the executive function, can be used by the President acting alone, i.e., without the counter-signature of the Prime Minister and the ministers concerned. These are the right to appoint 15 members of the Senate of the Republic (Art. 70) and two judges to the Constitutional Court (Art. 145), to designate the Prime Minister (Art. 102), to return laws passed by the Turkish Grand National Assembly for reconsideration (Art. 93), and to bring a suit of unconstitutionality against any law passed by the Turkish Grand National Assembly (Art. 149).

2. *The Council of Ministers:*

The Council of Ministers *(Bakanlar Kurulu)* is composed of the Prime Minister and the ministers. The Prime Minister is designated by the President of the Republic from among the members of the Turkish Grand National Assembly. The ministers are nominated by the Prime Minister and appointed by the President of the Republic (Art. 102). The legal existence of the Council of Ministers starts at the moment of such appointment, not at the date it receives a vote of confidence in the National Assembly. In contrast to the 1924 Constitution, the Constitution of 1961 does not require the ministers to be chosen from among the members of the Turkish Grand National Assembly. In practice, however, most of them are.

The list of the Council of Ministers thus appointed is submitted to both chambers and the government program is read before each chamber not later than a week after the formation of the Council of Ministers. However, the program is submitted to a debate and a vote of confidence only in the National Assembly. Debate on the program begins after two full days following the reading of the program, and the vote of confidence is taken after one full day following the termination of the debate. These also are instances of «cooling-off» periods provided by the Constitution. No special majority is required for the vote of confidence; an ordinary majority (i.e., a majority of those present and voting in the Assembly) is sufficient (Art. 103).

As the chairman of the Council of Ministers, the Prime Minister ensures coordination among the ministries and supervises the implementation of the general policy of the government (Art. 105). In modern parliamentary systems, he is the effective head of the executive branch. The fact that he is normally the leader of the majority party in the National Assembly confers upon him a degree of political influence far greater than that of his colleagues in the Council of Ministers. He also enjoys certain constitutional privileges not shared by the other ministers. For example, he alone may request a vote of confidence in the National Assembly, after consultation with the Council of Ministers (Art. 104). Similarly, he alone has the right to request the President of the Republic to call new elections for the National Assembly under the conditions provided by Article 108 of the Constitution.

In a parliamentary system, the ministers assume two kinds of political responsibility. One is the «collective responsibility» for the general policy of the government, shared jointly and equally by all ministers. If the Council of Ministers falls as a result of a vote of censure, no individual minister can stay in office claiming that he has not personally approved of, or participated in, the government policy censured by the National Assembly. In addition, each minister is individually responsible for matters within the jurisdiction of his own ministry and for the acts of his subordinates (Art. 105). Thus, the National Assembly may choose to declare, through an interpellation, its lack of confidence in an individual minister rather than unseat the entire Council of Ministers, in which case only the minister concerned loses his position, without any legal requirement for the rest of the Council of Ministers to do the same. However, this is a very rare occurrence in modern parliamentary systems. Apart from this political responsibility, the ministers are also held criminally responsible for offenses connected with their office. As we have seen above, such responsibility is ascertained through a parliamentary inquiry, and in the case of impeachment, the minister is tried by the Constitutional Court.

The Constitution has taken certain measures to increase governmental stability by strengthening the Council of Ministers vis-à-vis the National Assembly. For example, while the vote of confidence taken following the formation of a new Council of Ministers does not require more than an ordinary majority, a vote of censure (either at the end of interpellation debates or as a result of a request of confidence by the Prime Minister) requires an absolute majority of the full membership of the National Assembly, i.e., 226 votes. «Cooling-off» periods mentioned above are other examples, designed to prevent hasty and emotional decisions on the part of the National Assembly and to provide some time for backstage negotiations and maneuvering which may save the life of a cabinet. However, the Constitution has permitted the executive branch to call new elections for the National Assembly (more commonly known as the power of dissolution) only under very exceptional circumstances. Thus, under Article 108 of the Constitution, the Prime Minister cannot request the President to dissolve the National Assembly unless the Council of Ministers has been voted out of office twice within a period of 18 months and has now received another vote of censure. This rather limited right of dissolution does not offer any help in cases of protracted government crises when no majority, coalition can be formed.

Upon the dissolution of the National Assembly in accordance with Article 108, the ministers resign and the Prime Minister forms a Provisional Council of Ministers *(Geçici Bakanlar Kurulu)*, in which all parliamentary party groups in the National Assembly are proportionally represented, and the ministers of Justice, Interior, and Transportation are chosen from among the independent members of the Turkish Grand National Assembly (Art. 109).

V. THE JUDICIARY

1. The Independence of the Judiciary:

One of the main differences between the Constitutions of 1924 and 1961 lies in the roles they accorded to the judiciary. The Constitution of 1924 established the judiciary as a separate and independent branch of government (Art. 8) and stated that the judges were independent in the trial of all cases and in the rendering of their verdicts. Even the all-powerful Grand National Assembly was not allowed to modify, postpone, or dispense with the decisions rendered by the courts (Art. 54). However, as in the case of civil liberties, the Constitution did not provide effective safeguards for these principles and left their interpretation to the will of the Grand National Assembly. Thus, it stipulated that judges could not be dismissed «under any circumstances or manner other than specified by law,» and that the qualifications of judges, their powers, responsibilities, compensations, and the manner of their appointment and dismissal were to be determined by special law (Arts. 55, 56). It would not be wrong to say that, under these provisions, the judiciary enjoyed independence from the political departments only to the extent that the Grand National Assembly wished to grant it such independence. In fact, prior to 1961, the laws pertaining to the organization and functions of the judiciary also contained several mechanisms exposing the courts to the undue influence of the executive branch.

Consequently, the Constitution of 1961 has taken special care to protect and safeguard the independence of the judiciary. One such measure is the provision that all judges may hold their office until they reach the constitutionally prescribed retirement age, namely sixty-five. They may not be dismissed, retired, or be deprived of their salaries even on account of the abolishment of a court (Arts. 133, 134). The Constitution has also established a «Supreme Council of Judges» *(Yüksek Hâkimler Kurulu)* charged with the personnel matters of the judges, such as appointments, promotions, transfers, disciplinary prosecutions, and dismissals. This body is composed of eleven regular and three alternate members, elected by the plenary session of the Court of Cassation *(Yargıtay)* from among its own members (Arts. 143, 144).

The jurisdiction of the Supreme Council of Judges is limited to the judges of the general courts *(adlî mahkemeler)*. Nevertheless, the Constitution has also provided safeguards for the judges of the other two court systems, namely the administrative and the military courts. Thus, the judges of the Council of State are elected by the Constitutional Court from among the candidates nominated, in equal numbers, by the Council of Ministers and by the plenary session of the Council of State itself (Art. 140). Similarly, the judges of the Military Court of Cassation *(Askerî Yargıtay)* are appointed by the President of the Republic from among the candidates nominated by the plenary session of the Military Court of Cassation (Art. 141). In other words, both Courts have nominating powers with respect to their new members and, in the case of the Council of State, the final appointment power also rests with another judicial body, namely the Constitutional Court. Furthermore, the Constitution states that personnel matters pertaining to the judges of both Courts are to be regulated by law «in accordance with the principles of the independence of the judiciary and tenure for judges» (Arts. 140, 141).

In the 1973 amendment of the Constitution, a new system of criminal courts, called the State Security Courts *(Devlet Güvenlik Mahkemeleri)*, was added to the judicial system to deal with cases involving the security of the State. These courts are composed of civilian and military judges; while they are supposedly part of the general courts system and subject to the review of the Court of Cassation, they do not conform to the principle of the independence of the judiciary. Judges of the State Security Courts are nominated by the Council of Ministers and appointed by the Supreme Council of Judges; the military judges serving on these courts are also nominated by the Council of Ministers and are appointed in accordance with the procedure provided in the law (Art. 136). The fact that a political body is thus given complete control over the nominations deprives the State Security Courts of much of their independence and exposes them to political influences. The Constitutional Court invalidated the law regulating the State Security Courts; since a new law on the subject had not been passed, these courts were not in operation at the time of this writing.

2. The Constitutional Court and Judicial Review of the Constitutionality of Laws:

The Turkish Constitution of 1961 established, following the example of certain post - World War II constitutions (notably, the German and the Italian), a system of judicial control of the constitutionality of laws. Among the drafters of the Constitution, there was virtual unanimity on the need for such a system. However, some debate took place regarding the type of court, its organization and composition, the method of selecting the judges, and access to the court; compromises were reached on most of these points.

The Turkish Constitution opted for a special court specifically designed to exercise judicial control over the constitutionality of laws, rather than granting such power to the general courts as in the case of the United States. However, in exceptional cases to be discussed below, general courts are also empowered to render a decision on the constitutionality of a particular law involved in a pending trial; but such decisions by the general courts are binding only on the individual case in question.

As to the organization and composition of the Constitutional Court, a compromise was reached to the effect that some of the judges were to be selected by judicial bodies and the rest by political departments. Thus, of the fifteen regular members of the Constitutional Court, four are selected by the Court of Cassation, three by the Council of State, and one by the Court of Accounts (*Sayıştay*) from among their own members. Three members are elected by the National Assembly and two by the Senate of the Republic. The President of the Republic selects two members, one of whom is selected from among three candidates nominated by the Military Court of Cassation. Of the five alternate members, two are selected by the Court of Cassation and one each by the Council of State and the legislative assemblies (Art. 145).

The Constitutional Court thus organized is accorded complete independence from the political departments. All judges of the Constitutional Court, whether they are selected by judicial or political bodies, hold their office until they retire at the age of sixty-five. The political departments (the legislative and the executive) have no removal power over the judges. Apart from age, their office may be terminated only upon conviction of an offense entailing dismissal from the judicial profession or for reasons of health. In the latter case, the Constitutional Court itself decides on the termination of the membership.

Access to the Constitutional Court can be secured in two ways : principal proceedings, i.e., those instituted by a governmental organ; and incidental proceedings, arising out of a pending trial. Principal proceedings *(iptal dâvası)* can be instituted by the President of the Republic, political party groups in each legislative chamber, political parties which have obtained at least ten per cent of the total valid votes cast in the last general elections for the National Assembly, or at least one-sixth of the full membership of each legislative chamber. Such access is also granted to the Supreme Council of Judges, the Court of Cassation, the Council of State, the Military Court of Cassation, and the universities, but only «in matters pertaining to their existence and functions» (Art. 149). Suits of unconstitutionality must be initiated within ninety days following the promulgation of the law in question in the Official Gazette (Art. 150).

In contrast to principal proceedings, incidental proceedings can be initiated by any individual and are not subject to any time limit. In other words, the individual may, during proceedings in regular courts, secure the judicial review of legislation which allegedly infringes upon his rights. However, access to the Court is dependent upon two conditions. First, such a plea of unconstitutionality *(anayasaya aykırılık itirazı)* must be put forward in the course of a pending trial; second, the regular court trying the case must itself determine whether the access to the Constitutional Court is justified. In the event that it does, the court adjourns the proceeding and refers the matter to the Constitutional Court, which must decide the matter within six months. If no decision is reached by the Constitutional Court within the six month period, the regular court itself decides upon the question of constitutionality. This is the only case where regular courts are empowered to pass judgement upon the constitutionality of laws (Art. 151).

The jurisdiction of the Constitutional Court includes the constitutionality of laws, law-amending ordinances *(kanun gücünde kararnameler)*, and the Standing Orders of the legislative assemblies. The Constitutional Court is also empowered to review and decide whether the procedural rules are complied with in constitutional amendments (Arts. 147, 64). When a law is invalidated by the Constitutional Court, it becomes ineffective as of the date of publication in the Official Gazette of the Court's decision. If the Court deems it necessary, it can set some later date as the effective date of its decision. However, this date cannot be more than one year from the date of publication of the original decision. Decisions involving invalidation are not retroactive, meaning that the invalidated laws are considered valid until the date of the implementation of the Court's decision. The legislative and the executive branches have no power whatsoever to modify or postpone the decisions rendered by the Constitutional Court (Art. 152).

In addition to its main function of reviewing the constitutionality of laws, the Constitutional Court also performs functions specifically accorded to it by the Constitution, such as trying impeachment cases (Art. 147) and deciding on the unconstitutional activities of political parties (Art. 57).

SELECTED BIBLIOGRAPHY

Aldıkaçtı, Orhan : **Anayasa Hukukumuzun Gelişmesi ve 1961 Anayasası**, (İstanbul 1973).

Sosyal, Mümtaz : **100 Soruda Anayasanın Anlamı** (İstanbul 1976).

Tunaya, Tarık Z. : **Siyasî Müesseseler ve Anayasa Hukuku** (İstanbul 1975).

Arsel, İlhan : «Constitutional Law,» pp. 21-48 in Tuğrul Ansay and Don Wallace, Jr. (eds.), **Introduction to Turkish Law** (Ankara 1966, Society of Comparative Law).

Dodd, C. H. : **Politics and Government in Turkey** (Berkeley : Univ. of California Press, 1969).

Frey, Frederick W. : **The Turkish Political Elite** (Cambridge, Mass. : M.I.T. Press, 1965).

Giritli, İsmet : **Fifty Years of Turkish Political Development, 1919-1969** (İstanbul, 1969).

Kemal, Karpat H. : **Turkey's Politics : The Transition to a Multi-Party System** (Princeton, N. J. : Princeton University Press, 1959).

Kili, Suna : **Turkish Constitutional Developments and Assembly Debates on the Constitutions of 1924 and 1961** (İstanbul : Robert College Research Center, 1971) (This book includes the texts of the Constitutions of 1876, 1924 and 1961).

Lewis, Bernard : **The Emergence of Modern Turkey** (London : Oxford University Press, 1968).

Özbudun, Ergun : **Social Change and Political Participation in Turkey.** (Princeton, N. J. : Princeton University Press, 1976).

Robinson, Richard D. : **The First Turkish Republic : A Case Study in National Development** (Cambridge, Mass. : Harvard University Press, 1963).

Texts :

Constitution of the Turkish Republic (Tr.: Balkan/Uysal/Karpat) (Ankara 1961).
The Turkish Constitution (Translated and Presented by the «Week», a weekly journal) (Ankara 1961).
Blaustein and Flanz (Eds.): **Constitutions of the Countries of the World, Turkey** (With the 1973 amendments) By Flanz and Arsel (Oceana, New York 1976).

CHAPTER 3

ADMINISTRATIVE LAW

Assoc. Prof. Dr. Rona AYBAY *

I. INTRODUCTION

A. Nature and Subject Matter of Administrative Law:

Administrative law is a branch of public law.[1] It is the body of rules which regulates the relations of the administrative authorities with private citizens, determines the legal status of State officials, and indicates the rights and liabilities of individuals in their dealings with these officials as representatives of the State. The procedure by which these rights and liabilities are enforced is also regulated by administrative law. In short, administrative law is the body of law built up around administrative actions and decisions.

Since statutes are often written in general terms, administrative authorities find it necessary and are permitted to take regulatory measures in order to apply the general rules to individual cases and problems. The legal rules which govern the methods and procedures under which these regulatory measures are taken also constitute a part of administrative law. Thus administrative law deals, primarily, with the status, powers, and activities of administrative authorities.

Apart from the classical or traditional functions of the State, such as maintaining order and security in the society, every State

---

* Faculty of Administrative Sciences, Middle East Technical University and the Hacettepe University. The author wishes to pay tribute to the late Professor *Tahsin B. Balta* who wrote the chapter on Administrative Law in the first edition of this book. Prof. *Balta*'s loss to the legal world will long be deeply felt.

[1] The Roman jurists under the influence of Greek philosophy, juxtaposing the state and individuals, divided the whole body of legal rules into public law *(jus publicum; kamu hukuku)* and private law *(jus privatum; özel hukuk)*. According to the famous definition by Ulpian, one of the great Roman jurists, «*public law is that branch of the law which focuses on the status of the Roman State, i.e., the interests of the community, while private law considers the interests of individuals.*» (Digest, 1.1.1.2)

The division between public and private law has served certain practical and pedagogical purposes for centuries and was utilized, especially by German scholars of the nineteenth century, to build a highly systematized body of law. Yet, it also is a fact that there are cases where elements of public and private law are closely interwoven. This may be observed especially in those fields of law which have emerged as a result of modern developments. Thus, some doubts have arisen as to the validity of the distinction between public law and private law areas.

is currently engaged in extensive activites in the fields of economics, education, health, communications, etc. Instead of confining itself to defence, public order, and a few other general matters, the modern State also provides elaborate social services through different agencies of the public administration. This is especially true in the case of a country like Turkey, which declares in its Constitution that it is a S o c i a l S t a t e , i.e. a State which is committed to undertaking new and greater responsibilities pertaining to the economic and social life of the country.

Obviously, the expanding functions of the State bring about new powers, and new powers require new kinds of political and legal control.

In order to carry out these extensive functions, the State needs vast cadres of personnel called administrative agents, (public functionaries or civil servants).

Civil servants have considerable discretionary authority *(takdir yetkisi)* for instance, the right to grant or refuse a licence. Thus they have power to interfere with freedom, even though they cannot punish in the way the courts can. Again, it is administrative law that governs the rights, duties, responsibilities, and procedures regulating the appointment of public functionaries.

There is a close connection between administrative law and public administration. Sometimes administrative law is understood to mean the law relating to public administration; yet public administration is only partly governed by administrative law. Certain organizations within the public administration, such as public enterprises, are governed, especially in their commercial transactions, by the rules of private law.

The State also needs financial means to carry out its functions and secures these through taxes and revenues. Administrative law, therefore, also covers the rules which are applicable to financial matters. That is to say, tax regulations are included in administrative law in its broadest sense.

B. General Characteristics of Administrative Law :

When it is compared with civil law, for instance, administrative law may appear as a n e w and d e v e l o p i n g   branch of law. This is a natural consequence of the fact that both modern societies and the administrative functions they require are constantly and rapidly changing. The effect of this continuing change can be seen in the field of administrative law more clearly than in other or older branches of law. This is why the administrative law may appear to be more d y n a m i c than many of the other branches of law.

Another important characteristic of administrative law is that it is u n c o d i f i e d. There is no single fundamental code which applies to the field of administrative law as a whole. This branch of law is so vast and complex that to regulate it by a single document is practically impossible. However, this should not be interpreted to suggest that administrative law is based on unwritten rules. In fact, almost every statute passed has some provisions falling within the scope of administrative law. This is a natural consequence of the fact that to be put into practice every statute needs some special administrative measures on the part of the administrative authorities.

Mainly because of the absence of a fundamental code embodying the general principles of administrative law, the role played by court decisions in the formation and development of administrative law is more important than in many other fields of law.

C. Development of Administrative Law in Turkey :

The early stages of the formation of administrative law in Turkey were related to the western-oriented reform movements, beginning with the *Tanzimat Fermanı* (Edict of Reorganization) of 1839. As a result of these reforms (especially during the 1860's), the foundations of the main administrative institutions of the present day, such as the Council of State and provincial and local administration, were laid down. The first courses on administrative law were introduced in the Law and Political Science *(Mülkiye)* Schools in 1890's.[2]

The real emergence of administrative law, however, came in the Republican era when a system of administrative courts, modelled on the French system, was established in 1927.

Although both the practices and court decisions have been heavily influenced by French administrative law, recent developments and cases decided by the *Danıştay* (Council of State) indicate that there is now a tendency toward creating a Turkish administrative law based on local realities, more independent from its French parent.

---

[2] İbrahim Hakkı Paşa's *«Hukuku İdare»* (Administrative Law) published in two volumes in 1891 and 1892 was the first book on this subject in Turkish.

II. SOME FUNDAMENTAL PRINCIPLES

Certain basic principles, such as the r u l e o f l a w and s e c u l a r i s m have had a formative effect on administrative law. These principles are either directly provided for in the text of the Constitution or are implicit in the spirit of the country's public law.

Some of these principles may be briefly summarized as follows:

A. The Rule of Law [3]:

When Article 2 of the Constitution describes the Turkish Republic as a S t a t e o f L a w *(Hukuk Devleti)* it refers to the concept of the rule of law as it is understood in Anglo - American jurisprudence. This, however, is not easy to define as a legal principle.

In a simple sense the rule of law has to do with a government providing legal security for the individual. In this sense, the rule of law requires that every action taken by the administration must be in strict conformity with law. This refers to the concept of the rule of law as opposed to the concept of the p o l i c e s t a t e which assumes that the government and its servants are not bound by law.

In a decision rendered by the Turkish Constitutional Court, the rule of law has been defined as:

> "... a State that respects human rights and establishes a just order of law whereby these rights are protected and maintained.
>
> All actions and functions of such a State must be in conformity with law and the Constitution. In a State bound by the principle of rule of law, the law absolutely prevails over all institutions of the State, including the Legislature".[4]

The principle of rule of law also means that the law must not give the government «too much» power. True, the public authorities in any State are set up to administer, but in a State bound by the principle of rule of law, the individual should not be regarded as a person who is only governed by the authorities. He is also in a position to benefit from and enjoy public services

---

[3] See Chapter 2, II 5 on the Constitutional Law.
[4] Decision rendered on the case related to the Law No. 6195; Dated Oct. 11, 1963, Official Gazette, Nr. 11572, dated 4.12.1963. 1 Anayasa Mahk. Kar. Der. 343 (348).

which, under the law, must be operated effectively through the participation of citizens. Thus, the real implementation of the principle of rule of law requires the existence of a democratic political system. Among other concepts which are closely and intimately connected with the principle of rule of law are h u m a n r i g h t s, e q u a l i t y, j u d i c i a l r e v i e w o f l e g i s l a t i v e a n d a d m i n i s t r a t i v e a c t s and t h e i n d e p e n d e n c e o f t h e j u d i c i a r y.[5]

In fact, these concepts may be regarded as the means through which the ideal of the rule of law can be put into practice.

B. Legality of Public Administration :

Article 6 of the Constitution prescribes that «the Executive function shall be carried out... within the framework of law.» In addition to the general principle of the rule of law, this provision provides for an effective limitation of possible arbitrary rule by the Administration :

(i) In contrast to the Legislative and Judicial branches which are referred to as p o w e r s, *(yetki)* (Arts. 5 and 7) the Constitution regards the Executive as a f u n c t i o n *(görev)* ;

(ii) The Executive branch and the institutions of public administration have to act in accordance with the statutes *(kanunlar)* enacted by the Legislature.

These characteristics reflect the concept of the superiority of Legislature and Judiciary over the Executive and deny the administration any «inherent» power. In order to exercise any authority, the administration must be specifically empowered by a law passed by the Legislature. This does not mean, however, that the administration does not possess any rule-making power.

C. Secularism[6] :

Secularism has been regarded as one of the most important achievements of the political and social reform program introduced in Turkey under the leadership of Atatürk, the founder of the Turkish Republic.[7]

In 1937, by an amendment to the 1924 Constitution then in effect, secularism was declared to be a constitutional principle.

---
[5] See the Constitution, Art. s. 2, 12, 114, 132, 133, 149, 151.
[6] See Chapter 2, II, 3 on the Constitutional law.
[7] «Reforms of Atatürk» are directly referred to in the Preamble of the present Constitution. The Preamble is an integral part of the text of the Constitution (Art. 156).

The present Constitution, which was enacted in 1961, recognized secularism as one of the fundamental characteristics of the Republic (Arts. 2; 153).

The 1961 Constitution contains lengthy provisions regulating matters related to the freedom of faith (Arts. 19, 57). Private individuals, societies, and political parties are explicitly prohibited from exploiting religion and religious feelings for political benefit; yet there is no direct provision which requires that the administration should uphold the spirit of secularism. This, however, may be inferred from the fact that the principle of equality recognized in the Constitution (Art. 12) requires a neutral position before any religious denomination on the part of the administration.[8] Yet, the fact that the Office of Religious Affairs *(Diyanet İşleri Başkanlığı)*, which deals only with Islam, is made a constitutional organ (Art. 154) raises some doubts about this neutrality. It should be mentioned, however, that the existence of such an Office incorporated in the General Administration may be justified by certain peculiarities of Turkish society, such as the fact that the overwhelming majority of the population is Muslim together with the economic and moral power possessed by the religious foundations which were inherited from the Ottoman Empire.

D. Indivisibility of Administration and Centralism :

Turkey is a unitary State, therefore there can be no political or administrative entity with «reserved powers» in the sense of federalism, within the boundaries of the Turkish Republic. The departments and units of public administration may take diversified forms as to their organization, functions, possessions and the personnel they employ, but they all constitute the same body of the Administration. «In terms of organization and functions, the Administration is a whole» (Cons., Art. 112/2). The harmony and cooperation between various parts of the Administration are to be regulated and secured by laws. The statutes related to the administrative structure may prescribe different types of organization for various parts, yet the principle of unity and indivisibilty of administration must always be taken into account.

The Constitution recognizes the principle of d e c e n t r a l i z a t i o n alongside c e n t r a l i z a t i o n as a basis for the

---

[8] On the other hand, Art. 119 prescribes that «... In the performance of their duties, civil servants... shall not discriminate between citizens on the basis of the latter's political views...»

organization and functions of public administration. As an outcome of certain historical developments, however, centralism has far more weight in practice.

The units of local administration are subject to the control of the central administration exercised through the power of «tutelage» *(idari vesayet)*. Tutelage is regarded as a means by which the unity and indivisibilty of administration is guaranteed. One may argue, that the extent of tutelage in its present form is excessive and therefore constitutes an undue burden on local administration. It should be mentioned, however, that despite difficulties, local administrations have developed considerably during recent decades.

III. ADMINISTRATIVE ORGANIZATION

A. Introduction :

The administrative structure consists of the administrative organization and its functions. Obviously, officials (civil servants and other personnel) and public funds and property are also needed to render the services expected of the administration.

Administrative organizations may acquire legal personality only by statute or on the authority expressly granted by statute.

At the core of administrative organization is the Central Administration *(merkezi idare)* which is also called the General Administration *(genel idare)*. Subsidiary units of administration are created under the principle of decentralization.

B. Central Administration :

The Central Administration which is responsible for the most fundamental functions has its central departments together with provincial and regional branches.

1. Central Departments :

The President of the Republic is in a position to discharge certain administrative functions in addition to his political powers and functions : e.g. to promulgate the laws passed by Parliament, to sign the decrees related to the appointment of high-ranking civil servants, and to ratify and promulgate international treaties.

Since the President of the Republic is not accountable for actions connected with his duties, the Prime Minister and the other ministers specifically concerned are responsible for the decrees of the President. The most important figure of central administration, therefore, is the Prime Minister. As the head of the Council of Ministers, the Prime Minister promotes cooperation among ministries which are organized on a functional basis, i. e. each ministry is responsible for a certain function throughout the country.

In this connection it is interesting to note that the most important powers and functions related to the Armed Forces are in the hands of the Chief of the General Staff, who is directly responsible to the Prime Minister. The Ministry of National Defence performs armed forces activities other than those of personnel, intelligence, operations, training and mobilization.[9]

Some organizations of public administration such as the State Planning Organization, the State Institute of Statistics, and the Office of the Religious Affairs are attached directly to the Prime Ministry itself.

The Council of Ministers usually meets under the chairmanship of the Prime Minister[10] and discharges certain functions of an administrative nature in addition to its purely political functions. The promulgation of regulations (*tüzükler*) and decrees related to higher positions in the civil service may be cited as examples of the administrative functions of the Council of Ministers. Although the Council of Ministers would, under normal circumstances be expected to discharge its functions in group meetings, there are many cases where the decrees of the Council of Ministers are individually signed by its members without any deliberation in formal Council meetings.

Each of the ministries is headed by a minister who is a member of the Council of Ministers. Ministers of State (ministers without portfolio) also take part in the meetings and decisions. Ministers retain their legislative seats while serving in the Council of Ministers.[11]

Ministries may be established by the decision of the Prime Minister. There has been an increase in the number of ministries,

---

[9] See Law Nos. 1324 and 1325, dated July 31, 1970.
[10] The President of the Republic presides over the Council of Ministers whenever he deems it necessary.
[11] Those who are qualified for election as deputies may be appointed as ministers even if they are not actual members of Parliament. They enjoy the same immunities as the members of Parliament while serving as ministers.

due mostly to political expediency rather than to actual needs of administration.[12]

The ministers are not merely politicians, but also, as public officials, they supervise and discipline the administration within their own spheres. Each ministry is staffed by civil servants, and there is an undersecretary *(müsteşar)* in each ministry serving as the top administrative assistant to the minister. Although the organization charts of ministries vary according to the nature and extent of the functions, usually the principal units are headed by general directors who are responsible to the undersecretary. Auxiliary units, such as the Office of Legal Advisor and the Board of Inspectors, are common to almost all ministries.

In addition to the ministries, certain consultative and auxiliary organs are part of the central administration; e.g. the National Security Council *(Milli Güvenlik Kurulu)*, the High Planning Council *(Yüksek Planlama Kurulu)*, the Council of State *(Danıştay)* [13]

2. *Provincial Administration :*

In terms of central administrative organization the country is divided into provinces *(iller)* based on geographical and economic factors and on the requirements of public service. Provinces are divided into sub-provinces (counties, *ilçeler)*, which are further divided into districts *(bucaklar)*. The administration of each of these divisions is headed by an official who is the local representative of the government and has authority over all the civilian branches of the central administration in his area, including the police.[14]

Provinces and sub-provinces may be established by statute. The present number of provinces is 67. There are considerable

---

[12] It is interesting to note that creation of a ministry (or a division or merger between ministries) does not need to be authorized by a new statute. Law no. 4951 states that «State agencies are divided into ministries upon recommendation by the Prime Minister and approval by the President of Republic.» Although the great majority of ministries have their organic laws *(kuruluş yasaları)*, several have been established according to the procedure mentioned above. By mid-1977 the number of ministers was 29, including seven Ministers of State, three of whom also had the title of «Deputy Prime Minister.»

[13] *Danıştay*, the supreme administrative court (see V, E, 2, a) is at the same time the highest advisory body to the government. It submits opinions on drafts of legislation referred to it by the Council of Ministers, studies drafts of regulations, renders opinions on problems assigned by the Prime Ministry, etc.

[14] The armed forces stationed in the province are obliged to render assistance to the administration in cases of emergency upon the request of the governor (Law on the Administration of Provinces, No. 5442).

discrepancies between the provinces in terms of population, area, and economic and social development.[15] The same is true of sub-provinces, the number of which currently stands at 572.

The head of a province is the governor *(vali)* who is appointed by the Council of Ministers. The governor represents the government and is responsible to each of the ministers for the general administration in his province. The head of a sub-province is the sub-governor *(kaymakam)* who is appointed by a joint decree signed by the President of Republic, the Prime Minister, and the Minister of Interior. The head of a district is the director *(müdür)*, appointed by the Minister of Interior, at the direction of the governor. Recent reports on the reorganization of public administration suggest that the district be abolished as an administrative unit because it has not served the purposes for which it was established.

The Constitution states that provincial administration is based on the principle of «deconcentration» *(yetki genişliği)* i.e., a limited degree of devolution of authority, under which the higher officials of provincial administration are authorized to initiate certain administrative acts and decisions independently of the hierarchical control of the central departments. This provision is included with the intention of reducing the disadvantages of strict centralism.

On the other hand, regional self - governing organizations *(bölge kuruluşları)*, comprising several provinces may be established for the purpose of carrying out specific public services.

C. Local Administration :

Local authorities at provincial, municipal, and village levels are units of local administration. They are created to meet common local needs of the inhabitants of provinces, municipal districts or villages. The units of local administration are public corporate bodies with financial autonomy. Their deliberative bodies are elected by universal suffrage. Jurisdiction over the acquisition or loss of status by popularly elected administrative organs may be exercised only by courts.

1. *The Province (İl) as a unit of Local Administration:*

There is a provincial local authority in each of the 67 provinces. i.e. each province is at the same time a unit of local administration.

---

[15] Each province is a constituency (electoral district) in the parliamentary elections and therefore any change in the existing boundaries between the provinces may easily be labelled as «gerrymandering» by those who oppose it.

The names and boundaries of provincial authorities correspond to those of the province as an administrative unit of the Central Administration. In addition to being the representative of the Central Administration in the province, the Governor *(Vali)* is the head and executive officer of the provincial local authority.

The deliberative body of provincial administration is the Provincial General Council *(İl Genel Meclisi)* which is composed of the councillors *(İl Genel Meclisi Üyeleri)* popularly elected in the sub-provinces. The number of councillors is in proportion to the population of sub-provinces. Elections are based on proportional representation, and candidates are usually nominated by political parties. Nevertheles, the Provincial General Council must not, under the law, concern itself with party politics.

All the resolutions passed by the Provincial General Council are subject to the approval of the Governor. The Governor puts forward his objections to those resolutions of which he disapproves before the Council of State, whose decision, which must be rendered within two months, is final.

The Governor cannot be removed from his office as the head of provincial administration by a vote of non-confidence passed by the Provincial General Council. In certain cases, however, the Council may appeal to the Ministry of Interior for the removal of the Governor. In the light of such an appeal, which must be passed by a two-thirds majority in the Council, the Ministry may at its discretion transfer the Governor.

On the other hand, the Council of State has the power to dissolve the Provincial General Council upon the appeal of the Ministry of Interior, on certain grounds specified by law.

Each year the Provincial General Council elects four [16] of its members to form the Provincial Commission *(İl Encümeni)* which acts as the Council's Standing Committee under the chairmanship of the Governor.

2. *Municipalities* (Belediyeler) :

Each municipality is a legal entity responsible for organizing and performing activities to meet local and common needs of the municipal area and its inhabitants. Municipalities are created in all urban areas with over 2,000 inhabitants and in provincial and

---

[16] In smaller provinces where the number of councillors is less than 8, two members are elected for the Commission.

sub-provincial capitals, regardless of population. A new municipality may be set up by a decree signed by the President of Republic.[17]

In recent years, and in spite of the inadequacy of their legal basis (Law of Municipalities dated 1930), the municipalities have been very active and responsive in dealing with urban and regional problems.

The functions of the municipalities are enumerated in the Law of Municipalities.[18] Certain functions, such as those of ensuring the good order and cleanliness of public facilities and issuing licences for them, inspecting food and beverages with respect to sanitary conditions, and combatting epidemic and contagious diseases, are obligatory for all municipalities.[19] The law classifies certain other functions, such as the construction of municipal theatres, cinemas and hotels as optional functions.

The organs of the municipal administration are the Municipal Council, Municipal Standing Committee, and the mayor.

The Municipal Council *(Belediye Meclisi)* is comprised of municipal councillors *(Belediye Meclisi üyeleri)* who are elected for a term of four years directly by the electorate. The conditions of eligibility to vote in municipal elections are the same as those for provincial general councils. The elections are based on proportional representation. The number of councillors may not be less than 12 and varies according to the population. Candidates are generally nominated by political parties.

The Municipal Council debates and decides on matters such as the budget, final accounts, city plans, classification of streets and assignment of names and numbers, rates of municipal taxes, and municipal police regulations.

In contrast to the resolutions passed by the Provincial General Council, which must be approved by the Governor, most of the

---

[17] The procedure by which a new municipality is created involves a number of stages that take place before the approval by the President of Republic : e.g. the decision of the Provincial General Council and the Governor's opinion on the matter, examination by the Council of State.

[18] Law No. 1580, dated April 4, 1930.

[19] The Law creates certain additional duties for those municipalities whose financial resources are supposed to be sufficient for more extensive services; e.g. municipalities with an income of TL. 200.000 are required to establish dormitories for orphans and to provide free birth and child care homes; municipalities with an income of TL. 500.000 or more are required to build stadiums and municipal recreation centers.

It should be mentioned, however, that due to decline in the value of the Turkish Lira since 1930, the figures indicated in the law do not correspond to present realities. Those duties which were originally envisaged as obligatory only for the largest municipalities have now become obligatory for all municipalities.

decisions passed by the Municipal Council go into effect without any approval. Certain decisions like the budget, however, are put into action only by the approval of the top civilian authority of the locality, and for some more important decisions, like the receipt of long-term loans, the approval of the Council of State is required.

The Municipal Council may be dissolved by the Council of State on grounds specified by law.

The Municipal Standing Committee *(Belediye Encümeni)* is comprised of the mayor, municipal department directors, and members elected by the Municipal Council from among councillors. Members of the Committee are responsible to the Council. Among the matters and subjects within the powers of the Standing Committee are to transfer budgeted funds, to prepare rates for public transportation, to determine maximum prices, and to proclaim municipal fines.

The Mayor *(Belediye Başkanı)* is the head and executive organ of the municipal administration and is elected by the local voters for a four year term. The election is based on the principles of direct vote, simple majority, and single ballot. A candidate for mayor may be nominated by a political party, or he may be an independent candidate.

Until 1963 the mayor was elected by two-thirds majority of the plenary session of the Municipal Council. However, under the present law, in exceptional cases the mayors of municipalities which are municipal capital *(il merkezleri)* are appointed by the Ministry of Interior, and those of other municipalities by the Governor [20]; but it should be noted that such appointments are very rare in practice.

The mayor, as the top executive and representative of the municipality, has certain powers such as, executing regulations and prohibitions of the municipality, issuing instructions and orders, managing municipal property, and collecting revenues.

3. *The Village* (Köy):

A village is a unit with under 2,000 inhabitants, set up within a larger administrative unit. People living in collective or separate dwellings and having common property such as mosques, schools,

---

[20] In such cases, governors and deputy sub-governors may be appointed mayor.

pastures etc., constitute a village. In order to set up a village authority, the community in question must have no less than 150 and not more than 2,000 inhabitants.[21] The competent authority for creating villages is the Ministry of Interior.

The organs of the village administration are the village-meeting, the Council of Village Elders, and the Village Headman.

The Village Meeting *(Köy Derneği)* is comprised of all eligible voters who are registered as residents of the village. This meeting elects the Village Headman and the Council of Elders and has such powers as determining monthly and annual fees of the Village Headman and other employees of the village administration.

The Council of Elders *(İhtiyar Meclisi)* has elected and ex · officio members. The number of elected members is four in villages with a population of less than 1,000 and six in those with more than 1,000 inhabitants. They are elected in direct elections, by secret ballot, and simple majority. Political parties are prohibited from nominating candidates. This, however, does not exclude indirect influences exerted by the political parties. The village *imam* and the school headmaster are ex-officio members of the Council of Elders. The Council meets at least once a week and decides on village activities to be performed by villagers or by hired workers, and determines the amount of money villagers should contribute for the purpose of village work projects. Among the functions of the Council of Elders is the settlement of cases arising from default of payment through amicable settlement or by arbitration.

The Village Headman *(Muhtar)* is elected for a period of four years by the inhabitants of the village by a majority vote on a single ballot. Political parties must not, under the law, nominate candidates in the elections for village headmen. The Headman is the head of the village administrative functions, organizes villagers for collective work. etc. The Headman is also entrusted with a few central governmental tasks.

4. *Town Quarters* (Mahalle Teşkilâtı) :

Quarters of a town within a municipality constitute a type of organization similar to the local administration. It should be mentioned, however, that the town quarter is not a unit of local

---

[21] However, there are at the moment a number of villages with over 2,000 inhabitants which still do not have municipal status (see supra note 17).

administration in the constitutional sense. The head of a town quarter is elected by the inhabitants of the quarter by secret ballot and simple majority. Various laws in force assign certain duties to the town quarters. Among these duties are issuing certificates of birth, marriage, death ; participation in police search of domiciles ; issuing documents certifying poverty, good conduct, and residence.

5. Gökçeada (İmroz) and Bozcaada Administration:

Under the Lausanne Peace Treaty of 1923 two Aegean islands, İmroz and Bozcaada are treated as a special administrative unit under a deputy governor. Both islands are townships attached to the Çanakkale province but the Provincial Local Administration of Çanakkale does not cover İmroz and Bozcaada. The islands have their own special administrative organs.

6. Local Administration Unions:

Groups of municipalities, village administrations and provincial local administrations may form unions to perform their legally assigned functions through collective action. The Union may be formed upon unanimous approval of a set of by-laws by the municipal council, council of Village Elders and Provincial General Assembly. The formation is final upon approval of the Governor. If the member local administration units are from different provinces, final approval rests with the Ministry of the Interior.[22]

The organs of Local Administration Union are the Union Council, Union Standing Committee and the Union President. The Union Council *(Birlik Meclisi)* enjoys the powers of Municipal Councils within the limits of the powers delegated to the Union. Each member unit is represented by two councillors in the Union Council.

The Union Standing Committee *(Birlik Encümeni)* is comprised of four members elected by the Union Council from among its own members. The Union President *(Birlik Başkanı)* deals with the execution of decisions, budgetary expeditures, direction of other union activities and presides over the Union Committee. The Union

---

[22] «The Union of the Municipalities of Marmara Region» *(Marmara ve Boğazlar Belediyeler Birliği)*, which was created by the twenty municipalities of the Marmara Region embracing greater Istanbul in March 1975, is a good example of comprehensive and coordinated approaches to area-wide problems. Among the purposes for which the UMMR was formed are to construct, coordinate and maintain the major urban services such as water supply, public transport, tourism and to control pollution of air and water.

President and the Assistant President are elected at the first meeting of the Union Council for a four-year term of office. These officials are appointed by the Governor of the Province in which the Union headquarters are located, if the provincial local administration has participated in the Union. If the Union covers more than one province, then the President and his assistant are appointed by the Minister of Interior.

D. Functional Autonomous Corporations and Organizations
(Hizmet Yönünden Yerinden Yönetim Kuruluşları) :

The management of certain public services are organized as autonomous public corporate bodies which are to some extent beyond the strict control of central administration. Among these autonomous organizations are the Universities, the Turkish Radio and Television Corporation, the State Economic Enterprises, and the professional organizations classifiable as public institutions, such as the Bar Associations.

The degree of autonomy these units enjoy varies according to the extent of tutelage *(idari vesayet)* the Central Administration has over them. In the case of Universities, for instance, the tutelage of the Central Administration is at a minimum level, and therefore Universities enjoy the greatest autonomy. They are administrated by the organs and officers elected by their academic staff [23] and their autonomy is guaranteed by the Constitution (Art. 120).

Under the original version of the 1961 Constitution, the Turkish Radio and Television Corporation *(T.R.T.)* was to be an autonomous public corporate body but by a Constitutional amendment introduced in 1971, the word «autonomous» was deleted and replaced by the word «impartial» (Art. 121). Thus, the extent of autonomy the T.R.T. enjoys has been reduced.

Public Professional Organizations such as the Bar Associations *(Barolar)* and Engineers and Architects Association *(Mühendis ve Mimar Odaları)* are created by law, and their administrative bodies are comprised of officers elected from and by the members. The Constitution provides that the central administration may not remove elected officers of the professional organizations without a court judgement. Under the law no person may actually practice

---

[23] Middle East Technical University is an exception to this rule; its highest administrative body, the Board of Trustees is comprised of 9 members appointed by the Council of Ministers. See Constitution, Art. 120/2; Law No. 7307, dated May 27, 1959.

his profession without becoming a member of the relevant Association, provided that there is one in the field. It should be mentioned that in order to avoid any flavor of totalitarianism, the Constitution states that the by-laws of professional organizations, and their administration and activities shall not conflict with democratic principles (Art. 122). Among the purposes and functions of the various Public Professional Organizations are to preserve professional ethics and dignity and to make efforts in the interest of the public for the development of that profession.

The State Economic Enterprises (*İktisadî Devlet Teşekkülleri; Kamu İktisadî Teşebbüsleri*) are created to regulate economic life and to contribute to the development of the country through production and distribution. The origin of SEE's goes back to the early 1930's when it became evident that, despite efforts to encourage and stimulate private enterpreneurs, the economic and social development attained lagged far behind the expectations. The new Republican régime, therefore, felt compelled to intervene in the economic field directly and began creating «public corporations» owned by the State.

The State Economic Enterprises enjoy autonomy in their commercial activities and are subject to private law in their dealings with other parties. The most important of those carry the title of a «Bank», as for example *Sümerbank* or *Etibank*.

The Board of Directors of an SEE is usually comprised of four members and a General Director who acts as the Chairman, all of whom are appointed by the Council of Ministers. In certain SEE's a workers' representative takes part in the Board of Directors with full membership rights.

Various attempts have been made to improve the organization and operation of the SEE's which have increased in number and scope since the 1930's. The present law relating to the State Economic Enterprises has been an outcome of these attempts, conducted in the light of the 1961 Constitution.[24]

---

[24] Law No. 440, dated March 21, 1964. It should be noted that studies on the organization and operation of the State Economic Enterprises are continuing with a view to improving them.
Upon the invitation of the State Planning Organization, in 1971, a study was conducted by a group of experts who made several suggestions and recommendations covering personnel questions, problems of organization, finance, marketing, etc. Among these suggestions particular emphasis was given to measures to be taken with the aim of minimizing the ever increasing trend toward greater government intervention.

E. Public Personnel and Functionaries
(Kamu Görevlileri ve Memurlar) :

The human element in public service is the government employee, i.e. the public personnel *(kamu görevlileri)* as the term is commonly understood in Turkey. This is a broad term covering officers and employees in the service of the State or in its affiliated bodies, other than political bodies. Among these are the public functionaries (civil servants - *memurlar*), «workers» *(işçiler)*,[25] contract personnel *(sözleşmeli personel)* and employees paid on a daily basis *(gündelikli, geçici personel)*.

Although the larger part of the public personnel, public functionaries in particular, are governed by Administrative law,[26] there are certain categories, such as «workers» who are subject to the private law.

Public functionaries are defined as persons permanently appointed to regular and continuing state functions required by the public services.[27] Thus, they constitute the «core» of the public administration.

Public functionaries are required to commit themselves with loyalty to the Constitution and to comply, faithfully, with laws of the Republic. Their employment and promotion are based on the merit system *(liyakat sistemi).* The legal status of the public functionaries is based on the idea of life-long profession (career) and they are provided with legal guarantees and safeguards; except in cases specifically prescribed by law, no public functionary may be separated from service or deprived of his salary or other rights.

As a natural outcome of this, public functionaries are not permitted to join political parties, and are required to refrain from any discrimination based on language, race, sex, political affiliation, or religion while carrying out their duties.

In addition, public functionaries are not entitled to rights of collective bargaining and strike. Nor are they permitted to establish or join trade unions. (Constitution Art. 119 as amended in 1971).

---

[25] The application of the term «worker» *(işçi)*, as opposed to «white collar officer» *(memur)*, is the subject of some dispute and ambiguity in Turkey. As a matter of fact, there are some blue-collar workers employed in the public service who are classified as *memur* and some white-collar workers classified as *işçi*.

[26] Public personnel such as judges, teaching staff of Universities and military personnel are entitled to special statutes regulated by separate laws.

[27] See, Constitution, Art. 117, and the State Personnel Law (No. 657, dated July 23, 1965) Art. 4. The Criminal Code introduces a broader definition to this concept which is valid only in the field of Criminal Law (Cr. C. Art. 279).

Turkish citizenship is a prerequisite for entry into government service as a public functionary, whether it be acquired by birth or naturalization.

Entry into government service is, as a rule, through competitive examinations. A probationary - period *(adaylık süresi)* precedes the final appointment. The criteria for promotion and functions are defined by statutes. The pay system is based on graduated salary scales which are linked to the yearly budget passed by the Parliament.

The functionary is required to enforce orders and instructions he receives from his superiors, unless he deems them contrary to the provisions of by-laws, regulations, statutes, or the Constitution. A functionary who considers the order he receives illegal, must inform the person issuing it about the matter. Nevertheless, if the superior insists on the performance of his order and reiterates it in writing, it must be carried out. In such a case, the subordinate will not be held liable for torts arising from the enforcement of the order.

It should be mentioned, however, that the subordinate who carries out an order, which by its very nature constitutes a crime, is not absolved from criminal prosecution.[28]

As to the tort liability for damages done by the public functionaries through the exercise of their duties, under the State Personnel law, the injured person may sue the concerned public agency, which in turn may seek redress from the functionary [29] (Article 13).

The State Personnel Law prescribes a number of disciplinary penalties *(disiplin cezaları)* for the functionaries who fail to carry out their duties properly.[30]

---

[28] See, Const. Art. 125. There are special statutes regulating the commencement and conduct of the criminal proceedings against public functionaries. For offences related to their functions a preparatory investigation *(hazırlık soruşturması)* and a preliminary investigation *(ilk soruşturma)* are conducted, either by superior authorities directly or upon obtaining their permission. (Law No. 1609, dated May 15, 1930, and law related to the prosecution of the public functionaries, dated 1913, which is inherited from the Ottoman period). See below Ch. 11, Part. 3 on Criminal Procedure.

[29] Nevertheless, the injured party retains the right to sue the functionary for the injuries he has personally done, under the provisions of Code of Obligations relating to torts.

[30] The following are among the disciplinary penalties which might be imposed (in their order of seriousness) :
The warning *(uyarma)*, i.e. a notification made to the functionary with the aim of drawing his attenition to the fact that he must show more care and consciousness while

In order to avoid any arbitrary imposition of disciplinary penalties, there are certain procedural safeguards specified in the Constitution which require that the defendant be notified in writing of the allegations in question and provided with an opportunity to defending himself. Disciplinary actions are not exempted from the jurisdiction of courts of justice (Const. Art. 118).

F. Public Possessions *(Kamu Malları)* :

It is obvious that public administration can not fulfill its functions and render the services expected of it without having adequate means and property at its disposal. Immovable (real) *(taşınmaz mal)* or movable *(taşınır mal)* belongings of the state and its affiliated bodies fall into two main categories : public possessions *(kamu malları)* and private possessions *(devletin özel malları)*.

Public possessions include *res* in common use *(orta malları)* such as streets, highways, parks, which anyone may use reasonably. There are also *res* locally in common use, such as village harvest places which are only open to their inhabitants. Among the public possessions are those properties allocated to the fulfilment of a specific public service *(belli kamu hizmetlerine ayrılan mallar)*, e.g. hospitals, schools, military installations, weapons, and other military equipment. These are to be used only for the requirements of that particular service to which they are assigned.

On the other hand, in the absence of evidence to the contrary, no private ownership is possible in public waters or in places unsuitable for cultivation or in the springs issuing forth from them. (C.C. Art. 641). As for the mines and other natural resources, the Constitution states that the «natural wealth and resources shall be under the jurisdiction and at the disposal of he state.» [31]

All of the monuments and movable or immovable antiquities are, by virtue of law, owned by the State. Their excavation is subject to governmental authorization and supervision.[32]

---

performing his duties; the reprimand *(kınama)*; the temporary salary step delay *(kısa süreli durdurma)* and the long-term step delay *(uzun süreli durdurma)*, i.e. to delay the step increase *(kademe ilerlemesi)* for a certain period; suspension *(geçici olarak görevden çıkarma)*, i.e. to suspend the functionary from government service without pay for a temporary period varying from one month to six months; and discharge from government service *(devlet memurluğundan çıkarma)*.

[31] «The right to explore for and exploit them shall be vested in the state. Exploration and exploitation by the state in co-operation with private industry or directly by private industry shall require specific legislative authorization» (Constitution, Art. 130).

[32] Under the Law No. 1710, dated April 25, 1973, relating to antiquities *(Eski Eserler Kanunu)* the export of antiquities is prohibited.

Private possessions of the State and its affiliated bodies *(devletin özel malları)* such as property inherited by the State (C.C. Art. 448), are governed, as the term suggests, by private law. Nevertheless, they are immune from seizure *(haciz)* and the bodies that own these properties may sell or rent them only through certain procedures specified by laws.

IV. EMERGENCY POWERS OF ADMINISTRATION

It is a generally accepted principle of law that in time of war or other cases of public emergency threatening the life of the nation, any state may take measures to maintain order, dictated by the exigencies of the situation.[33]

In the event of a calamity or an impending threat of calamity such as a flood, an earthquake, or epidemic diseases, the authorities also may take emergency measures and impose restrictions and obligations.

The Constitution envisages that in cases of emergency forced labor and financial obligations, including the seizure of property, may be imposed upon citizens.[34] The procedures relating to the proclamation, enforcement, and termination of these obligations, however, must be specified and regulated by law. There are various statutes applicable in times of emergency. Among these is law no. 7269,[35] under which the governors and sub-governors in the calamity areas may call upon the able-bodied males for forced or compulsory labor.

The law relating to civil defence[36] provides for the recruitment of people to be armed against enemy infiltrations; this law does not exclude women from the service. Further, the law relating to currency control,[37] which authorizes the Council of Ministers to

---

[33] See, the European Convention on Human Rights (Art. 15); International Covenant on Civil and Political Rights (Art. 4); American Convention on Human Rights (Art. 27).

[34] Art. 123, Since the text of Art. 123 refers to citizens, one may ask whether aliens are altogether exempted from the imposition of emergency measures. It should be noted, however, that the rights and liberties enjoyed by aliens in Turkey, may, under the Constitution (Art. 13), be restricted in accordance with international law. This general rule may be applicable in cases of emergency, and measures enforced may affect all persons in the locality where the emergency administration is in force.

[35] Dated May 15, 1959 *(Umumi Hayata Müessir Afetler Dolayısiyle Alınacak Tedbirlerle Yapılacak Yardımlara Dair Kanun).*

[36] Law No. 4654, dated August 7, 1944.

[37] Law No. 1567 as amended by law no. 6250, dated February 15, 1954. The constitutional validity of this law, which has been in operation since 1930, was challenged before the Constitutional Court in 1963. The plaintiffs claimed that the powers given to the Council of Ministers under this law amounted to the delegation of legislative power, which is prohibited by the Constitution (Art. 5). The Court, however, refused to declare the law unconstitutional, 1 *Anayasa Mahk. Kar. Der.* 132.

issue decrees for the purpose of protection of the value of Turkish currency, is usually regarded as an emergency law.

Another state of emergency which was introduced by a constitutional amendment in 1971 is related to universities; in cases where the freedom of learning and teaching in universities is endangered, and should such danger not be averted by the University authorities, the Council of Ministers may by decree take over the administration of Universities and communicate it to Parliament, without delay, for approval (Art. 120).

As for martial law *(Sıkıyönetim)* which involves radical curtailment of freedoms, transfer of police duties to the military, as well as the transfer of the administration of criminal justice to the military courts, the Constitution introduces detailed provisions in Article 124. The Council of Ministers is vested with the power to promulgate martial law in one or more regions or in the whole of the country for a period of time not exceeding two months. The Council of Ministers may declare martial law in the event of war, in a situation likely to lead to war; in case of a revolt or of a forceful and open uprising against the motherland and the Republic, or in the event of definite indications of widespread acts of violence directed toward suppressing the free democratic order or the basic rights and freedoms recognized by the Constitution.

A proclamation of martial law must at once be communicated to Parliament, which must be summoned if necessary. The Parliament, in a joint session of the two Houses, may abolish, shorten or extend the promulgation for two months at a time.

It is important to note that martial law does not excuse or justify any breach of the existing law. In other words, martial law is not a state of «no law at all». Consequently, the measures taken by the martial law authorities are also subject to judicial review.

Whether the promulgation of martial law itself is subject to judicial review, however, is an open question. Theoretically speaking, under the existing Constitution, no administrative act can be excluded from judicial review; i.e. there is no room for acts of policy *(actes de gouvernement,* as the French call it) *(hükümet tasarrufu).*

Yet, both the Constitutional Court and the Council of State refuse, on procedural grounds, to examine the validity of the proclamation of martial law.

The Council of State holds that such a proclamation, especially after it has been approved by the Parliament, becomes a legislative act (an Act of Parliament), and, therefore, falls beyond the jurisdiction of the Council of State which may solely hear administrative law cases.[38]

On the other hand, the Constitutional Court declares that, although approved by the Parliament, the promulgation of martial law is not a law (statute) and therefore the Constitutional Court has no jurisdiction over it.[39]

V. CONTROL OF PUBLIC ADMINISTRATION

A. Political Control :

The public administration is under the control of Parliament, which is in a position to supervise the administration from the point of view of expediency *(yerindelik)* as well as legality *(hukuka uygunluk)*. This political control is based on the principle of ministerial responsibility, and it operates through such means as questions *(soru)*, interpellation *(gensoru)*, parliamentary inquiries *(meclis soruşturması)*, etc.[40]

It is important to note, however, that due to the party system, under which there is little chance of winning a seat in Parliament without party support, members of the party (or coalition) in power are unlikely to withdraw their support from the government. Therefore, in most cases the pressures leading to the resignation of a government or of a minister is unlikely to come simply from parliamentary control. The practical effect of the control carried on by the Parliament is closely connected with the opposition's efforts at publicizing the issues through the mass media. Therefore, this may be regarded as an aspect of control of public administration exercised by exposing culpable official conduct to public opinion.

If as many people believe, the best antidote to maladministration is publicity, then the importance of the role played by mass media in general, and the press in particular, in controlling the public administration is self-evident.

---

[38] *Danıştay Dava Daireleri Kurulu* E. 1970/442, K. 1970/445, rendered in July 3, 1970.
[39] Decision rendered on the case related to the promulgation of martial law in Istanbul area in July 1970, dated, Nov. 17, 1970, 8 Anayasa Mahk. Kar. Der. 443.
  The jurisdiction of the Constitutional Court is limited to cases specified in Art. 147 of the Constitution. These do not include the promulgation of martial law.
[40] See Chapter 2, on Constitutional law.

B. Administrative Control :

Every public organization has a mechanism through which it is controlled internally. As a natural result of the hierarchical nature of administrative organization, the subordinate is under the supervision of his superior, (hierarchical control; *hiyerarşi denetimi*). The superior has the power to alter or stop the enforcement of the actions initiated by the subordinate on grounds of legality or expediency. The superior may resort to disciplinary actions as well.

Another type of control is external control(*dış denetim*) which is exercised by one public organization over another, e.g. tutelage (*idari vesayet*) under which certain decisions and actions of local administration need to be approved by the central administration.[41]

C. Financial Control :

The Board of Inspectors of the Ministry of Finance [42] inspects and supervises all government agencies and public organizations from a financial standpoint. Such agencies are also subject to the supervision of their own inspectorates.

On the other hand, the Court of Accounts *(Sayıştay)* (Constitution, Art. 127) is in charge of examining and auditing, on behalf of the Parliament, all accounts of revenues and expenditures of government departments.[43] The Court of Accounts reports to the Parliament which has, under the Constitution, final control. The members of the Court of Accounts are chosen by the Parliament; they enjoy guarantees and safeguards similar to those prescribed for the judges.

The Court of Accounts also has judicial power over the accounting officals of government agencies and can hold them responsible for irregularities and illegalities in their work.

The State Economic Enterprises are not subject to the financial control of the Court of Accounts. Instead, the High Control Board (*Yüksek Denetleme Kurulu*) which is a body attached to the Office of the Prime Minister, investigates and controls them. The State

---

[41] See above II, D and III, C.
[42] The Ministry of Finance exercises an overall control in financial matters by means of preparing and presenting budgets to Parliament.
[43] By a constitutional amendment introduced in 1971, the following paragraph was added to Art. 127 of the Constitution :
«The procedures for auditing on behalf of the T.G.N.A., the state properties in the possession of the Armed Forces, with due regard to the principles of secrecy demanded by the national defence services, shall be regulated by law.»

Economic Enterprises are also controlled from the standpoint of productivity and rationality of their operations.

The reports prepared by the High Control Board are presented to the Office of the Prime Minister. These reports are eventually examined by the Parliament. The Parliament decides whether the managing body (Board of Directors) of each State Economic Enterprise is to be «acquitted» *(ibra)* or held *responsible*.[44]

D. Citizens' Complaints :

The Turkish system of law does not recognize any official comparable to the *ombudsman* of Scandinavian countries or the *Parliamentary Commissioner* of Britain. However, the Constitution provides for a procedure by which citizens may petition the competent authorities and the Parliament with requests or complaints concerning themselves or the public (Article 62).

The right to petition Parliament is widely used by citizens who believe that they have sustained injustice as a result of maladministration. Petitions are examined by a standing committes consisting of seven members from the Senate of the Republic and eighteen members from the National Assembly. The committee's decisions are final unless appealed by a member of Parliament to a Plenary Meeting of both Houses. Although these decisions are not legally binding upon the administrative authorities, they are regularly followed in order to avoid clashes with Parliament.

It should be noted, however, that in cases where a judicial remedy is available, or the administrative remedies have not been exhausted, the Parliament does not intervene. The law also prohibits legislative initiative through the exercise of the right to petition Parliament.[45]

E. Judicial Review :

1. The Principles :

The system of judicial review of administrative acts and actions in Turkey is, primarily, based on the constitutional principle of rule of law.[46] In fact, the constitutional provision which states that

---

[44] Law relating to the control of State Economic Enterprises by the T.G.N.A., Law No. 468, dated May 12, 1964 *(Kamu İktisadi Teşebbüslerinin T.B.M.M. nce Denetlenmesi Hakkında Kanun)*.

[45] The law relating to the right to petition Parliament, No. 140, dated December 26, 1962 *(Türk Vatandaşlarının T.B.M.M. ne Dilekçeyle Başvurmaları... Hakkında Kanun)*. Art. 5/I, d. Art. 13.

[46] See, above II, A.

«judicial review may be sought for all the acts and actions of the administration» (Art. 114, as amended in 1971) is regarded as the practical aspect of the rule of law observed in the field of administrative law.

The Constitution envisages a system under which Turkish public administration is completely subject to judicial review. If administrative power is used in a way not authorized by law, the courts are expected to protect and compensate the individual. Some effective remedy must be available against every sort of excess or abuse of power. Accordingly, no adminstrative act can be excluded from judicial review. If the statute is silent, the general rule prescribed in the Constitution applies, i.e. legislative silence does not mean that judicial review is precluded.[47]

The Constitutional Court has never hesitated to annul a statutory provision which appeared to preclude judicial review.[48]

It should be mentioned, however, that the effective judicial control over administrative acts, introduced by the 1961 Constitution, gave rise to some criticism. During the extraordinary regime, commencing with the Memorandum of 12 March 1971, those circles that opposed judicial review seemed to gain some ground. Some constitutional amendments introduced during this extraordinary period were aimed at limiting the powers of the judicial branch, and among these was the amendment to Article 114 relating to the judicial review of administrative acts. The first paragraph of the article read

> "In no case can any action or act of the administration be left beyond the review of judicial organs."

was replaced with;

> "Judicial review may be sought for all the acts and actions of the administration."

On the other hand, a new paragraph was inserted into the article:

> "Judicial power cannot be exercised in such a manner as to restrain the fulfilment of the executive function

---

[47] However, in the case of the proclamation of martial law by the Council of Ministers, which is considered an administrative act in Turkish law, there is no court to quash it or declare it void, because no court believes that it has jurisdiction over this proclamation. Thus, the proclamation becomes a kind of acte de gouvernement which theoretically may not exist under the Constitution. (See, above IV).

[48] In a number of statutes passed before 1961, there were finality clauses, i.e. certain administrative acts were declared to be final and conclusive and / or not subject to any form of review. Later, these were invalidated by the Constitutional Court.

carried out in conformity with the forms and principles prescribed by law. Judicial decisions cannot have the nature of administrative acts."

The reaction of the Council of State to this amendment has been strong, and amounted, in a sense, to disregard it. The Council of State believed that the amendment to Article 114 of the Constitution did not bring about any real change in its powers. In fact, one may very well argue that the change which the amendment introduced was related to the language rather than the essence or substance of the matter. As for the sentence added to Article 114 prohibiting the Court from making any decision of an administrative nature, the Council of State considered it a superfluous provision in the Constitution. Because it was obvious that no court could make administrative decisions,[49] and, as the Council of State had never done so in the past, the Council of State concluded that there was no need to change the line it had been following in determining the extent of its jurisdiction.

2. *Administrative Courts:*

The traditions of Turkish law require that there should exist an independent branch of law under which an individual could seek redress for an injustice committed by a public official or body. This branch is Administrative Law, and as a general principle, all cases governed by administrative law fall within the competence of administrative courts.

Administrative Courts constitute a separate system which includes the Council of State *(Danıştay)*, the Military Administrative Court *(Askeri Yüksek İdare Mahkemesi)*, the Court of Accounts *(Sayıştay)* and the subordinate administrative courts.

a) The Council of State:

The Council of State is, in its judicial capacity,[50] the main and highest administrative court. It is the court that has general jurisdiction over administrative cases; administrative cases are referred to the Council of State where another administrative court

---

[49] It should be noted, however, that certain functions carried out by the courts have always been considered acts of an administrative nature, e.g. the examination of the accounts of the guardian *(vasi)* by the competent Justice of the Peace Court (C.C. Art. 407). Nevertheless, the clear intention of the constitutional amendment was not to limit this type of functions.

[50] See, above III, B, 1 for the non - judicial functions of Council of State. Also see, Ch. 1 IV D on the Sources of law.

is not specifield by law. It is also a «Court of Cassation» or final court of appeals for cases decided by the subordinate administrative courts.

The judicial divison of the Council of State consists of ten judicial chambers *(dava daireleri)*. Each chamber acts as a court and has five members including the president. The jurisdiction of each chamber is defined by the law on the Council of State.[51] Certain cases specified by law, such as cases involving a challange to the legality of a regulation *(tüzük)* or a decree issued by the Council of Ministers, are heard by the General Assembly of the Judicial Chambers *(Dava Daireleri Kurulu)*. The General Assembly of the Judicial Chambers consists, under the chairmanship of the first President of the Council of State, of the presidents of the judicial chambers together with one member from each of them. The General Assembly of Judicial Chambers, which acts as a separate court, also has the duty of reconciling the conflicting judicial decisions of the Chambers of the Council of State.

Under the Constitution, members (justices) of the Council of State are elected by the Constitutional Court upon the joint nomination of the government and the Council itself. They fully enjoy the tenure provided for judges by the Constitution, i.e. they may not be dismissed and, unless they so desire, may not be retired before the age of sixty five, etc..

The personnel of the Council of State also includes «the spokesmen of the law» *(kanun sözcüleri)* who, like the French «commisaires de gouvernement» give their own opinions about judicial cases to the Council. The law regulating the Council of State requires that in the decisions rendered the name and opinion of the «rapporteur» should be indicated. Rapporteurs are usually the assistant members *(yardımcılar)* of the Council of State.

b) Subordinate Administrative Courts :

There are mainly two kinds of subordinate administrative courts. One is the administrative council of the provinces and sub-provinces *(İl ve İlçe Yönetim Kurulları)* and the other is the judicial commissions for taxation.

The Administrative Councils of the provinces and sub-provinces are composed of high ranking functionaries in the area, and they exercise certain judicial functions in addition to their administrative

---

[51] Law No. 521, dated December 24, 1964, as amended by Law No. 1740, dated June 18, 1973.

duties. The Administrative Councils of sub-provinces have strictly limited jurisdiction. The Administrative Council of Provinces, on the other hand, hear certain cases such as those involving the legality of the acts and actions of sub-governors and district directors.

It should be noted, however, that judicial decisions of the Administrative Councils are subject to the correction of the Council of State by way of appeal. Yet, due to the fact that their members are functionaries who do not enjoy the tenure provided for the judges in the Constitution, these Councils may hardly be regarded as courts in the constitutional sense.

The same considerations are valid for the judicial commissions for taxation, which are composed of functionaries who have financial background. The commissions for taxation have two levels; the commission of first degree is called the Committee of Tax Appeals *(Vergi İtiraz Komisyonu)*, and the superior commission is called Committee of Cassation for Taxes *(Vergi Temyiz Komisyonu)*. The Council of State may review the decisions rendered by these Committee by way of appeal.

c) Court of Accounts :

The Court of Accounts *(Sayıştay)*, which functions primarily as a financial control body, also has certain judicial powers over the accounting officials of government agencies and may hold them responsible for irregularities in their accounts.[52]

The Organization of the Court of Accounts is similar to that of the Council of State; it is composed of Chambers *(daireler)* each having four members and a President. The highest body in the Court of Accounts is the General Assembly of the Court of Accounts *(Sayıştay Genel Kurulu)* which consists of all the Presidents and members of the Chambers. Among the functions of the General Assembly is the unifacation of conflicting decisions rendered by the Chambers. The Court of Accounts also has a Board of Appeals *(Temyiz Kurulu)*, which examines the decisions of Chambers by way of appeal.

d) Military Administrative Court :

The Military Administrative Court is an innovation introduced by constitutional amendment in 1971.[53] Judicial review of

---
[52] See, above V, C, law No. 832, dated February 21, 1967.
[53] Amendment to Art. 140 of the Constitution, dated September 20, 1971; Law relating the Military Administrative Court, law No. 1602, dated July 4, 1972.

administrative acts and actions concerning military personnel rests within the jurisdiction of the Military Administrative Court. Formerly, it was the Council of State which had the power to review the administrative acts and actions affecting the military personnel.

Members (justices) of the Military Administrative Court are all military personnel, either military judges or high ranking officers of the Armed Forces. There are three Chambers in the court, each having seven members and a president. Under the law, the military judge members must form the majority in each Chamber.

Decisions of the Military Administrative Court are not to be reviewed by the Council of State.

3. *Remedies*:

The law relating to the Council of State provides for two remedies available for the individual who believes that he sustained injustice from maladministration: action for annulment *(iptal davası)* and full remedy action *(tam yargı davası)*.

a) Action for Annulment:

An action for annulment is the principal remedy against every illegal administrative act; the plaintiff does not need to prove that he has been adversely affected directly in his rights and property by the administrative act he challenges. Theoretically, any individual can bring an action for annulment against an administrative act which may indirectly or possibly have an adverse effect on his interests.

It should be noted, however, that whether an individual has standing in an action for annulment is not always easy to determine. The peculiarities of the case play an important part, and the Council of State seem to favour a restrictive approach on standing.

The subject matter of an action for annulment is the examination of the administrative act in question from the point of view of legality. Theoretically, the Court does not try to find out whether the challenged administrative act is a reasonable one. If the administrative act is found illegal for reasons related to the administrative procedure and/or substantive law, then it will be quashed. The ruling of the Court annulling the administrative act has retroactive effect.

The Court does not have the power to remand cases to the relevant administrative agency, nor can it modify the challenged administrative act.

The decisions taken or rules made by the administrative agencies may be challenged through an action for annulment even before they are actually enforced. The only condition for ripeness of the case is that the challenged act must be an enforceable one; i.e. it must be administratively final. The existence of administrative remedies, such as the appeal to the superior administrative authorities, does not prevent an action for annulment, provided that the challenged act is final and enforceable.

Actions must commence in 90 days, beginning from the notification of an act by an official or publication of a rule-making act or other general act.

Commencement of an action for annulment does not automatically suspend the challenged administrative act, except in certain tax cases. But the Court may, upon the request of plaintiff, suspend the enforcement of the act in question by issuing an injunction to that effect *(yürütmenin durdurulması kararı)*. This, of course, is a provisional injunction which will have binding effect until the final decision is rendered, or until it is annulled by the Court before the final decision.

b) Full Remedy Action:

A full remedy action may be brought by a plaintiff who claims that his rights were violated or property was damaged by an illegal act or action of the administration. It is mainly used to recover damages or for other pecuniary claims.

While action for annulment can be brought only against administrative acts *(idari işlemler)*, full remedy action is available for both administrative acts and actions *(eylemler)*.

The time limit for the full remedy action is one year, running from the date of sustainment of damage or notification.

SELECTED BIBLIOGRAPHY

Balta, T. B. : **İdare Hukukuna Giriş** (Ankara 1968/1970).
Balta, T. B. : **İdare Hukuku, I - Genel Konular** (Ankara 1970/72).
Duran, L. : **İdare Hukuku Meseleleri** (İstanbul 1964).
Giritli, İ. : **Amme İdaresi Teşkilâtı ve Personeli** (İstanbul 1975).
Gözübüyük, A. Ş. : **Türkiye'nin İdarî Yapısı** (Ankara 1976).
Gözübüyük, A. Ş. : **İdari Yargı** (Ankara 1977).
Onar, S. S. : **İdare Hukukunun Umumi Esasları** (İstanbul 1966).
Versan, V. : **Amme İdaresi** (İstanbul 1974).
Aybay, R. : **Some Contemporary Constitutional Problems in Turkey,** 4 British Society for Middle Eastern Studies Bulletin 21 ff. (1977).
Mıhçıoğlu, C. : **The Civil Service in Turkey,** 16 Siyasal Bilgiler Fakültesi Dergisi 89 ff. (1964).
Presthus, R. V. / Erem S. : **Statistical Analysis in Comparative Administration : The Turkish Conseil d'Etat** (Cornell University Press 1958).
Public Administration Institute for Turkey and the Middle East : **Turkish Government Organization Manual** (Ankara 1966).
Soysal, M. : **Local Government in Turkey** (Ankara 1967).
Versan, V. : **Central and Local Government in Turkey,** 10 Annales de la Faculté de Droit d'Istanbul 266 ff. (1960).

CHAPTER 4

LAW OF PERSONS[1]

Prof. Dr. Tuğrul ANSAY [*]

I. GENERAL

Law exists to regulate the relations of persons, and such persons are the subjects of rights and duties imposed and given by law.

Persons include, in addition to human beings, legal (or juristic) persons, such as clubs or corporations. In modern law every human being is considered a person, and hence a legal person. The ancient, classification of slaves and citizens does not exist in modern law.

Although all persons are subject to rights and obligations, the extent of these rights and obligations may not be the same for all persons. Similarly, the capacity of persons may also differ.

II. BEGINNING AND END OF PERSONALITY

A layman may think that the personality of a human being starts at the moment of birth, and this is also the general rule of law (C. C., Art. 27 I). A child is born when it is completely separated from its mother's body and is then alive, if only for a few moments. However, for the lawyer even an unborn child may have a degree of personality. Thus, article 27 II of the Civil Code says that a child may be the subject of rights after it is conceived, if it is subsequently born alive; and in the law of inheritance, a child conceived, but not yet born, may be a legal heir if it is born alive (C. C., Art. 524, also Art. 584).

The personality of a human being ends at death. A dead person cannot be the subject of rights.[2] Upon a person's death his estate passes to his successors. By means of a last will made during his life, a person may dispose of his property, and such a will becomes effective at his death.

---

[*] University of Ankara, Faculty of Law.
[1] Civil Code, Arts. 8 - 81.
[2] On the corpse of a dead person, See Dural, 30.

A missing person may be declared dead by a court after the expiration of a certain period of time, if no news has been received from him during such time *(gaiplik kararı)*. A person may also be declared dead if he has been lost in an accident or circumstances in which lives may be lost, such as a ship collision, and if no news has been received from him since then (C. C., Arts. 31 - 34). In both cases, an application must be made to the court. This may be made five years after the date of last hearing of any news in the case of a missing person, and one year after the date of an accident in the case of a lost person. The judge thereupon collects information, by publication of a notice seeking the same, about the disappeared person. Not earlier than one year after the publication the judge may declare the person dead (C. C., Art. 34 I). The decision of the court is *nunc pro tunc*, that is to say, the person will be deemed dead from the date of last news or accident.

The rights of inheritance are the same as upon an ordinary death.[3] The succession, however, has a tentative nature for all heirs. They must return the inherited property if the missing or lost person comes back within periods of time specified by law (C. C., Arts. 526, 527).

Article 28 II of the Civil Code provides that if several persons have died or been declared dead and it cannot be proved that one has lived longer than another, it is presumed that they all died at the same time. Because of this presumption, none of these persons can acquire anything by way of succession from each other.

III. REGISTRY OF PERSONAL STATUS (Nüfus Kütüğü)

The facts of birth, marital status and the sex of a person, children and religious denomination are registered in the Registries of Birth, Death and Marriage, which are kept by the state.[4] The birth, death, marriage and divorce registries are mainted by the Census Officer *(Nüfus Memuru)*. Birth, death, marriage and other facts related to personal status are proved by these registrations (Census L., Art. 13), although the state assumes no legal liability for the accuracy of the registers (Census L., Art. 54). Birth, marriage or death certificates issued by the registrars are also used for proof.

---

[3] See Chapter 7 on the Law of Succession.
[4] Census Law *(Nüfus Kanunu)*, Law No. 1587, dated May 5, 1972.

IV. PERSONS AS SUBJECTS OF RIGHTS ; CAPACITY

A. Persons as Subjects of Rights (Haklardan istifade ehliyeti) :

Turkish law distinguishes the ability to be the subject of rights (in German : *Rechtsfaehigkeit*) from the capacity to act (in German : *Handlungsfaehigkeit*).

All persons, even an unborn child, as noted above, are today the subject of rights (C. C., Art. 11). For example, a two year old child, or an eighty year old man may inherit property, have money deposited in his name in a bank, be a creditor or debtor, own a house, bring a suit in court. However, because of a lack of capacity, discussed below, in most of these cases somebody else will act in the name of the child (and possibly the eighty year old man).

In legal history we find people such as slaves, who were not the subject of legal rights, or whose rights were severely limited; the French law also knew the so called «civil death» as a result of which all legal rights were lost. The Turkish Constitution, in the chapter regulating fundamental rights and duties, expressly states that «every individual is entitled, by virtue of his existence as a human being, to fundamental rights and freedoms, which cannot be usurped, transferred or relinquished» (Art. 10).

The equality of all persons as subjects of rights is further expressed in the Constitution in article 12 : «All individuals are equal before the law irrespective of language, race, sex, political opinion, philosophical views, or religion or religious sect. No privilege shall be granted to any individual, family, group or class».

Notwithstanding this principle, some differences exist between the rights of men and women. Thus, for example, if a woman is appointed as a guardian by a judge, she may refuse the guardianship, whereas a man may not (C. C., Art. 366). In the law of succession, male children are preferred to female ones in the distribution of agricultural land. In family law too, there are differences between husband and wife : The domicile of the husband becomes the domicile of the wife; she bears the family name of her husband; in cases of disputes in family matters the views of the husband may prevail. The minimum age for marriage is different for a girl and a boy.[5]

---

[5] See Chapter 6 III B 1 on Family Law.

Foreigners do not always have the same rights as Turkish nationals. A foreigner, for example, may not own real property within the country as freely as a Turkish national.[6]

Societies *(dernekler)* are fully subject to legal rights and obligations. Article 45 of the Civil Code states this rule in the following way: «Legal persons have the capacity of having rights and incurring obligations except those rights and obligations which are inseparably bound up with human nature, such as sex, age or family relationship». Business associations, on the other hand, are not subject to rights and obligations outside of the scope of their business [7] (Comm. C., Art. 137).

B. Capacity to Act (Fiil ehliyeti, kullanma ehliyeti):

1. Definition:

Capacity to act means, on one hand, the capacity to enter into transactions and, on the other hand, the capacity to be liable for wrongs or torts.

Capacity to enter into legal transactions (in German: *Geschaeftsfaehigkeit, muamele ehliyeti*) indicates the ability to enter into legally valid transactions (C. C., Art. 9). The legal validity of a transaction, for example of a contract, depends on the capacity of the persons party to the transaction. The same is true for the validity of a unilateral declaration, such as sending a notice.

To have the capacity to be liable for torts means that a person may be legally liable if he damages the body, person, or property of another [8] *(haksız fiil ehliyeti)*.

2. The Degree of Capacity:

Turkish law recognizes different degrees of capacity and incapacity. A person may be wholly unable to enter into legal transactions; or he may possess a limited capacity to do so. Modern law aims to confer full legal capacity as widely as possible and in general to create legal incapacities only where there are natural incapacities also.

a) Full capacity: Those who are of age *(reşit)* that is to say, have reached their majority, which is completion of 18 years of age and are able to make mature or fair judgments *(mümeyyiz)* are fully capable of entering into transactions. A person who has

---
[6] See below VIII; Ansay, *American-Turkish Private International Law* (New York, 1966).
[7] See Chapter 5 on Legal Persons.
[8] See Chapter 9, Part 3 on the Law of Obligations.

reached his majority is also presumed to be of mature judgment. Such persons will be bound by the contracts they sign, and they will be liable for tort if they give damage to somebody else or his property.

(1) Capacity to make fair judgments *(temyiz kudreti)*: According to article 13 of the Civil Code «persons who are not able to act reasonably because of minority, mental sickness, mental weakness, drunkenness or causes similar to these do not have the ability to make fair judgments». To act in a fair manner or reasonably is a vague concept. It changes from person to person, and from time to time. However, as the Code indicates, there are certain obstacles to the ability to make fair judgments. These are:

(a) Minority: Infants are completely incapable of making fair judgments. At what age a child starts to act reasonably is a question of fact, and therefore, must be determined in each case by the judge. Sometimes a 14 year old child might be more mature than a 16 year old. Again, a child may be able to make fair judgments with respect to certain transactions in which he has had some experience. Thus, a child who works in his father's shop is probably able to make fair judgments on selling goods there, but he will not be able to appreciate the nature of a guaranty contract.

(b) Mental sickness: Certain mental sicknesses, such as epilepsy, hysteria etc. may at times destroy the ability to make fair judgments. Again, the court may have to determine the facts in particular cases.

(c) Mental weakness such as imbecility, drunkenness, severe sickness with fever and other similar grounds may deprive a fully grown man of his legal capacity.

(2) Age: In order to have full capacity, a person must have his or her majority *(rüşt)*. According to article 11 of the Civil Code, a person ceases to be a minor when he is 18 years old. In exceptional cases persons may acquire majority upon marriage or court decision at less than 18.

(a) Marriage confers majority (C. C., Art. 11 II). The marriage age is 17 and 15 for boys and girls respectively. Under extraordinary conditions, a 15 year old boy or 14 year old girl may marry with the permission of the court (C. C., Art. 88 II); they would thus acquire majority.

(b) A minor who has completed his 15th year, may, upon his application and with the consent of his parents, be declared by the court to be of full age (C C., Art. 12). This may be useful when a minor is working and earning his own living, so as to permit the minor and third persons to enter into valid transactions.

b) **Full incapacity** *(tam ehliyetsizlik)*: Persons who do not have the ability to make fair judgments, even temporarily, are fully incapable of entering into transactions and any transaction of such persons is null and void. The person without capacity, the other party to the transaction, a judge, on his own motion, may declare such transaction void at any time. Therefore, for example, if a contract of sale of a bicycle is void, because one of the parties to it lacks capacity, the other party may state the contract void, although the fulfillment of the contract might in fact have benefited the party without capacity. Inasmuch as the purpose of the concept of capacity is to protect incapable persons, such a result seems unfair. The modern view is therefore to treat the transactions of incapable persons as merely voidable by the person without capacity and the Turkish Supreme Court has refused to declare a contract null and void stating that the result was against the principles of objective good faith.[9]

Incapable persons must act through a statutory representative, such as a parent or guardian. Legal personalities always act through their legal representatives, such as partners, directors and officers.[10]

Incapable persons are also generally not held liable for damages to others. However, in certain cases, equity may require that an incapable person be responsible for the results of his acts (C. O., Art. 54). Thus a drunken person may be liable for his tortious acts (C. O., Art. 54 II). Furthermore, tortious liability not based on negligence or fault, but based on causal relation [11] exists even in cases of full incapacity. Thus if tiles from a house owned by an incapable person fall and injure a pedestrian on the street, the incapable person will be held liable (C. O., Art. 58).

---

[9] C.C., Art. 2. The decision of the General Assembly on the Unification of Judgments of the Court of Cassation *(İçtihadı Birleştirme Kurulu Kararı)*, dated March 9, 1955. Akipek, 76.
[10] See Chapter 5 on Legal Persons.
[11] See Chapter 9, Part 3 on the Law of Obligations.

c) Limited capacity (*Mahdut ehliyet*) :

(1) Minors who are mature : Maturity, that is the ability to make fair judgments is ordinarily associated with majority. But in some cases a person who has reached his majority may not be mature, and on the other hand, a minor, as suggested above, may be able to make fair judgments.

(2) Persons who have been interdicted, that is to say put under guardianship *(vesayet)* because of thriftlessness, habitual drunkenness, imprisonment, or voluntarily, have limited capacity if they are able to make fair judgments.

Persons with limited capacity, like fully incapable persons, act through their statutory representatives. But they themselves have capacity to do certain acts : They may enter into transactions by which they merely benefit without incurring obligations or liabilities. They may, for example, accept gifts, which a fully incapable person may not. They may also enter into transactions related to their business, provided they are given permission to operate such a business (C. C., Arts. 284, 396).

Persons with limited capacity may enter into certain other transactions with the approval *(muvafakat)* of their statutory representative (C. C., Arts. 394, 16 I. For example, the sale of movable property) which may be given either for a specific transaction or a class of transactions. Such approval may take the form of ratification *(icazet)* of a prior transaction. The representative's approval may be explicit or implied, as by fulfilling obligations previously incurred by the interdicted person.

Transactions without the consent of the statutory representative are voidable by the incapable person. The other party is bound by the transaction except that he may ask the statutory representative to give his approval within a certain period of time, or may ask the court to fix a time. If approval is not given within such time, the transaction ceases to be binding on such other party (C. C. Art. 394 II).

A transaction may also be approved by the minor after he comes of age.

Persons who have limited capacity have full tortious liability.[12]

---

[12] During bankruptcy proceedings, the bankrupt merchant has limited capacity, Law of E. and B., Art. 191 (As a rule, only merchants may go into banktuptcy in Turkey). A married woman might be prohibited by her husband from operating a business, but this does not take away her capacity (C.C., Art. 159).

V. DOMICILE

A. In General :

Every person has a domicile *(ikametgâh)*. Although a person's domicile is often the same as his residence, which is the place where one is living, it is not legally the same as residence.

Domicile has many applications in law; for example, a person is generally sued in a court located in his domicile, and in private international law, choice of law may be based on the party's domicile.[13] In the law of taxation the domicile of a person is also important. Pecuniary obligations must be paid at the creditor's domicile [14] (C. O., Art. 73).

B. Domicile of Choice :

Domicile is the place where a person lives or resides with the intention of remaining there. The two elements of domicile are, therefore, living in a place and the intention to continue to live there; in other words, to make it one's home. A family living in Ankara which moves to Istanbul during the summer months does not acquire a new domicile, since they have the intention to come back to Ankara. Notwithstanding this general principle, presence in a place for the purposes of attending a university or in a hopital for medical treatment, and in the case of foreigners, possession of a residence permit,[15] have been considered bases for domicile for jurisdictional purposes.[16]

C. Domicile by Operation of Law :

In some cases the law determines where the domicile of a person should be. A married woman for example, has her husband's domicile.[17] Turkish law allows the wife to have a domicile other than her husband's, when the domicile of the husband is not known or the wife is legally separated.[18]

Minor children have the domicile of their parents. A person under guardianship is deemed to be domiciled at the place where

---

[13] Turkish private international law refers to the law of nationality in most cases. See, Ansay, *American - Turkish Private International Law* (New York, 1966).
[14] For the domicile of a legal person see Chapter 5 on Legal Persons.
[15] 2. H.D. (2nd Division, Supreme Court) Febr. 22, 1952, in Berki/Ergüney, *Yabancılar Hukuku ve Kanun İhtilâfları* 119 (Ankara, 1963).
[16] S. Ş. Ansay, *Hukuk Yargılama Usulleri* 87 (Ankara 1960). C. C. Pr., Art. 20, Contrary to C. C., Art. 22.
[17] C. C., Art. 21. The decision of the General Assembly of the Court of Cassation on the Unification of Judgments, dated March 16, 1932.
[18] S. Ş. Ansay, *Hukuk Yargılama Usulleri* 87, 88 (Ankara 1960); C. C., Arts. 161, 162.

the guardianship court is located (C. C., Art. 21). With the permission of this court, the person under guardianship may acquire a domicile of choice (C. C., Art. 362).

D. Rules :

Every person must have a domicile. If a person does not acquire a domicile, the law attributes a domicile to him. This will usually be the domicile of his parents. If a person travels a lot, or if it is otherwise impossible to fix a domicile, his residence may be treated as his domicile (C. C., Art. 20 II).

A person may have only one domicile. Merchants may have several domiciles, if they own more than one commercial enterprise (C. C., Art. 19 II and III).

VI. NAMES

Every person must have a first name and a family name.[19]

The first name is given to a person by his parents (C. C., Art. 264 III). In case of conflict between the father and mother, the father has the right to choose the name (C. C., Arts. 263, 264 IV).

Children bear the family name of their fathers (C. C., Art. 259). The wife also takes her husband's family name (C. C., Art. 153 I). In case of divorce she may resume her former family name (C. C., Art. 141 II).

A person may request a change of his name only on justifiable grounds [20] (C. C., Art. 26).

VII. NATIONALITY

Nationality *(tabiiyet, uyrukluk)* is the tie which binds a person to the state, and a person may demand the protection of the state to which he belongs.[21] All persons have nationality with the rare exception of stateless persons.

(1) Nationality by birth : Turkish nationality is mainly acquired through blood relation to the father. Thus a legitimate or illegitimate but legally recognized child of a Turkish father is

---

[19] Law on Family Names, dated June 21, 1934, Art. 1. Merchants also have trade names. Those persons who alone or with others operate a commercial enterprise are called merchants. They are subject to the provisions of the Commercial Code, which requires, among other things, that the enterprise must have a trade name. Business associations must also carry a trade name (Comm. C., Arts. 18, 41, 44, 45).

[20] See below IX. «A person aggrieved because of the change of a name may object to the decision of alteration within one year from the date of cognizance» C. C., Art. 26 III.

[21] Legal persons are also under the protection of the state. T. Ansay, *American - Turkish Private International Law* (New York 1966).

Turkish.[22] In addition, legitimate children born to a Turkish mother and not acquiring the nationality of the father by birth, as well as all illegitimate children born to Turkish mothers, are Turkish.[23]

Children born of non-Turkish parents do not acquire Turkish nationality by reason of birth on Turkish soil. An exception is the case of children born in Turkey and not acquiring at the time of birth the nationality of either their father or mother; they are Turkish at birth.[24]

(2) Acquisition of nationality other than by birth: Foreign women acquire Turkish nationality at the time of marriage to a Turkish men, if they make a declaration of intention to this effect to the marriage officer.[25]

Any foreigner may acquire Turkish nationality by means of naturalization *(telsik)*. Persons who have lived in Turkey more than five years and have all the qualifications required by the law may apply to the Ministry of Interior, and upon the recommendation of this Ministry, the Council of Ministers may grant Turkish nationality.[26]

VIII. PROTECTION OF PERSONALITY (Kişiliğin korunması)

A. In General:

The concept of personality involves not only rights and obligations and capacity, but also, among other things, bodily integrity, health, freedom, name, reputation and the right to privacy.

Persons are legally entitled to protect their personalities. A person is legally protected, to give a few examples, against insults, the disclosure of certain secrets and the publication of personal pictures. So too, the law protects personality by refusal to enforce promises not to marry in one's lifetime and lifetime employment agreements.

There are legal safeguards of personality against others and against oneself:

B. Protection of Personality Against Others:

A person is safeguarded, first of all, against attacks and offenses by others by the Criminal Code.

---

[22] Nationality Act. of 1964 *(Vatandaşlık Kanunu = TNA)*. Law No. 403, dated, Febr. 11, 1964, Art. 1 and 2; Constitution, Art. 54.
[23] Art. 1 a and b of the TNA.
[24] Art. 4 of the TNA.
[25] Art. 5 and 42 of the TNA.
[26] Arts. 6-8 of the TNA.

For example under article 456 I of the Criminal Code, whoever causes another bodily pain or injures the health or causes mental disorder without the intention of killing, shall be imprisoned for six months to one year. Articles 179 and following regulate felonies against personal liberty and article 480 I libels and slanders.[27]

The Criminal Code is not always an adequate protection principally because criminal sanctions are applicable only when the offense is intentional, and also because it does not compensate the injured party (any fines being payable to the state). Protection under the civil law includes, among other remedies, compensation.

According to article 24 of the Civil Code «a person whose personal interests have been illegally attacked may demand from the court the rejection of the attack». Thus, a person whose life is in danger, or whose person or property are being damaged or threatened, may demand from the court the prohibition of the attack, that is to say, relief in the nature of an injunction *(tecavüzün men'i davası)* (C. C., Art. 24 I).

Acts against a person's honor and dignity may also be prevented or stopped under this article of the Civil Code. Thus, a person may apply to the court when his honor or dignity is damaged by way of accusations, libels, slanders, wrong information or improper criticism. Article 24 is, therefore, one of the basic means of protection against attacks published in newspapers.

Disclosing secrets, such as private letters, or listening in on telephone calls of others, or improperly publishing pictures of a person are also considered acts against personality.[58] The publication of news about well known persons such as politicians, musicians, and scientists will not be considered acts against personality. Pictures of movie stars may also be freely published.[29]

The protection of the right of a person to his name is specifically regulated in article 25 of the Civil Code which states that «acknowledgment of this right may be requested from the judge, by a person whose name causes controversy. A person aggrieved by

---

[27] According to Art. 480 I of the Criminal Code, «whoever, in a manner that will allow three or more persons to hear such imputations imputes to a person a specific act such as is harmful to his honor or dignity or subjects him to people's hostility and insult, shall be punished by imprisonment for 3 months to 3 years and be given a heavy fine of 200 to 2000 liras».

[28] These are also offenses against privacy, Art. 195 ff. of the Criminal Code.

[29] It is generally considered that blood tests given to drivers to determine the percentage of the alcohol in the blood are not attacks against personality. Akipek 142.

the infringement of his name, may request the prohibition of this violation».

An example of protection of personality is seen in the field of restrictive trade practices and economic pressures such as boycotting or establishing cartels and trusts which reach a point where they threaten the economic existence of a person.[30] Unfair competition is also separately regulated by the Commercial Code (Art. 56 ff.) and Code of Obligations (Art. 48).

As noted above, compensation may also be demanded in the case of an attack on personality. There are two types of damage which can be compensated:

(1) Material *(maddî)* damage : If as a result of a negligent or intentional illegal act material injury is caused, the damage must be compensated.[31]

(2) Immaterial (moral, *manevî)* damage : In some cases, the attack may have permanent effects on the person, and therefore, the amount of the material compensation may not cover the actual damages. For this reason, in specific instances, if the damage is particularly grave (C. C., Art. 49 and C. C., Art. 25) the judge may decide on the payment of additional compensation. Thus, in case of divorce the judge may decide on the payment of compensation for immaterial damage by the spouse who has caused the divorce, to the other spouse, if his or her «personal interests are severely damaged» (C. C., Art. 143 II).

Instead of or in addition to immaterial damages the judge may require an apology and its publication in a newspaper.

One of the most basic ways of protecting the personality is legitimate self - defense. Provisions in the Code of Obligations (Art. 52) and Criminal Code (Art. 49) state that a person will not be liable for damages to another, inflicted in self - defense of the personality (Legitimate self - defense = *meşru müdafaa).*

C. Protection of Personality Against Oneself :

In addition to the protection of the personality against third persons, it is also protected against the person himself. Long experience has shown that persons themselves sometimes agree to restrictions on their own personality under outside pressure. In order to protect the weaker against the stronger article 23 of the Civil Code states : «No one can renounce, even partly, his

---
[30] See also Criminal Code, Art. 201.
[31] See Chapter 9, Part 3 on the Law of Obligations.

capacity to be the subject of rights or his capacity to enter into legal transactions. No one can renounce his freedom or restrict himself in its use in a degree offensive to law or morality».

As mentioned above, no person may sign a contract and promise not to marry in his lifetime, nor can a person agree to be a slave. No person may promise not to bring a suit in court or never to dispose of his property. No person may promise not to change his domicile in his lifetime or not to change his political ideas or religious beliefs. Lifetime employment contracts are not binding as they are deemed to constitute the renunciation of the freedom of the employee; such contracts are not completely void, but are deemed binding only for ten years; afterwards they may be terminated at any time by the employee (C. O., Art. 343. Also see C. O., Art. 536).

Persons may limit their freedoms, if these limitations are not against law or morals (C. C., Art. 23 II). There are some examples of such permissible limitations of freedom in the Civil Code and Code of Obligations (C. C., Arts. 83, 266, 306, 784, C. O., Art. 139, 396, 496 III). Certain contracts in restraint of trade are possible. But they are «only valid within such appropriate limits of time, place and subject matter as will not unreasonably impede the economic future of the employee» (C. C., Art. 349).

SELECTED BIBLIOGRAPHY

Akipek, Jale G. : **Türk Medeni Hukuku, Şahsın Hukuku,** Cilt : 1, Cüz : 2 (Ankara 1961).
Dural, Mustafa : **Türk Medenî Hukukunda Gerçek Kişiler** (İstanbul 1977).
Özsunay, Ergun : **Gerçek Kişilerin Hukukî Durumu** (İstanbul 1977).
Velidedeoğlu, H. V. : **Türk Medeni Hukuku** (İstanbul 1963).

CHAPTER 5

LEGAL PERSONS, SOCIETIES AND ASSOCIATIONS

Prof. Dr. Tuğrul ANSAY *

I. GENERAL

Human beings come together in groups to achieve common objectives. The purpose of accomplishing something together will determine the nature of the group.

Several persons may accidentally come together. The passengers in a transatlantic plane are there for the common purpose of flying over the ocean. When several students study in the same class, there is again a common purpose, which is to learn and receive a diploma. Students may elect some of their members to prepare a year book. These elected students also work for a common purpose.

Sometimes individuals bring their capital or skill together to achieve a common purpose, fulfill the formalities required by law and obtain a legal personality.[1] Such collaboration is legally called either a society or association, depending on the nature of the purpose of the founders. If the founders do not intend to make and share profits, the institution is a society; an example of a society is a club. If on the other hand the intention is to share profits, there exists an association. If the legal formalities required to obtain a legal personality are not fulfilled, the association thus formed is called an ordinary partnership.

Not only human beings, but legal personalities are the subjects of rights. They can also enter into transactions, own property, have their own name and a legal domicile.

Several persons may come together and form a society. Such society will have a different legal personality from the personalities

---

* Faculty of Law, University of Ankara.

[1] Legal personality *(hükmi şahsiyet, tüzel kişilik)* or legal person *(hükmi şahıs, tüzel kişi)* is used in civil law countries such as Turkey, in contrast to natural person or human being. In fact a natural person is considered a person in law because the law says so, and therefore in the real sense of the term natural persons are also legal persons. Yet in order to make the distinction, two terms, real and legal, are used. A corporation is legal personality. In English texts the terms incorporated and unincorporated distinguish legal personality from the absence of one. The term corporation is mainly used, in American law, to describe a business corporation *(anonim şirket.* See, below VI C).

of the persons who form the society. Thus where (A), (B) and (C) form a chess club, the club is a separate person, (D), different from (A), (B) and (C). (A), (B) and (C), as the members of the club, may appoint directors, who will administer the affairs of the club and represent the club. If an authorized director signs a contract in the name of the club, the club itself will be deemed to have signed the contract. The club can bring a law suit in court through its representatives. It may have its own property and its own debts. In short, a club can do the things, at least in law, that natural persons can. Of course, unlike a natural person, it cannot eat, sleep or marry.

The famous English legal scholar Blackstone compared a legal personality to the River Thames: «The River Thames is still the same river, though the parts which may comprise it are changing every instant»[2]. The life of a legal person may be perpetual; the death or withdrawal of members, or the addition of new members from time to time need not impair the continuity and identity of the body.[3]

II. THEORIES OF PERSONALITY [4]

There are several legal theories which attempt to explain the nature of a legal person.

1) The fiction theory regards legal persons as fictions. In this theory, legal persons are not really persons, like human beings, but are merely treated as if they were persons. They are creations of the lawgiver. This theory has certain practical consequences. Since personality is given by the state (the lawgiver), the state must approve the existence of a legal person and the state is free to limit the rights of a legal person.

2) The theory of collective property entirely rejects the idea of a legal person and holds that «the idea of fictitious personality is a conception which, though simple, is superficial and false, and one which conceals from our eyes the persistence in our own time of collective property side by side with individual property».

3) *Jhering* finds the human beings behind the legal personality, rather than the personality, as the real subjects of rights. Thus the members of a club, the stockholders of a corporation and the

---

[2] *Commentaries on the Laws of England*, 468 (Vol. 1, 16th ed. London 1825).
[3] In Turkish law, however, this may not be true for partnerships and other business associations where the identity of the persons forming the same is important to the purposes of the organizations.
[4] See, in general, M. Wolff, *On the Nature of Legal Persons*, 54 Law Quarterly Review 494 ff (1938) and Hallis, *Corporate Personality* (London 1930).

beneficiaries of a foundation (*tesis* or *vakıf*) are the real subjects of rights, and not the club, corporation or foundation.

4) Finally, the realist or organic theory, considers legal personalities to be social realities. In this view, legal personalities exist even without their recognition by the law. Law, by recognizing them merely makes them a legal reality.[5] Just as real persons have organs such as hands, eyes and brains, legal persons too, have organs, such as boards of directors and general meetings of members or stockholders, without which a legal personality could not exist. According to this realist theory, the approval of the state is not necessary to form a legal personality. So too, according to this theory, legal persons like real persons, have broad capacity to enter into transactions.

III. CLASSIFICATION OF LEGAL PERSONALITIES

A. Associations of Persons and Dedication of a Fund to a Specified Purpose :

1. Associations of Persons :

The first class of legal personality is composed of persons who come together to achieve a common purpose. The members or stockholders form the will of the legal person and make decisions by means of their resolutions at general assemblies or through the directors. Societies and business associations are examples of this type of legal personality.

2. Foundations :

Foundations are an example of a legal person formed by the allocation of a fund or property for a specified purpose. A donor of funds forms a foundation, and his intentions shape the organization and administration of the foundation.

B. Public, Private and Mixed Legal Persons :

Public legal persons include territorial entities such as villages, municipalities, provinces (Constitution, Art. 116) and functional ones, such as universities.[6]

As noted above, private legal persons include those which have a non-profit sharing purpose (societies, *dernekler*), and those which have a profit sharing purpose (business associations, *ticaret şir-*

---

[5] Otto Gierke, *Die Genossenschafftstheorie und die deutsche Rechtsprechung* 614 ff. (Berlin 1887); Hallis 137 ff.
[6] See Chapter 3, III, D on Administrative Law.

ketleri). There are also labor unions, political parties, bar associations and others which are subject to special laws.

Legal persons of a mixed character are those which are formed with state participation by special enactments, but which are partly subject to the provisions of the private law: An example is the state economic enterprises *(iktisadî devlet teşekkülleri)*[7].

IV. ORDINARY PARTNERSHIP   (C. O., Arts. 530 - 541)

The simplest form of association is the ordinary partnership *(adi şirket)*. It does not have a legal personality separate from the partners. Its formation is easy; it may be formed for profit making or non-profit making purposes. Its purpose may be a temporary one; for example, when two persons jointly buy a lottery ticket an ordinary partnership is formed.

An ordinary partnership is defined in the Code of Obligations as an association of two or more persons who agree to undertake to bring their skill or capital to attain a common object (C.O., Art. 520). If, for example, (A) and (B) buy a truck to carry goods from Istanbul to Ankara and share the profits, they have an ordinary partnership. Joint ventures are subject to the provisions of the ordinary partnerships.

The ordinary partnership is generally administered internally by the partners themselves. Each partner may individually perform the ordinary business of the partnership and has the power to represent the partnership against third persons (C.O., Art. 552 III). The partners in an ordinary partnership have co-ownership rights [8] in the partnership property (C.O., Art. 534). All partners are jointly liable against third persons because of the transactions of the partnership, and their liability is unlimited.

V. SOCIETIES

A. General:

Societies *(dernekler, cemiyetler)* are legal persons formed by at least seven persons who unite their knowledge and activities continuously for a non-profit sharing purpose (Law of Societies Art. 1). They are regulated by articles 53-72 of the Civil Code and the Law of Societies of 1972.[9]

---

[7] See Chapter 3, III, D on Administrative Law.
[8] See Chapter 8, VI on the Law of Property.
[9] Law No. 1630, dated Dec. 22, 1972, Some of the provisions of this Law have been annulled by the Constitutional Court.

Non-profit sharing purposes include charitable, political, scientific, artistic purposes and others. Three or more musicians may form a society to improve musical education in the country, or a society may be formed for the purpose of giving aid to poor students or for medical purposes, such as an aid for cancer society.

Although societies are non-profit sharing, that is to say they are not formed to earn profits for their members, they may operate commercial enterprises. A society of vegetarians may open a restaurant for its members, where non-members may also come and eat. Societies which operate a commercial enterprise are subject to the laws governing merchants. They must fulfill the obligations of a merchant (Comm. C., Art. 18; C. C., Art. 54 II) and must register their enterprises in the commercial register. If, eventually, the economic profit making purpose becomes predominant, then the laws governing ordinary partnerships will be applied to them.

Societies against law and morals (C.C., Art. 45), against the authority or unity of the state, based on religion or sects, family, group or race, as well as political societies with merely local purposes (Law of Soc., Art. 4) are prohibited.[10]

The permission of the Council of Ministers is necessary to form societies which have international or military training purposes (Law of Soc. Arts. 6 and 10).

If the purpose of a society is to benefit the public, an application may be made to the Council of State *(Danıştay)*, and such a society may be established upon the approval of this Council and the Council of Ministers *(Kamuya yararlı dernek,* such as *Kızılay* or *Çocuk Esirgeme Kurumu)*. Societies formed with such approval will have certain tax privileges, and bequests to them are also to a certain extent tax-free. They are also freed from the normal limitations on the sources and amount of property which a society may own (See, Comm. C., Art. 18).

B. Formation :

The freedom to form a society is guaranteed by the Constitution, which states that every individual is entitled to form societies without prior authorization (Const. Art. 29 I). The formation of a society, as opposed to some other forms of legal personalities, is rather easy and free of formal requirements. Seven or more

---

[10] Student associations may not deal with politics (Law of Soc., Art. 35).

persons need merely to prepare the society's by-laws, sign the same, and submit it to the highest local authority, for the society to acquire legal personality (C. C., Art. 45 Law of Soc., Art. 3). No prior authorization from the government is necessary, nor is any registration or publication a prerequisite. However, an application should be made to the highest local governmental authority with four copies of the by-laws after the society is formed (Law of Soc. Art. 8). Furthermore, the by-laws of the society should be published in a newspaper within fifteen days following such application (Law of Soc. Art. 12). A registration is also necessary (Law of Soc. Art. 14).

C. Capacity of Societies :

As far as the capacity of societies is concerned the Turkish law has inclined to accept the realist theory. Therefore societies may enter into transactions, acquire and alienate all kinds of property, and, generally may do every thing which a real person may do, except those things peculiar to human beings. A society is liable in tort for damage to third persons caused by its organs or agents during the performance of their duties [11] (C. C., Art. 48). The capacity of a society is however limited by the purpose of the society.[12] If a society is formed for the advancement of research in nuclear physics, the society will not have capacity to sign contracts for sporting purposes. Transactions outside the scope of a society's purposes are null and void [13]; and the dissolution of a society may be demanded if it is engaged in activities outside its purpose. A society may own immovable property only to the extent necessary to achieve its purposes (Law of Soc., Art. 52).

D. By - Laws :

The by-laws are the document by which a society declares its purposes; it must also state the facts of its organization and the sources of its finances (C. C., Art. 53). According to article 7 of the Law of Societies the following must be included in the by-laws :

(a) The name and principal office of the society.
(b) Its purposes and subject matter.
(c) The names, professions, addresses and nationalities of the founders.

---
[11] Özsunay 61 ff.
[12] See, Akipek 270, Law of Soc., Art. 35 I a.
[13] Akipek 259.

(d) Conditions to become a member and to resign from the society.
(e) How branches may be formed, how they will be administered and represented and the limits of their authorities.
(f) Formation, duties, powers, notice requirements etc. of the general assembly of members.
(g) Formation, powers and the number of the directors on the Board of Directors and Board of Controllers.
(h) Annual dues.
(i) Procedures for amendment of the by-laws.
(j) The method of dissolution.

E. Organization :

Societies, like other legal personalities, have the capacity to enter into legal transactions only if their organs, that is to say, General Assembly and Board of Directors, have been constituted in accordance with the requirements of law and of the society's by-laws (C. C., Art. 47). As noted in (D) above, the method of formation and the functions of the organs must be stated in the by-laws (Law of Soc. Art. 7). There are statutory and optional organs. Statutory organs are the General Assembly and the Board of Directors. In addition to these, the Law of Societies require the Board of Controllers as a third organ.

1. General Assembly:

The meeting of the members is called the General Assembly *(genel kurul)*. The assembly, which acts by means of resolutions which it passes, in the ultimate authority of a society (C. C., Art. 57).

a) **Powers of the General Assembly :** The most important powers and duties of the General Assembly are enumerated in the Civil Code and the Law of Societies. They include, among others, ratification of the budget which is submitted by the Board of Directors, examination of the balance sheet, control of the administration and the audit of the accounts, acceptance of new members and the dismissal of old ones, election of the members of the Board of Directors and, if necessary, their dismissal (C. C., Art. 58; Law of Soc., Art. 24).

b) **Meetings :** The General Assembly meets as provided in the by-laws. But it must meet at least once every two years (Law of

Soc., Art. 18). In practice by-laws usually require meetings once a year.

The General Assembly meets upon notice from the Board of Directors given as required by the by-laws. One fifth of the members may also require the Board to call a meeting of the General Assembly. If the Board fails to do so, the members may apply to the court (C. C., Art. 57, Law of Soc., Art. 18).

Meetings will be held with a simple majority of the members if a quorum does not exist at the first meeting called, those present at a subsequent meeting will constitute a quorum (Law of Soc. Art. 21).

c) Resolutions: Only those matters stated in the agenda of the meeting may be discussed. The agenda *(gündem)* is announced with the notice of the meeting (Law of Soc., Art. 19), and is prepared by the Board of Directors. However, matters which are proposed by at least one tenth of the members shall be included in the agenda (Law of Soc., Art. 23).

Resolutions are ordinarily passed by the majority vote of the members who are present at the meeting (C. C., Art. 60). The by-laws may, however, stipulate other percentages of the vote required to pass a resolution.

Each member is entitled to only one vote (Law of Soc., Art. 16).

Resolutions against obligatory provisions of the law or against the by-laws may be declared void by a court upon the demand of any member (C. C., Art. 68).

2. Board of Directors:

The second statutory organ is the Board of Directors *(idare meclisi)* which is elected by the General Assembly and consists of at least three persons (Law of Soc., Art. 25).

The Board's duty is to administer the society internally and to represent it on its relations with third persons (C. C., Art. 62, Law of Soc., Art. 25). The Board is responsible for keeping the books, preparation of the budget, balance sheet and annual reports; it calls the members to the meeting of the General Assembly.

3. Control:

There must be at least three controllers elected by the General Assembly. They not only audit the accounts of the society, but also control it's administration (Law of Soc., Arts. 27, 51). An additional government control also exists.[14]

F. Membership (Azalık, üyelik):

1. Acquisition:

Persons over 18 and able to enter into legal transactions [15] may join societies. Those foreigners who are domiciled in Turkey are also entitled to become members in turkish societies (Law of Soc., Art. 15). As the Constitution states, «no individual can be coerced into becoming a member of a society or into becoming his membership» (Art. 29 II).

The by-laws of a society may bring special qualifications for membership, such as membership in a certain profession, status as a university student, residence in a certain district etc.

Persons become members of a society upon the approval of the Board of Directors, if nothing contrary is stated in the by-laws (C.C., Art. 58 I, Law of Soc., Art. 15 III).

2. Termination of Membership:

a) Resignation: Members may resign from a society by giving the society notice; no more than six months notice can be required (C. C., Art. 63 and 66). The resignation may be effective immediately if it is so stated in the by-laws.

b) Dismissal:

(i) The by-laws may enumerate the grounds for dismissal from a society. For example a member may be dismissed, if he does not pay his dues for two consecutive years, or, if he fails to attend five consecutive general meetings.

The by-laws may give the General Assembly or the Board of Directors the right to dismiss a member without a particular reason. This right should not be misused.[16]

(ii) If there is no provision in the by-laws on dismissal, a member may be dismissed only by a resolution of the General Assembly for reasonable grounds (C. C., Art. 65 II), such as acting against the purpose of the society, or continuous non-payment of dues.

---

[14] For this extermal control, see Law of Soc., Arts. 40 ff.
[15] See Chapter 4 on the Law Persons.
[16] Akipek 315; Özsunay 174.

(iii) In each case a member may appeal his dismissal to a court.[17]

3. Membership Rights:

Members are entitled to attend general meetings, to speak and vote at them, to go to court to challenge resolutions which are against the law or by-laws, to call general meetings (one fifth of the membership required), to demand the inclusion of new items in the agenda of general meetings (one tenth of the membership required). As noted above, members have the right to resign from the society.

4. Membership Duties:

Members must not act against the purpose of the society. Another duty of the members is to pay membership dues, which may not exceed 1,200 TL. annually (Law of Soc., Art. 7 h).

VI. BUSINESS ASSOCIATIONS [18]

A. General Classification:

Certain types of associations are classified in the Commercial Code as business associations *(ticaret şirketleri)*. They are General Partnerships *(kollektif şirket)*, Limited Partnerships *(komandit şirket)*, Limited Partnerships in which the Capital is Divided into Shares *(sermayesi paylara bölünmüş komandit şirket)*, Corporations (or Stock Companies, *anonim şirket*) Limited Liability Companies (Partnership with Limited Liability, *limited şirket*) and Cooperatives [19] *(kooperatif)*. All these associations have a legal personality which is different from those of the persons who create them. All of them are «merchants» (Comm. C., Art. 136) and, therefore, must fulfill the obligations of «merchants».[20]

---

[17] Özsunay 173; Akipek 315. Court of Cassation, General Assembly Decision on the Unification of Judgments *(İçtihadı Birleştirme Kurulu Kararı)*, Oct. 4, 1950. Official Gazette *(Resmi Gazete)* Oct. 7, 1950.
[18] On terminology see, Conard, *Forming a Subsidiary in the European Common Market*, 59 Michigan L. Review, 1-48, 8 ff. (1960).
[19] Cooperatives are regulated by a special law : Law on Cooperatives, Law No. 1163, dated April 24, 1969.
[20] There are two types of merchants : real persons and legal persons. If a real person alone or with others operates a commercial enterprise he is a merchant. All business associations and societies operating a commercial enterprise, are also merchants (Comm. C., Arts. 14 and 18). Merchants must register themselves, must have trade names, must keep commercial books etc. See Chapter 4 on the Law of Persons, footnote 19.

B. Persons versus Capital:

1. Business Associations where Persons are Important:

In the case of associations where the identity of the persons who are the members is important to those dealing with the association, the members will usually have unlimited liability. In such a case, the partners will generally know each other personally and should have the utmost confidence in each other. For that reason, there will usually be no more than four or five partners. Because of their unlimited liability partners are interested in the administration of the association. The transfer of partnership rights is made difficult and the death of a partner has significant effects on the continuity of the partnership.

a) A general partnership is an example of an association where the persons are important. It is formed by two or more persons who enter into a written partnership agreement. Their signatures are authenticated by the notary public and the partnership should be registered in the Commercial Registry. Upon this registration it acquires legal personality.

Each partner has the right and duty to participate in the partnership administration (Comm. C., Art. 160). This power may however be given to one or several partners or to an outsider as a manager.

The partnership has capacity to enter into transactions within the scope of the stated purposes of the partnership; otherwise the transactions are not valid. The signature of one of the partners is sufficient to bind the partnership in its transactions with outsiders.

Partners have unlimited liability; the death or dismissal by the others of a partner causes the dissolution of the partnership, if nothing contrary is stated in the partnership agreement.

b) A limited partnership has two types of partners, those who have unlimited liability and those who have limited liability.

2. Business Associations where Capital is Important:

In business associations where capital rather than the identity of the association's members is the more important factor, the members have, generally speaking, limited liability.[21] Here, the amount of money contributed or promised by the shareholders, rather than the personal wealth and reputation of the partners, is significant. There is a fixed minimum capital which the association

---

[21] Although the Corporate Bodies Tax Law treats a cooperative like a business corporation, the liability of its shareholders may sometimes be unlimited.

must have for the security of its creditors. Shareholders are liable to the association and may be assessed up to the amount they promise to bring to the association. Beyond that, creditors of the association may not demand anything from the shareholders.

Since the capital brought by the members rather than the identity of the shareholders themselves is important, there may be numerous shareholders. This may be particularly desirable for the purpose of capital formation. Thus small capital holders, with as little as 500 TL. (the minimum par-value of a corporate share) may subscribe to a corporation. The transfer of shareholders' rights is made easy and the death of a shareholder does not effect the life of the association. Since the number of the shareholders may be large and since they are not necessarily experienced in business, the administration of the association is not in the hands of the shareholders but rather of the administrator or board of directors.

C. Corporations (Anonim şirketler) :

1. In General :

Corporations have limited liability and may have numerous shareholders. Because there is a public which must be protected against the misuse of limited liability and shareholders who must be protected against the abuse of other shareholders and directors, the law regulates corporations in detail and the state may, on occasion, intervene in their affairs.

2. Formation :

Unlike the formation of a society which can be simply formed even without registration, the formation of a corporation is made difficult. The following formalities must be fulfilled :

(1) There must be at least five incorporators and the minimum capital of a corporation is fixed at 500.000 TL. This capital is either contributed by the incorporators themselves, or else public participation may be solicited.

The articles of incorporation must be prepared in accordance with article 279 of the Commercial Code and the signatures of the incorporators must be authenticated by a notary.[22]

(2) The Ministry of Commerce must approve the incorporation. Usually the Ministry not only checks to see whether the purposes of the corporation conform to the general economic policy of the

---

[22] For the notary see Chapter 11, Part 1, III E on the Law of Procedure.

government, but also inquires whether the requirements of the Commercial Code have been fulfilled.

(3) A court inspection of the legality of formation is required.

(4) The registrar of the commercial registry, too, must check the validity of the incorporation formalities, when an application is made for registration.

The corporation acquires legal personality at the time of registration in the commercial register. Founders are liable for any damage to shareholders or outsiders by their negligence prior to such registration. Their liability is joint and unlimited, and they may also be held criminally liable (Comm. C., Arts. 305 ff.).

3. *Organization:*

a) General Assembly *(Umumî heyet, genel kurul)*:

(1) The shareholders constitute the General Assembly. The stated capital of a corporation is divided into shares, each with a par value of at least 500 TL. The persons who own or hold these shares are called shareholders. Shareholders exercise their rights with regard to the affairs of the corporation in the General Assembly, which must meet at least once a year (Ordinary General Assembly, *adî umumî heyet*). Each ordinary share entitles its holders to at least one vote at the General Assembly.

(2) In the ordinary General Assembly, the shareholders discuss and approve certain matters such as the annual report, balance sheet and budget. They elect the directors and controllers, and may remove them, and may authorize the distribution of dividends.

(3) Those shareholders who disagree with the resolutions of the General Assembly may bring a suit to annul such resolutions as are against the law, by-laws or good faith. They may also bring suits against directors who negligently damage the corporation or shareholders. Certain other rights, such as demanding an extraordinary meeting of the General Assembly, appointment of a special auditor, are given to minority shareholders representing at least one tenth of the stated capital of the corporation.

(4) Shareholdings may be transferred by the transfer of the share certificates issued to represent the shareholders' rights. There are two types of certificates: registered and bearer certificates *(nama ve hamile yazılı hisse senetleri)*. The names of the owners of the registered shares are stated in the corporate books and such shares are transferred by endorsement. The buyer's name

must then be registered in the corporation's books. For the transfer of bearer shares, mere delivery is sufficient.

b) Board of Directors *(İdare meclisi, yönetim kurulu)*: The Board of Directors consists of three or more persons who are called directors. They are elected by the shareholders for terms of not more than three years each. The internal administration of a corporation is their responsibility. They prepare the annual report, balance sheet and budget. They also represent the corporation in its dealings with others. The signature of at least two directors, in the absence of a contrary provision in the by-laws, is necessary in such dealings. Usually a manager (and in larger corporations other officers) is appointed by the Board for the administration of the regular business of the corporation.

The directors are authorized to enter into transactions within the subject matters stated in the by-laws of the corporation, which also show the corporate capacity. Those transactions which are outside of the scope of business of the corporation are null and void as being beyond its capacity *(ultra-vires)*.

c) Controllers (Comptrollers = *Murakıplar, denetçiler)*: There must be at least one controller in each corporation. Controllers have the duty to control [23] the affairs of the corporation by checking the legality of transactions undertaken by the directors and managers and auditing the accounts of the corporation.

D. Foundations (Vakıflar):

1. In General:

Unlike a society or association, a foundation is a legal personality to which a fund has been granted for a specific purpose (C. C., Art. 73). Therefore, in a foundation, it is the property that is important; there are no members, partners or shareholders.

Under the Turkish law there are two types of foundations. Those which were formed during the old Muslim Law period and are regulated by special laws. The Civil Code [24] regulates the newer foundations which may again differ according to their purposes. Those which are formed for the public benefit have certain privileges.[25]

---

[23] This exact function is not known in American corporate or English company law.
[24] Arts. 73-81, as amended by the Law Nr. 903, dated July 13, 1967.
[25] Özsunay 240 ff.

2. Formation:

Foundations may be formed by real or legal persons.

The purpose of a foundation may be economic or non-economic; it must, however, be specific. If a person grants his two houses merely for charitable purposes, there is, usually, no valid foundation. Foundations may however be set up for several purposes related to each other such as to train and educate young men. The purpose, such as to send the best students each year from a particular university to a specific foreign country, must continue over time.

Property, money or credits must be set apart for the purposes of the foundation, and the amount allocated must be sufficient to achieve the purpose (C. C., Art. 80 A).

The intention to form a foundation must be expressed either in a deed, authenticated by a notary, or last will.

In order to acquire legal personality the foundation must be registered by the court (C. C., Arts. 45 and 74). There is also a central registry at the General Directorate of Foundations.

3. Organization:

A foundation is administered by its Board of Directors *(mütevelli heyeti)*, usually appointed by the founder himself. This is an obligatory organ (C. C., Art. 77), without which a foundation may not function. One director is sufficient. A Board of Consultants *(müşavere heyeti)* or Board of Founders *(müessisler heyeti)* may be additional organs.

4. Control:

Foundations in Turkey are subject to state supervision, this is done by the General Directorate of Foundations *(Vakıflar Genel Müdürlüğü)* (C. C., Art. 78).

The Directorate, first of all, controls the operation of the foundation to see that it accords with the will of the founder. It is also entitled to demand the removal of a director by the court, to make necessary changes in the organization and even the purposes of the foundation when it is necessary for the preservation of the foundation's property or its continued functioning (C. C., Arts. 79, 80). For example, the purpose of a foundation, which is formed to encourage research in finding a cure to prevent cancer may be changed, if a cure should be found.

SELECTED BIBLIOGRAPHY

Akipek, Jale G. : **Türk Medeni Hukuku, Şahsın Hukuku,** Cilt : 1, Cüz : 2 (Ankara 1961).

Ansay, T. : **Bankacılar İçin Şirketler Hukuku Bilgisi** (Ankara 1978).

Özsunay, E. : **Medenî Hukukumuzda Tüzel Kişiler** (Istanbul 1974).

Velidedeoğlu, H. V. : **Türk Medeni Hukuku, Şahsın Hukuku,** C : 1, Cüz : 2 (Istanbul 1963).

Velidedeoğlu, H. V. : **Türk Medeni Hukuku,** pp. 226 ff. (Istanbul 1963).

Ansay, T. : **Legal Aspects of Foreign Investment, Turkey** (in : Legal Aspects of Foreign Investment, Ed. : Friedmann, Boston 1959) pp. 543-561.

Ansay, T. : **Public and Private Enterprises in Turkey** (In : Public and Private Enteprises in Mixed Economies, Ed. : W. Friedmann, London 1974), pp. 135 - 191.

CHAPTER 6

FAMILY LAW

Prof. Dr. Tuğrul ANSAY [*]

I. IN GENERAL :

The family is the primary group in the society. The smallest family unit consists of husband and wife and the children. There are larger types which include other persons : parents, brothers, sisters, aunts, uncles, and in-laws.[1]

The Turkish Constitution refers to the family as the basic institution of Turkish society (Art. 35) and requires its protection. The Civil Code contains provisions regulating the family as an institution. The Code primarily deals with the small family consisting of the husband and wife and the children. It also includes provisions regarding the larger type of families, such as those concerning the duty to maintain ascendants in the direct line as well as brothers and sisters. According to article 318, the person who is regarded by law or agreement or tradition as the head of a group of persons living together in one household as a family is held to have a certain authority over them.

The traditional family in Turkey is a rural, religiously oriented, large family.[2] Only recently, Turkey's industrialization has tended to cause a change towards the small, nuclear family. The Turkish Civil Code, modeled on the Swiss Civil Code which was designed to regulate the affairs of small families, brought with it provisions which do not always lend themselves well to the Turkish concepts of traditional family life. As a result, for a considerable part of the population, there has been some contradiction between their traditional social practice and the law.

---

[*] Faculty of Law, University of Ankara.
[1] René König, *Sociological Introduction*, International Encyclopedia of Comparative Law, Vol. IV (1974).
[2] Stirling, *Turkish Village* (University of Kentucky Press, Lexington 1965); Benedict, *Ula, An Anatolian Town*, (Leiden 1974) pp. 146 ff. ; Güçbilmez, *Yenimahalle ve Kayadibi, Karşılaştırmalı bir köy araştırması* (Ankara 1972); Timur, *Türkiye'de aile yapısı* (Ankara 1972); Kongar, *İzmir'de kentsel aile* (Ankara 1972)

II. ENGAGEMENT:

A. Agreement to Marry:

The first step toward marriage is the engagement *(nişanlanma)*. It indicates that two persons of opposite sexes have promised to marry. Since the marrige may not be performed without fulfilling certain formalities, there is always a preliminary stage, known as the engagement, before the marriage.

In Turkey the engagement is more than a promise of marriage. Because of social mores, engagement may still be considered an important stage during which the girl and the boy have a socially acceptable opportunity to come to know each other intimately.

It is generally accepted that the engagement has a contractual nature.[3] The parties express their willingness to engage. This expression is usually made orally and symbolized by the exchange of rings.[4]

B. Breach of Engagement:

Marriage is the expected outcome of the engagement. But engagement itself does not constitute an enforceable contract. It does not compel any of the parties to marry, and it does not prevent a marriage with someone else. Liquidated damage agreements for breach of promise are null and void (C. C., Art. 83). Yet, there are certain legal consequences attributed to the breach of engagement.

1. One of the consequences of the breach of engagement is the reciprocal return of the gifts given by the fiancées during the engagement. This is done even when one of the parties has caused the breach. If gifts no longer exist, compensation may be demanded under the provisions of unjust enrichment (C.C., Art. 86). According to judicial practice, return of the gifts given by the parents may also be demanded.[5]

In addition to the return of gifts, damages may be recovered against a party who breaks the engagement without reasonable cause. Compensation covers material and/or immaterial damages.

2. Material damages: Material compensation may be demanded from the party who caused the breach of engagement. The extent of the compensation is limited. The innocent party may demand compensation for expenses and losses incurred in good faith in

---

[3] See below, Ch. 9.
[4] Ceremonies are not an essential part of a valid engagement. Tekinay, 18.
[5] Tekinay, 31 ff.

contemplation of marriage (C. C., Art. 84). These may be expenses such as renting an apartment, purchasing furniture, or resignation from employment in anticipation of marriage. According to the circumstances, the compensation may be reduced to the level of actual damage. Furthermore, not only the damages of the fiancées, but also those of the parents or persons acting as parents, who have incurred expenses, may be recovered.

3. Immaterial damages : Compensation for moral damages may also be recovered if one of the parties acts culpably and the other party innocently suffers gross injuries because of breach of engagement. The social environment to which the injured party belongs and the duration of the engagement are factors determining the degree of the injury.[6]

Suits related to breach of engagement should be brought within one year after the breach of engagement (C.C., Art. 87).

III. MARRIAGE :

A. In General :

The status of husband and wife begins with the enactment of marriage *(evlenme)*. Marriage, legally is considered a contract. Conditions similar to those required for a valid contract, including the agreement of the parties, are necessary for a valid marriage. But because of the importance of the family as an institution of society and due to the effect of marriage on persons who are not parties to the contract of marriage, the marriage and its enactment are specially regulated in the Civil Code.

B. Conditions for a Valid Marriage :

For a valid marriage certain conditions should exist :

1. Capacity to marry : Only those persons who have sufficient mental capacity to make fair judgements are allowed to marry. Mental illness is, therefore, a bar to marriage. In addition, a person must have reached the minimum age of 18 to marry. In exceptional cases, however, the age of marriage is reduced to 17 for the bridegroom and to 15 for the bride, with the consent of both of the parents or the guardian. Under extreme situations and for good and sufficient cause, consent to marry can be given by the competent judge if the bridegroom is at least 15 and the bride at least 14 years of age (C.C., Arts. 88 and 90).

---

[6] Tekinay, 50.

2. Absence of consanguinity: Marriage between close relatives is prohibited. Close relatives are defined in article 92 of the Civil Code.[7]

3. Already existing marriage: Monogamy is one of the essential principles of Turkish family law. A second marriage cannot be entered into unless the first is terminated.[8]

4. Adoptive relationship: An adopting parent is not allowed to marry his or her adopted child. But this impediment is not absolute. If the persons, notwithstanding the adoptive relationship, have married, the marriage will be held valid. The adoptive relationship between the adopting parent and the adopted child, however, comes to an end upon the marriage (C. C., Art. 142).

6. Sickness: Certain sicknesses enumerated in article 123 of the Law of General Hygiene,[9] constitute a bar to marriage.

The persons legally eligible to celebrate marriages should determine that the requirements for a valid marriage exist prior to performing the ceremony. The last three impediments discussed above, however, are not absolute. A marriage which is celebrated before the expiration of the waiting period, in spite of those certain sicknesses or within an adoptive relationship, will not be dissolved.

C. Celebration of Marriage:

Only civil marriages performed by authorized marriage officers are allowed in Turkey.

The celebration formalities commence with the submission of the necessary documents by the parties to the mayor (or to the village elders = *ihtiyar heyeti*). The civil authorities then determine impediments to the marriage by posting a notice concerning the parties' intention for a period of fifteen days at the municipality where the parties are domiciled and where their birth registrations are kept.

If no objection is raised within this period of time, a certificate of eligibility will be issued which entitles the parties to request celebration of marriage at any time within six months without repeating the preliminary formalities.

---

[7] Between a parent and a child or other descendants, between a sister and brother, between a person and his or her aunt or uncle, between parent or other ancestor, child or other descendant of the husband and the wife or *vice versa*.

[8] Divorce, death, or the declaration of marriage as void are grounds of the termination of a marriage (C. C., Art. 93).

[9] *Umumî Hıfzısıhha K.*, Law No. 4593, dated April 24, 1930.

The marriage ceremony is performed by the mayor,[9a] or, more frequently, by his appointee. The ceremony must be performed in the presence of two witnesses who are of age, usually in the town hall. The authorized person asks the parties the same question, that is, whether they are willing to marry each other. Upon hearing affirmative answers, he, then, declares the marriage to be enacted (C. C., Art. 109). But the marriage is deemed enacted from the moment when the parties have expressed their intention to marry.[10] After completion of the ceremony, the marriage officer issues a certificate of marriage. The marriage is also entered in the register of personal status of the husband and wife.[11]

Only after the celebration of the civil marriage is a religious *imam* marriage permitted. Contrary acts by imams are punishable offenses (Cr. C., Art. 237 III, C. C., Art. 108). Still, there are marriages performed by the imams without the prior civil celebration. Although such marriages are not legal, amnesty laws are periodically enacted which allow the registration of «consensual marriages» if a child has been born out of such a relation and if no marriage impediment between the parties exists. The most recent of these laws is dated June 20, 1974 [12] and is valid five years.

D. Marital Duties Between the Spouses :

1. According to the Civil Code, spouses owe each other fidelity, support, assistance, and have the duty of cohabitation; they should do their best for the happiness of the family.

The term fidelity is understood to mean that the couple should be faithful to each other in all respects (C. C., Art. 151 III). One example of the breach of fidelity is adultery.

The spouses have the reciprocal duty to support the family. Both of them should contribute to the cost of maintaining the household in proportion to their respective means (C. C., Art. 151 II).

In addition to material support, each spouse is also obliged to perform services for the other. They help each other in solving the problems of the family. The most important duty of assistance is to take care of one's spouse in the event of illness (C. C., Art. 152).

[9a] The Census Law (No. 1587, dated May, 5, 1972) has transferred all powers relating to the celebration of marriage to census officers. The transitory period will last until Sept. 1, 1979 (Art. 15).

[10] İçt. Bir. Kur. Kar., June 14, 1965, Tekinay, 94 - 95.

[11] See Ch. 4, III.

[12] Law No. 1826, promulgated on June 20, 1974. Previous Laws : Nos. 2330, 4727, 5524, 6652.

The duty of cohabitation indicates that the spouses are under the obligation to live together and maintain marital relations.

2. Equality between the husband and wife:

As in the laws of the Western nations, there is an equality of rights and duties of the spouses. This principle is stated in the Constitution as, «all individuals are equal before the law irrespective of sex» (Art. 12), and the same is maintained in the Civil Code which is older than the Constitution. But due to the concepts prevailing in Switzerland during the enactment of the Swiss Civil Code, the Swiss - inspired Turkish Civil Code contains exceptions to the rule of equal treatment of the spouses. The constitutionality of such rules has not yet been challenged. According to the Civil Code, for example, in cases of dispute, the views of the husband are decisive. He is also described as «the head of the family». The husband determines the place where the family should live. The wife carries the family name of her husband (C. C., Arts. 152 - 154). She may acquire the nationality of her husband, but he cannot acquire her nationality. Similarly, the children carry the family name of the father and acquire his nationality. The wife normally has legal standing to represent the family only for the continuing needs of the family (C. C., Art. 155 I).

As a counterpart of the superior position of the husband within the family, the duty of support also falls primarily on the husband. He is obliged to furnish his wife and children with everything necessary for their needs, according to his ability (C. C., Art. 152 II). The wife, however, should help the husband to fulfill these duties. Her contribution is made through her work in the home, or from her private resources (C. C., Art. 153 II).

IV. MATRIMONIAL PROPERTY SYSTEMS:

The husband and wife are free to regulate their pecuniary relations during the marriage within the limits prescribed by law. An arrangement may be made by a notarized agreement entered into before or after the marriage.[13] The spouses may choose one of the following property systems: separation of property, joint property, or common property. In the absence of an agreement on the matrimonial property system, the system of separation of property shall apply (C. C., Art. 170). Since the spouses usually do

---

[13] If done after the marriage, the ratification of the court is necessary (C. C., Art. 173).

not think much about the monetary aspect of their future life at the time when they marry, marriage contracts regulating the matrimonial system are rather rare. As a result, separation of property is the common system in Turkey.

1. The system of separation of property *(mal ayrılığı,* C. C., Arts. 186-190) : Under this system each spouse retains the ownership and administration of all his present or future property and has the free enjoyment and disposition of both capital and income. Similarly, both spouses retain control of their individual earnings.

Each spouse remains solely responsible for his own debts incurred either before or after the marriage. Yet each spouse (usually the wife) must contribute «reasonably» to the expenses of the household. The contribution of the wife to the household does not oblige the husband to return it or compensate her in the future.

2. The system of joint property *(mal birliği,* C. C., Arts. 191-210) : Under this system, all property owned by the spouses at the moment of marriage and all properties acquired during marriage, other than property explicity excluded by the marriage contract, constitutes joint property of the family, although husband and wife do not lose individual title to it. The husband, however, has a usufructuary right [14] in the joint property, and he administers it. The spouses may also have their separate property, which is not part of the joint property of the family.

3. The system of common property *(mal ortaklığı,* C. C., Arts. 211-236) : Under the common property system, the property of the spouses becomes family property, and the spouses own this property in common according to the general rules of co-ownership.[15] But as a rule, the husband administers the family property. The spouses may retain individual ownership in their reserved property which does not become a part of the family property.

V. DIVORCE AND JUDICIAL SEPARATION :

A. General :

Marriage may be terminated by the death of one of the spouses or by the declaration of a judge. The judge may either declare the marriage void or decide to grant a divorce *(boşanma).* Annulment of a marriage by court decision is rare. There are, however, many

---
[14] See Ch. 8 VIII B on the Law of Property.
[15] See Ch. 8 VI on the Law of Property.

divorces. The grounds of divorce are stated in the Civil Code. Incompatibility is a general ground for divorce, and is by far the most common one. There are also some specific grounds.

B. Grounds for Divorce:

1. The general ground of divorce is incompatibility *(şiddetli geçimsizlik, imtizaçsızlık)*. If there is severe incompatibility between the spouses that makes common life unbearable, either spouse may sue for a divorce. The judge in his discretion determines whether there is severe incompatibility. Continuous disagreement, arguments, loss of trust, lack of sexual capacity have been found as causes of incompatibility.[16] The spouse who is more responsible for the incompatibility is not entitled to bring a divorce suit (C. C., Art. 134 II).

2. Adultery *(zina)*: One of the oldest grounds for divorce is adultery. Adultery is voluntary sexual intercourse by a married person with someone other than one's spouse. Adultery is, on the one hand, a breach of fidelity and a specific ground for divorce, and at the same time, it is a criminal offense (Cr. C., Arts. 440-444). A divorce action should be brought within six months of the time of discovery of the adultery. A divorce suit on this ground is not admissible if five years have lapsed since the act of adultery. A spouse who consents to the other spouse's adultery may not bring an action for divorce on the ground of such adultery (C. C., Art. 129).

3. Plots against life, grave assaults and insults: A plot against life is an attempt by one spouse to murder the other. Grave assaults are threats or attempts to do bodily harm to the other spouse, by force or violence. Unlawful beating or other physical violence and insults also constitute a ground for divorce (C. C., Art. 130).

4. Crime and dishonorable life: The conviction of a spouse for a humiliating crime, such as theft, but not a political crime, dishonorable conduct, such as habitual drunkness, are grounds for divorce (C.C., Art. 131).

5. Desertion *(terk)*: Since cohabitation is one of the obligations of the spouses in the family, desertion is a ground for divorce. If one of the spouses leaves the matrimonial home to escape from the duties of the marriage, and does not return or offer justification

---

[16] See, Velidedeoğlu, 215 ff (1965); Tekinay, 153.

for the absence, there is a desertion. In order to become an acceptable ground for divorce, desertion must last at least 3 months (C. C., Art. 132).

6. Mental illness: Mental illness is a bar to marriage if it exists before the marriage. It is also a specific ground of divorce, under certain conditions, if it appears after the marriage. A mentally ill person must be under care and treatment continuously for a period of at least three years immediately preceeding the date of the petition, and this illness must be incurable. Furthermore, such illness should make normal married life unbearable for the other spouse (C. C., Art. 133).

C. The Role of the Judge in a Divorce Suit:

The Turkish Civil Code has made divorce by collusion or mutual agreement difficult (C. C., Art. 150). The judge is theoretically not bound to accept the accusations of the parties. Yet, in most cases, the court grants a divorce if both spouses demand it by mutual consent. If there is no agreement, the divorce proceedings may be protracted. The judge must therefore take the steps necessary to protect the interests of the persons involved, including the children and to determine the amount of an interim allowance (maintenance, *tedbir ve iştirak nafakası*) (C. C., Art. 137) to be paid by one of the spouses, usually the husband, to the other spouse.

D. Judicial Separation:

The spouse who has the right to bring a divorce suit may demand judicial separation. The judge may also order judicial separation if there is a possibility that the spouses could live together again in the future. Judicial separation may be obtained on almost the same grounds as divorce, and the court relieves the petitioning spouse from the duty of cohabitation. The husband and wife relationship continues despite judicial separation. A widow, therefore, may have a claim against her separated husband's estate for maintenance after his death, although no similar right accrues to a divorced wife (C. C., Arts. 138-140).

E. Legal Consequences of Divorce:

There are many legal consequences of divorce. Some of them are p e r s o n a l in nature: The wife may resume her maiden name, she will have her own independent domicile, both spouses keep the majority acquired by marriage (C. C., Art. 141). She may, however, keep the nationality of her husband which she has acquired by marriage.[17]

There are also f i n a n c i a l consequences of the divorce for the spouses. One party may claim compensation for material and moral damages from the other party who has caused the breakdown in the marriage, resulting in divorce. This compensation may be paid periodically. The spouses may also get an allowance after the divorce. This is called «maintenance» *(yoksulluk nafakası)*. Maintenance is payable only for one year if one of the spouses is in need and is blameless in the divorce action and the other spouse has sufficient means to pay (C. C., Arts. 143 ff.).

Divorce also has consequences for the children. Upon the divorce, the parental authority over the children will be given by the judge to one of the spouses. The other party, to whom the parental authority is not given has, however, to contribute according to his financial capacity to the expense of raising the children. This is called «allowance of participation» *(iştirak nafakası)*. The court has continuing jurisdiction to enter new orders for the children's welfare based on changed conditions (C. C., Art. 148, 149).

VI. PARENT AND CHILD :

A. General :

Normally, biological relationship creates kinship between the parent and the child. But the parent-child relation may also come into existence through adoption or through the presumption that a child born to a married woman is that of her husband. Kinship may also be divisible according to whether the mother and father are married or not.

B. Legitimate Child :

1. Birth during the marriage:

A child born to a married woman is legitimate. There is a strong presumption of legitimacy for children who are born not more than 300 days after the dissolution of a marriage. Yet the husband is entitled to contest the paternity if the birth takes place within 180 days after the marriage. The husband, or in the case of his death, his heirs, must normally bring this suit of rejection within one month after they take notice of the birth.[18]

---

[17] Nationality Act, Art. 8. See Ch. 4, fn. 22 on the Law of Persons.
[18] C. C. Arts., 242 I, 245. In case of the suit of the child, see, Tekinay, 342.

2. Legitimation:

A child who is not considered legitimate because of a defect in the marital status of the parents may be legitimized subsequently. One of the methods of legitimation is the marriage of the parents after the birth of the child (C. C. Art., 247). This legitimation is automatic, even without the official acknowledgement (consent) of the father and mother. Yet the parents are required to notify the population or census officer *(nüfus memuru)* of their domicile about their child born out of wedlock.

Children of persons who have promised to marry may also be declared legitimate by the judge if marriage does not take place because of the death or loss of capacity to marry of one of the parties (C.C., Art. 249).

Finally, certain amnesty laws in Turkey make the legitimation of children possible. These laws were especially enacted to legitimize the status of thousands of children who were born of *imam* marriages. As noted earlier, such marriages are not legal, and, as a consequence, the children born of such consensual marriages are not legitimate. According to the amnesty laws, the children will be registered as legitimate if they were born to parents who were living together continuously as husband and wife. Under the provisions of the last such Law, dated June 20, 1974, even the children of fathers who are legally married to women other than the child's mother will be registered as legitimate children. Children, however, who were born out of an occasional relation may not be registered as legitimate.

C. Illegitimate Children (Nesebi sahih olmayan çocuklar):

Children born outside of marriage, and who are not considered legitimate under the conditions described above, are illegitimate. There is no full equality between the legitimate and illegitimate children of a father.[19]

The biological relation between the illegitimate child and its mother is obvious to determine. The fact of the birth will reveal who the mother is (C. C., Art. 290 I).

The relationship between the child and its father, may be established in two different ways:

1. By the a c k n o w l e d g e m e n t *(tanıma)* of the father a legal relationship is established between the father and the child. This

---

[19] See below, Ch. 7, II B 1 on the Law of Succession. An illegitimate child may be put under the authority of a guardian instead of the parent (C. C.. Arts. 311 - 313).

unilateral recognition by the father must be made in **notarized form**. Children born through the adultery of a married woman or man or to persons who are prohibited from marrying, may not be declared illegitimate by way of acknowledgment (C. C., Art. 292).

Recognition becomes effective without the consent of the child. But it may be challenged by the mother, child, or by an interested person if it is proved that the person who declares recognition is not the real father, if the recognition is against the interest of the child, or if the recognition is prohibited (C. C., Art. 293). Refusal must be made within three months after the notice of recognition.

2. The second method of legitimation is by court decision *(babalığa hüküm)*. There are certain prerequisites for such a decision. First, the man should have promised to marry the mother; furthermore, their sexual intercourse should have been an unlawful act, and the mother's seduction should have been accomplished by an abuse of authority. The paternity of a married man cannot be established. Finally the blood relation between the father and the child should be determined. Here, scientific tests are being used, but there is also a strong presumption that the child is from that man who had sexual relations with the mother between 300 and 180 days prior to birth. Instead of a suit for the establishment of paternity with all its legal consequences, a paternity suit only for the support of the child may also be brought. This suit may primarily be brought by the child and mother. It should be brought within one year after the birth.[20]

D. Adoption :

Adoption *(evlat edinme)* is the creation of a parent-child relationship by contractual agreement, and, under the Turkish Civil Code, it is primarily intended as a device to enable childless persons to raise children. Therefore, only persons who have no descendants may adopt a child. The adoptive parents must be at least 40 years old and must be at least 18 years older than the child. Even a single person may adopt a child. In the case of a married couple, both spouses must give their consent (C. C., Arts. 253-255).

The adoption should be made with the approval of the judge in notarial form. The supervision of the court is required for the protection of the best interests of the child.

---

[20] C. C., Art. 296. For details see, Tekinay, 453 ff.

The adoptive parent acquires parental authority over the child and gives the child his family name. The contractual relation creates legal consequences only between the adoptive parents and the child. The child has the same rights of inheritance in the estate of adoptive parents as legitimate issue (C. C., Art. 257), but adoptive parents may not inherit from their adopted child. The child also remains a member of his natural family.

Adoption may be terminated by mutual consent of the parties or by court decision for grave reasons (C. C., Art. 258).

E. Parental Authority:

The power of the father and mother over the person and property of their minor children is called parental authority *(velayet)*. This authority is, as a rule, exercised jointly by the parents. In case of disagreement, however, the opinion of the father prevails (C. C., Arts. 262, 263). When one of the parents is unable to exercise this authority for reasons such as absence, the other spouse exercises the parental authority solely. In the event of divorce, parental authority is vested by court order in one of the parents, usually in the mother. In the case of illegitimate children, the court again decides whether the natural mother should have the parental authority.

The rights and powers derived from and attached to parental authority may be divided in two groups: those relating to the child's person and those relating to his property.

(1) Powers and duties over person: The parents name the children, they represent them, and raise them. They decide where the children should live. They are responsible for the care, protection and education of their children, which also includes the right of discipline (C. C., Arts. 267 and 273).

(2) Powers and duties over property: The parents also have the right and duty to administer the property of their minor children (C. C., Art. 278. With few limitations). They have a usufructuory right [21] in the property of the children until the children reach their majority age, or until they live separately with the consent of parents. The child's income must be spent primarily for his education (C. C., Arts. 280 ff.).

The abuse of parental power is under the judicial control. Parental authority may sometimes be taken away by court decision

---

[21] See Ch. 8, VIII B on the Law of Property.

from both of the parents or from only one of them, in case of mental sickness, abuse of authority, or lack of capacity (C. C., Art. 274), and a guardian is appointed by the court to replace the parents.

VII. GUARDIANSHIP, CURATORSHIP, STATUTORY ADVISORS

A. Guardianship :

1. In general :

Every minor child who has lost both his parents and is not under parental authority is provided with a guardian *(vasi)* to protect his interests. Lunatics, mental defectives, prodigals or spendthrifts are also provided with guardians. Criminals imprisoned for one year or more are placed under interdict and provided with a guardian (C. C., Arts. 354 - 357). An individual can also be placed under interdict at his own request and provided with a guardian (voluntary interdiction = *ihtiyarî hacir*).[22]

The judge appoints the guardian initially for four years and supervises him continuously. The judge may terminate the guardianship.

2. Powers and duties of the guardian :

The guardian acts as a supervisor upon the minor or other interdicted persons. It is his duty to provide for his wards' maintenance and education. He represents them in legal transactions and administers their estates. He is not, however, permitted to perform all acts. He does not, for example, have the power to make any donations of his wards' property. He cannot establish a foundation with their property. He cannot put the minor or other interdicted persons under a legal responsibility as a guarantor (C. C., Art. 392).

B. Curatorship :

In cases where the interests of the guardian or parent and the minor or the ward are in conflict, when an impediment prevents the guardian from doing his duties, or in some specific and temporary instances, the judge appoints a curator *(kayyım)* to represent these persons.

In cases when a person has disappeared for a long period of time, when he cannot administer his property himself, where the

---

[22] «Those persons of full age who can prove that they are incapable to conduct their affairs properly because of old age, physical infirmity or inexperience», C.C., Art. 358.

rights of succession are not clearly determined, or when a society or association lacks directors or other officers, an administrative curator is appointed by the Court (C.C., Art. 377).

C. Statutory advisor :

In order to give advice to a person who is particularly lacking capacity a statutory advisor *(kanunî müşavir)* may be appointed by the court for bringing an action and conciliation, purchase and sale of immovable property, signing a negotiable instrument, making a credit transaction, or donation, or signing of a guaranty contract.[23]

The role of a statutory advisor is not as wide as a curator. It does not involve the total administration of the estate of a person.

SELECTED BIBLIOGRAPHY

Akıntürk, T. : **Aile Hukuku** (Ankara 1975).
Tekinay, S. S. : **Türk Aile Hukuku** (İstanbul 1971).
Velidedeoğlu, H. V. : **Türk Medeni Hukuku,** Cilt : 2, Aile Hukuku (İstanbul 1965).

---

[23] C. C., Art. 379, Comp. Art. 379 II, also gives the power of administration.

CHAPTER 7

LAW OF SUCCESSION[1]

Prof. Dr. Tuğrul ANSAY *

I. IN GENERAL

All systems of law that recognize private ownership of property also recognize that such ownership should pass at the death of the owner to others. The law of succession (*miras hukuku*) deals with the passage of a person's property rights at his death.

It is a generally accepted rule that, in the absence of express provision made by a deceased person, his estate will, by operation of law, go to his close relatives upon his death. This is so because of the importance placed on the family and the duty of the members of the family to support each other. Persons are free however, by will or otherwise, to dispose of their property to persons other than their relatives, within the limits permitted by law. A particular indirect limitation placed on the power of disposition is the existence of death duties or inheritance taxes which even in westen countries, where the concept of private ownership is most widely recognized, are relatively high.

Under Turkish law, which is based in this respect on Swiss law, persons are generally free to dispose of their property at their death. They may execute wills, by which they leave their property to such real or legal persons as they choose. This so called «testate succession» has some limits. Notwithstanding the provisions of a will, close relatives of the deceased are entitled to a certain portion of the estate, called the reserved portion.

In the absence of such disposition, the estate of a deceased person will pass, in the proportions prescribed by law, to his relatives, or if there are none, to the state. This is called «intestate succession».

II. INTESTATE SUCCESSION

A. Parentels :

If the deceased (*muris, müteveffa*) has failed to make a will or otherwise provide for the distribution of his estate at his death,

---
* Faculty of Law, University of Ankara.
[1] Civil Code, Arts. 439 - 617.

it will be distributed among his next of kin. For this purpose, the blood relatives of a deceased person are divided into groups which are called parentels (Diagram 1). The first parentel consists of the descendants *(füru)* of the deceased, the second of his parents *(usûl)* and their descendants, the third of his grandparents and their descendants. The fourth parentel is the state [2] (subject to a usufruct [3] is the surviving great grand parents of the deceased or their children). The rights of a surviving spouse and how they relate to parentels is discussed below.

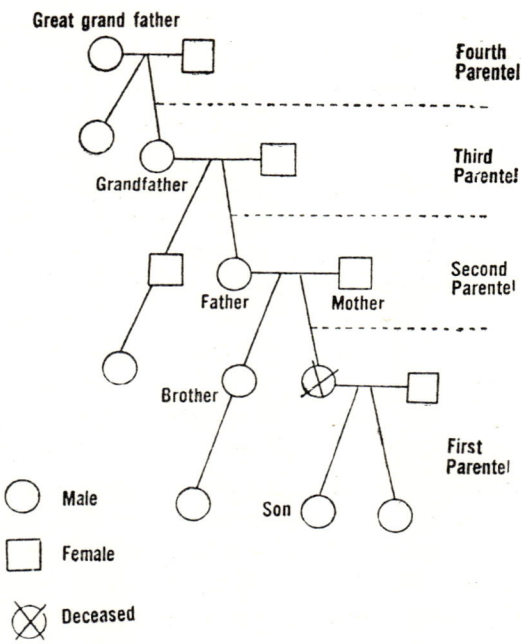

Diagram 1

The following rules apply to the operation of the system of parentels:

First, as long as one member of a parentel is living at the death of the decedent, the more removed parentels will be eliminated. Thus, if the deceased leaves one child, parents or grandparents of the deceased, as well as their descendants, will

---

[2] However, the state, unlike the other parentels, is never liable for the debts of the estate in excess of the amount of the estate.
[3] See Chapter 8, VIII B on the Law of Property.

not receive anything. Secondly, among the members of each parentel those nearest in degree take priority over those further removed, and any predeceased person in any degree will be represented by his or her descendants (Diagram 2). For example, if (D) is survived by one child, a son, he will be his sole successor. But if this son had died before (D), then the surviving children of (D)'s son, but not, for example, (D)'s parents, will take the estate. Thirdly, surviving successors in the same degree of closeness to the deceased in the same parentel, participate in the estate equally. Also, there is equality among male and female successors. Therefore, if (D) dies intestate, leaving two sons and one daughter, each of them will receive one third of the estate

Diagram 2

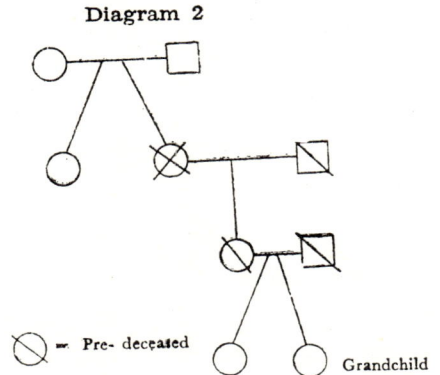

Diagram 3

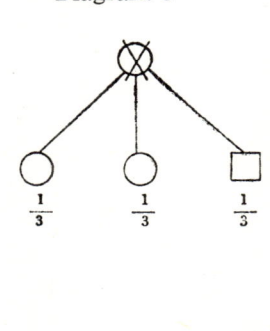

Diagram 4

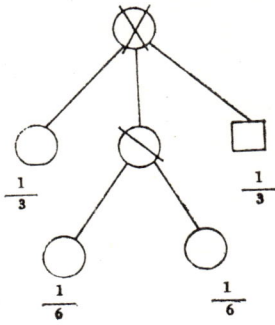

(Diagram 3). If one of the sons had predeceased (D), leaving two children, his share will go to them, making each of their shares one sixth of the whole estate (Diagram 4).

B. Other Persons who may Inherit:

1. Illegitimate Children:

Illegitimate children have the same rights of inheritance from their mother as legitimate children. Illegitimate children recognized by their father or whose paternity is established by a court [4] may inherit from their father, but only one half as much as a legitimate child does (C. C., Art. 443). For example, when D, a man, leaves two legitimate children and one illegitimate (for example, recognized) child, the legitimate ones will each receive 2/5 of the estate and the illegitimate child 1/5 (Diagram 5).

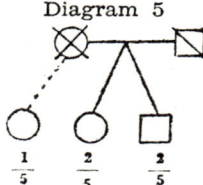

Diagram 5

2. Adopted Children (C. C., Art. 447):

Adopted children are treated the same as the legitimate natural born children of the deceased. Therefore they receive the same amounts as the other children of the deceased. An adopted child is however not an intestate successor of relatives of his adoptive parents and the adoptive parents will not take from the adopted child if he predeceases them (C. C., Art. 447 II). An adopted child may be an intestate successor of his real parents and may thus inherit from both his adoptive and real parents.

3. The Surviving Spouse (C. C., Art. 444):

The surviving spouse shares the estate with the living blood relatives of the deceased, if any. Her or his portion varies according to the closeness of the other successors of the deceased with whom she or he has to share the estate. If there are close relatives, such as children, the surviving spouse receives less; if there

---

[4] See Chapter 6 on Family Law.

are only distant relatives she receives more. Furthermore, the surviving spouse has the choice of ownership or usufruct [5] of the estate or a combination of the two. For example, if the surviving spouse inherits together with the descendants (children, grand children etc.) of the deceased, she gets either one fourth of the ownership (Diagram 6a) or a usufruct of one half of the estate (Diagram 6b).

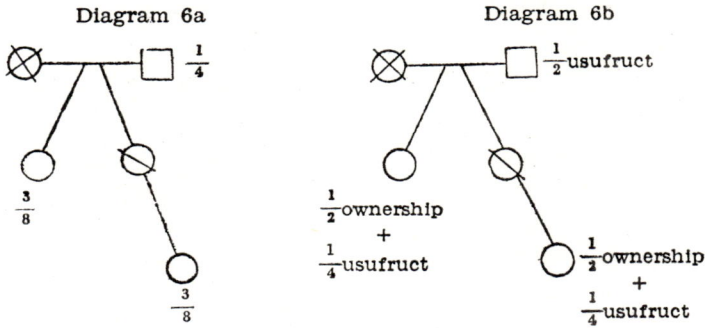

In the case of usufruct, the ownership passes to the descendants and the surviving spouse takes one half the rents, interest, dividends etc. If the surviving spouse takes with the second parentel, she receives ownership of one fourth of the estate plus the usufruct of another half of the estate. If she takes with the third parentel she gets ownership of one half and usufruct of one fourth of the estate. If there is no third parentel, she becomes the sole legal successor and takes the whole ownership.

III. TESTATE SUCCESSION

A person may dispose of his property as of his death by executing during his lifetime a will or by entering into an agreement of inheritance.

A. Wills:

A will *(vasiyetname)* may be defined as a unilateral legal transaction expressing the intention of a person, made according to the conditions required by law, which becomes effective as of the death of the person. The subject matter of a will may not be limited to the disposition of property. Thus by his will, a person may also recognize his child (C. C., Art. 291).

---

[5] See Chapter 8, VIII B on the Law of Property.

1. Capacity:

In order to execute a will a person must have capacity to make fair judgments. Any person who has completed the age of 15 is deemed to have capacity to make a will (C. C., Art. 449), if he is also able to make fair judgments. This differs from the normal age at which one has capacity to enter into transactions.[6] Mistake, fraud or duress make a will void [7] (C. C., Art. 451).

2. Form:

A will must be made in a form required by law. It may take the following forms:

a) The authentic or official will *(resmî vasiyetname)* : This is a will which is prepared by an official such as a notary [8] or a Peace Court judge [9] pursuant to the directions of the testator.[10] The testator then reads the text and accepts its contents by signing it. Thereafter, the will is dated and signed by the official himself. Finally, the testator, in the presence of two witnesses [11] expresses that he has read the text and that it is his last will. The witnesses also sign a statement on the will that they found the testator capable of executing the will and that he accepted in their presence its contents.

If the testator is not able to read, the text is read to him by the official in the presence of witnesses. When it is approved by him, he will sign it. If he is unable to sign, then it is signed by the official and by two witnesses.

Such an authentic will is preserved at the office of the notary or Peace Court judge, and a copy may be given to the testator at his request.

The authentic will provides security in that it is less likely that such a will will be declared void after the death of the testator, as is frequently the case with other forms of wills. Another advantage of an authentic will is that it may be made by a person who is unable to read or write. On the other hand, the authentic will entails notarial expenses and does not have the privacy of the holographic will.

---

[6] See Chapter 4 on the Law of Persons.
[7] See Chapter 9 on the Law of Obligations.
[8] See Chapter 11 on the Law of Procedure.
[9] See Chapter 11 on the Law of Procedure.
[10] Testator (male) or testatrix (female) means the maker of a will.
[11] Certain persons (husbands, wives, children and other descendants, parents and other ancestors etc.) are not qualified to act as witnesses to an authentic will (C. C., Art. 483).

b) The holographic will *(el yazısı ile vasiyetname)* (C. C., Art. 485) : The holographic will is completely written by the testator himself. It must include the place of preparation and the date, again in his own handwriting, and it must be signed by the testator himself. Even a letter, if it meets these requirements and clearly shows the intention of a person, may constitute a valid holographic will.

It is easy to prepare a holographic will. It may be prepared anywhere, and it enables a person to keep the contents of his will secret. It does not require any witnesses.

c) The oral will *(şifahi vasiyetname)* (C. C., Art. 486) : Only in exceptional circumstances, when it is impossible to execute an authentic or holographic will, will an oral will be considered valid. Thus, for example, a soldier in the battle field may make an oral will. Here the testator must express his will to at least two witnesses who must in turn write out and sign the will as soon as possible and submit it to a court, expressing that the testator was capable of making his will and that it was made under extraordinary conditions.

3. Revocation of Wills:

Since the execution of a will is a unilateral transaction made without the approval of other persons, the testator may revoke his will wholly or partly at anytime *(vasiyetnameden rücu)*. The revocability of a will is one of its essential characteristics, and the testator cannot before his death deprive himself of the power to revoke it.

A will may be revoked in several ways. It is revoked by making a new will. If the new will is inconsistent with the former one, it replaces the earlier will.[12] The new will need not be in the same form as the earlier. For example, an authentic will may be revoked by a holographic will. A new will which is only supplementary to an existing will and only partly alters the existing one without revoking it entirely, is called a codicil.

Other ways of revoking a will in whole or part are : By burning, tearing or otherwise destroying it intentionally, or unintentionally, if in the latter instance its contents cannot be otherwise proved (e. g. by means of another copy) or by crossing out or otherwise cancelling all or part of a will. The disposition by the testator in his lifetime of an article of property specifically bequeathed in a will

---

[12] N. Ayiter, 56.

constitutes a partial revocation of the will, that is to say with respect to such bequest.

4. Beneficiaries :

Beneficiaries designated in wills are called legatees (except that beneficiaries of real property are also called devisees). There are two sorts of legatees :

a) Universal legatees *(mansup mirasçılar,* appointed legatees) (C. C., Art. 463) : Universal legatees receive all or a fraction of the estate, and like statutory or intestate successors, they may be obliged to pay the debts of the estate.[13] There may be several universal legatees.

b) Particular (specific) legatees *(musalehler)* (C. C., Art. 464) : Particular legatees are the recipients of specific bequests or legacies, that is to say, a specific article of property, say a certain watch, all the testator's furniture etc., or a sum of money.

5. Conditions and Charges :

A legacy may be left subject to a condition or charge *(şart ve mükellefiyet)* (C. C., Art. 462). The legatee receives a legacy, but is under the obligation of performing some act, such as the repair of a building or helping needy students. In the case of such a condition, the legatee may not acquire the property until the fulfillment of the condition. For example if (A) bequeaths his house to his cousin (B) on the condition that (B) completes his university education successfully and receives his degree, (B) may not demand the delivery of the house until he receives the degree.

6. Appointment of Executor [14] :

A testator may appoint in his will one or more executors *(vasiyeti tenfiz memuru)* to carry out his will (C. C., Art. 497).

The executor, in order to carry out the will, must administer the estate, pay its debts, and distribute the remainder of the estate as directed by the will or otherwise required by law (C. C., Art. 498 II).

Executors are subject to supervision by judges of the Peace Court and may be dismissed by them.

---

[13] See below V E.

[14] The executor of a will, or administrator where there is no will, has a somewhat lesser role in the administration of estates than under Anglo-American law. This is due to the greater functions of the heirs or successors under Turkish law, See V below.

B. Agreement of Inheritance (C. C., Arts. 474 ff.) :

A testator may, instead of making a will, enter with another person into an agreement of inheritance *(miras mukavelesi)*. For example, a husband and wife may conclude an inheritance agreement under which they appoint their son as the ultimate successor to both their property. Unlike a will, the agreement of inheritance is not a unilateral disposition, but a bilateral contract. As a consequence, its makers are, to a certain extent, bound by the agreement and the agreement is not revocable unilaterally by either of the parties. They may, however, by mutual agreement, terminate the agreement of inheritance. If the beneficiary of the agreement acts against the testator (for example, by committing a felony against the testator), the testator may cancel the agreement as to such beneficiary (C. C., Art. 493).

The parties to an agreement of inheritance must express their will and sign the agreement in front of a notary or Peace Court judge and two witnesses (C. C., Art. 492).

IV. RESERVED PORTION

A. General (C. C., Art. 453) :

A testator is not wholly free to dispose of his entire estate as he pleases. The law limits his freedom in favor of his close relatives, by means of the «reserved portion» *(mahfuz hisse)*.[15] This portion is reserved for certain relatives of the deceased. Not all persons who would be entitled to inherit by intestate succession have reserved portions. Only the descendants, father and mother, brothers and sisters and the surviving spouse have rights to such a portion. The amount of the reserved portion depends on the closeness of the surviving heirs to the deceased.

(1) Descendants : Their reserved portion is three quarters of their statutory share. Thus, if the amount of the estate to be distributed is, for example, 80,000 TL., and if four children are the successors, the intestate share of each would be one fourth or 20,000 TL. Therefore, in the event of a will, the reserved portion of each child is three fourths of this amount, or 15,000 TL. This leaves the deceased free to dispose of the remaining 20,000 TL. of his estate (Diagram 7).

(2) Parents : Their reserved portion is half of their statutory share (Diagram 8).

---

[15] This is not known to all legal systems. See, Rheinstein, *The Law of Decedents' Estates*, 59 ff., 63 (Indianapolis 1955).

(3) Sisters and brothers : Their reserved portion is one fourth of their statutory share.

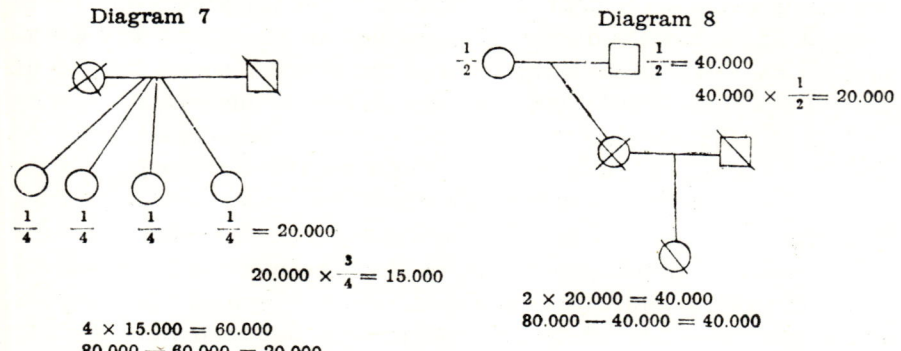

Diagram 7

$\frac{1}{4} = 20.000$

$20.000 \times \frac{3}{4} = 15.000$

$4 \times 15.000 = 60.000$
$80.000 - 60.000 = 20.000$

Diagram 8

$\frac{1}{2} = 40.000$

$40.000 \times \frac{1}{2} = 20.000$

$2 \times 20.000 = 40.000$
$80.000 - 40.000 = 40.000$

(4) Spouse : If he or she is the sole heir, the reserved portion is half of the statutory share. If there are other heirs, then the reserved portion is the entire amount of the statutory share (C. C., Art. 453).

Example : When a man dies with an 80,000 TL. distributable estate, leaving a wife and three children, the statutory share of the successors would be 20,000 TL. each.[16] The reserved portion of the children is therefore 15,000 TL. and of the wife 20,000 TL. This leaves 15,000 TL. which the deceased is free to dispose of by will (Diagram 9).

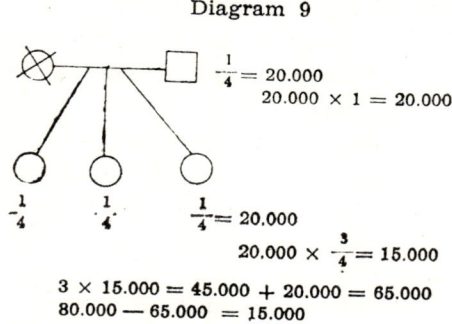

Diagram 9

$\frac{1}{4} = 20.000$
$20.000 \times 1 = 20.000$

$\frac{1}{4} = 20.000$
$20.000 \times \frac{3}{4} = 15.000$

$3 \times 15.000 = 45.000 + 20.000 = 65.000$
$80.000 - 65.000 = 15.000$

B. Reduction of Dispositions :

The value of the estate is determined at the time of death. If the dispositions made by the testator's will exceed the amount left after the reserved portions, such dispositions will be reduced (*mira-*

---

[16] See above II A.

sın tenkisi). Dispositions made during the testator's lifetime are also subject to reduction in certain circumstances.[17]

C. Debarment from Inheritance (C. C., Arts. 457 - 460) **and Loss of Inheritance Rights** (C. C., Art. 520) :

A successor of the deceased who commits a felony against the decedent or his next of kin or close friends, or negligently fails in fulfilling a statutory duty to the decedent during his life time or to his family may be debarred from inheritance *(mirastan iskat)* by a testamentary disposition of the deceased (C. C., Art. 457). The share of such a person will pass to the other successors of the deceased as if the debarred person had died prior to the decedent (C. C., Art. 458).

In some cases, such as where the successor intentionally kills or attempts to kill the decedent, he loses his inheritance rights automatically *(mirastan mahrumiyet)* (C. C., Art. 520).

V. TRANSFER OF ESTATE *(Mirasın intikali)*

A. General :

The mechanics of inheritance is one of the main concerns of the law of succession. Under Turkish law, the property of the deceased passes to his heirs (statutory successors) in the case of intestate succession or to his legatees in the case of a will, at his death. But who are these persons ? They may not be living in the same house, or even in the same town or country. If the deceased executed a will during his lifetime, this must be discovered and the validity of the will be determined.

These matters may take more than a few days to be resolved. During this time somebody must care for the assets of the deceased; the household of the deceased must have money to buy food, pay the rent and other expenses; and the business of the deceased, if any, must be run. If the deceased has debts, by whom and how will they be paid ? The law of succession provides the answers to these questions by means of the principles discussed below :

B. Universal Succession :

The most important principle of the Turkish law of succession is the principle of «universal succession» *(küllî tevariis)*, by which is meant that on the death of a person his entire property passes

---
[17] See, C. C., Arts. 512 and 507 on the method of reduction.

immediately and automatically to his universal legatees or heirs. Such persons become the owners of all the property of the deceased, although they may not know of the death, the property or its whereabouts. As for specific legatees under a will, they have the right to demand the delivery of their specific bequests from the heirs or universal legatees (C. C., Art. 541).

C. Legal Status of the Heirs Before Partition of the Estate :

If there is more than one heir, the estate becomes the common property of all of them until the partition of the estate (C. C., Art. 581). The heirs (also universal legatees, C. C., Arts. 539, I, 541) form a «community of heirs» (C. C., Art. 581). All of them must act together, as in the case of co-ownership,[18] and no one of them is entitled to dispose of a single article of property in the estate without the concurrence of the others. Transactions on the estate, which are made individually, without the approval of the others, are void, except in the case of acquisition by *bona fide* third persons. Suits by the estate must be brought in common, and suits against the estate must state the names of all successors as defendants. The heirs have no statutory power to represent each other. However, they may give such power of representation to one of the heirs (or the administrator or executor). The creditors of any one of the heirs must wait until the partition of the estate and may not levy on any property in the estate (C. C., Art. 543).

Administrative acts with respect to the estate, however, require only the approval of the majority of the heirs and for the preservation of the estate each heir may take necessary protective measures himself.

D. Determination of Heirs :

Although the physical partition of the estate may be effected by the heirs themselves, the state determines who the heirs are.

Upon the application of an heir (or legatee), the Peace Court of the last domicile of the deceased determines who the eligible heirs (or legatees) are and their shares in the estate and issues a certificate of inheritance [19] *(veraset ilâmı)* (C. C., Art. 538).

The same court will initiate the necessary steps for the protection of the estate (C. C., Art. 531). Thus, if any of the heirs is under

---
[18] See Chapter 8, VI A on the Law of Property.
[19] The certificate of inheritance may also in some circumstances be issued by a court located where a successor resides (C. C. Pr., Art. 11 III). N. Ayiter, 164.

guardianship, or away, or if any of the heirs demands it, or in order to prevent someone absconding with property, the judge may order all the property of the estate put in a room, lock it under seal, or have an inventory made of the property included in the estate.

In cases where one or more of the heirs is abroad, and does not have a representative to act in his name, or if there are doubts as to the existence of other heirs (C. C., Art. 533), the judge may order official administration of the estate (*terekenin resmen idaresi*). If the deceased has named an executor in his will, such executor must be appointed by the judge to administer the estate. However, if the deceased had a guardian, this person will be appointed to continue administering the estate of the deceased.

E. Debts of the Estate :

Under the rule of «universal succession» all rights and liabilities of the deceased pass to the heirs at the time of death. The heirs are successors not only to the assets of the deceased person, but also to his debts. Moreover, the heirs are fully liable for the debts, although exceeding the value of the estate's assets, to the extent of their personal wealth (C. C., 539). An heir may, however, disclaim his share of the estate within three months of the date he learns of the death of the deceased. The heirs may also demand official liquidation of the estate when none of them is prepared to take the estate.

1. Official Inventory :

If there is a question whether the debts exceed the assets, the heirs may ask the judge within one month after the date of death (or such later date as the heirs hear of the death) (C. C., Arts. 546, 548) to have an official inventory made (C. C., Art. 559). All creditors are asked to state their claims within a certain period of time which should not be less than one month (C. C., Art. 561 II). The inventory of assets and debts is then open for inspection for at least one month (C. C., Art. 563). If the heirs accept the estate on the basis of this inventory,[20] they will not be liable for debts of the estate not shown in it.[21]

Where the State takes an estate, for lack of heirs, its liability does not exceed the amount which it receives (C. C., Art. 571).

---

[20] If they do not want to accept the estate they must indicate this within one month of the completion of the invertory (C. C., Art. 566).

[21] In certain exceptional cases this may not be so; in those cases, however, the liability of the heirs will not exceed the amount which they received from the estate, C. C., Art. 559.

2. Official Liquidation (C. C., Arts. 572 ff.):

If the heirs think that the debts of the estate are more than the assets, they may demand, within the three months during which they are entitled to disclaim the estate, an official liquidation *(resmî tasfiye)* of the estate. In this case, the estate of the deceased is kept separate from the properties of the heirs and they will not be liable for the debts of the estate.

The creditors of the deceased, if they believe the collection of their debts requires it, may also demand an official liquidation.

The official liquidation is directed by the judge of the Peace Court [22] or by a liquidator appointed by him (C. C., Art. 574).

F. Disclaimer of Inheritance:

Although the estate passes automatically to the heirs of the deceased, and they become heirs in common, they are, as noted above, entitled to disclaim the estate *(mirasın reddi)*. In case of disclaimer, the estate passes to the next closest relatives of the deceased, who in turn may also disclaim the estate (C. C., Art. 551). If all successors disclaim, then the state becomes the sole successor being liable for the debts of the estate up to the amount which it received (C. C., Art. 571).

VI. PARTITION AND DISTRIBUTION OF THE ESTATE
(C. C., Arts. 581 ff.)

A. Distribution by the Heirs:

After the debts of the deceased have been paid and his last will otherwise fulfilled, the estate will be (partitioned and) distributed among the heirs *(mirasın taksimi)*. The heirs agree among themselves how this should be done. Property may be distributed in kind, or sold and the proceeds distributed. If there is immovable property, such as land or a house in the estate, written approval of all heirs is necessary; otherwise oral agreement and delivery of the goods is sufficient (C. C., Art. 611 I).

B. Distribution by the Court:

If the heirs cannot agree (C. C., Art. 583), or if a creditor requests it (C. C., Art. 588), a suit may be brought in court for the distribution of the estate. The law governing distribution by the

---
[22] See Chapter 11, Part 1 on the Law of Procedure.

court (C. C., Arts. 589 ff.) includes certain provisions regulating the partition of agricultural lands (C. C., Arts. 597 - 601).

SELECTED BIBLIOGRAPHY

Ayiter, Nuşin : **Miras Hukuku** (Ankara 1974).
İmre, Zahit : **Türk Miras Hukuku** (İstanbul 1968).
İnan, Ali Naim : **Miras Hukuku** (Ankara 1969).
Kocayusufpaşaoğlu, N. : **Miras Hukukuna Giriş** (İstanbul 1966).
Velidedeoğlu, H. Veldet : **Türk Medenî Hukuku** (İstanbul 1963).

CHAPTER 8

LAW OF PROPERTY[1]

Prof. Dr. Tuğrul ANSAY *

I. IN GENERAL

In civil law rights are classified as real rights (rights *in rem*) and personal rights (rights *in personam*). A personal right is a right which exists only against a certain person or persons. Thus if (A) agrees to buy a radio from (B) for 400 TL., (A) has a right against (B) for the delivery of the radio and, in exchange, (B) has a right against (A) for the payment of 400 TL. (A) has no rights to go to (C) or (D) and demand the delivery of the radio. This is called a personal right of (A). A real right, on the other hand, is a right in property which may be claimed against any person. Therefore, if (A) owns the radio nobody can get it from him without his consent. (A) may keep the radio, may sell it, may lend it or destroy it.

Real rights are classified according to the breadth of the powers their holders enjoy. Ownership is the broadest real right. If somebody owns property, he may mortgage, sell, bequeath, lend or use or even destroy it. But, as will be discussed below, even ownership is not an unlimited right today.

Other real rights are mainly servitudes *(irtifak hakları)* usufruct *(intifa hakkı)* and mortgage *(rehin)*.[2] As will be seen below, in the case of a mortgage, the mortgagee has a real right in the mortgaged property. Therefore, if the mortgaged property is sold to somebody else, the mortgagee may assert his rights against the new owner or owners; but he has no right to sell or lend the mortgaged property.[3]

II. PROPERTY

The subject matter of real rights is property. The word «property» has different meanings. It indicates, in the first place, the

---

* Faculty of Law, University of Ankara.
[1] Civil Code, Arts. 618 - 935.
[2] In order to distinguish these real rights from ownership, they are sometimes called restricted real rights.
[3] See below VIII D.

thing subject to real rights. When I say «this book is my property, or when Mr. (A) says, «my property consists of books, an automobile, a house, furniture» the first meaning of property *(eşya)*, is indicated. Property also means the real right involved. If we say the property in the radio passed to (B), we use the word property as indicating «ownership» *(mülkiyet)*.

Property is generally classified into movable and immovable property.

1. Immovable Property (real property):

Those kinds of property which cannot be moved, such as land and buildings, are called immovable property [4] *(gayrimenkul mal)*.

Mines, too, are immovable properties, although they are not subject to private ownership.[5] Rights which are registered in the Land Registry as independent and permanent rights (e. g. *üst hakkı*) are also considered immovable property [6] (C. C., Art. 652).

2. Movable Property (personal property):

Property which can be carried from one place to another is movable property *(menkul mal)*. In addition, such things as electricity, gas and steam, which are not considered as immovable, are movable property.

III. OWNERSHIP

A. The Meaning of Ownership:

As indicated, ownership is the most extensive real right over property. It is a legal relationship between persons and things which gives persons control over things. It may be broadly defined as the right of a person to possess, use, enjoy, and dispose of a thing. The same has been stated in article 618 of the Civil Code as follows:

«The owner of property may, within the limits of law, deal with the property as he pleases, and exclude others from interfering with it in any way». This statement has positive and negative implications:

1. The Positive Aspect:

The positive aspect of ownership lies in the right to deal freely with property, a freedom subject to limits prescribed by law. This

---

[4] Land is defined in the Regulation of Land Registry *(Tapu Sicili Nizamnamesi)*, Art. 3.
[5] Mining Law *(Maden Kanunu)*, No. 6309, dated March 11, 1954 as amended with the Law No. 271, dated July 11, 1963.
[6] A ship has a special status. It is treated as both movable and immovable property.

aspect of ownership is safeguarded by the Turkish Constitution. «Every individual has property and inheritance rights».

Of course, an owner of property cannot do everything he wants with it. There has been a shift away from the «absolute» nature of ownership which existed in the past. Due to modern social trends, the owner of property is under some obligation to consider the interests of the community, and this view has been expressed in the new Turkish Constitution:

«These (property and inheritance) rights may be limited by law only in view of public welfare».

«The exercise of a property right may never be against the public welfare» (Art. 36 II and III).

«The State will take necessary steps to achieve the cultivation of lands productively and to distribute lands to peasants who own insufficient or no land at all. With these aims laws may define the extent of lands according to their kind and to the different agricultural areas. The state will facilitate the ownership of agricultural machinery by peasants...» (Art. 37).

The following are some examples of limitations on the absolute freedom of ownership:

Land is subject to taxation; immovable property is subject to taking by the State or a public utility by eminent domain, with compensation paid to the owner for its value; [7] the use of land is limited in the public interest by zoning laws, city planning, building codes and the like; [8] an owner may not use his land so as to interfere with the rights of others, e. g. so as to become a nuisance; [9] the landowner is obliged to permit the passage of wires or waterpipes through his land for the benefit of neighboring landowners; [10] the owners of neighboring land have rights of passage to main roads if no other way to reach them exists [11] (C. C., Art. 671).

2. *The Negative Aspect:*

The negative aspect of ownership is the ability to avoid interference with one's ownership rights. Thus the owner may, for example, demand the restitution of possession, if his property is wrongfully taken away from him. He may also demand compensation for injury to his property rights.

---

[7] Constitution, Art. 38, C. C., Arts. 684, 685. Oğuzman / Seliçi, 421.
[8] Oğuzman / Seliçi, 448 ff.
[9] Neighborhood rights, C. C., Arts. 2, 656, 661.
[10] Provided that compensation is paid in advance, C. C., Art. 668.
[11] Other limitations on immovable property: C. C., Arts. 661, 666, 668, 673, 674 ff.

B. Ownership and Possession :

To determine the owner of a particular piece of property is not always easy. A person may rent his house to another or he may lend his tape recorder for a couple of days. In such cases third persons may think that the tenant or the person who has borrowed the recorder are its real owners, since such persons have physical control, that is to say possession, of these properties.

There is, in fact, a close relationship between ownership and possession. Ownership may be defined as physical control over a thing based on a legal ground, whereas possession is the actual physical control of the thing (C. C., Art. 887). Under the Civil Code possession is the evidence of ownership (C. C., Arts. 898 and 905). When a person has possession of either movable or immovable property, there is a presumption that he is the owner of it. Generally, ownership may be transferred by transfer of possession (C. C., Arts. 687 and 633), although there are exceptions to this rule.

Ownership is an aggregate of rights in a piece of property. Possession, on the other hand, is primarily a matter of fact. If a bracelet is stolen from its owner by a thief, the owner's rights remain intact; the thief acquires no right to the bracelet as against the owner. But the possession of the owner, and with it the evidence of his ownership rights, are gone for the time being.

It is possible that possession may be lawfully acquired, and yet not accompanied by ownership. An owner who lends or rents and delivers a car to another person parts with possession, but does not cease to be the owner. The same is also true of one who delivers goods to another in order that the latter may perform services upon them. Such voluntary transfers of possession, where the owner does not lose his ownership rights regardless of the loss of actual physical control, are generally called bailments.

IV. POSSESSION (Zilyetlik)

A. Elements of Possession :

If the concept of possession is analyzed, two elements may be found :

1. Physical Control :

Physical control means the right to control the thing possessed (C. C., Arts. 887, 890). Such power does not necessarily mean a physical proximity between the person and the property. I am the possessor of the suit which I wear. I am also the possessor of my furniture which I left in my summer house, although I am hundreds of miles away from it. I am the possessor of the newspaper I buy until I leave it at the restaurant or throw it into the waste basket. When I leave my hat in a restaurant checkroom while eating, I do not lose possession of it.

Possession of immovable properties may be acquired by means of registration in a Land Registry kept by the State.

2. *Intent*:

Possession may not generally be acquired without the intent (*zilyetlik iradesi*) to acquire it.[12] But this intent may be of a general character; it need not refer to the specific thing in question. For example, a sleeper into whose hand a stick is placed does not thereby acquire possession. The owner of a house, however, acquires possession of a newspaper placed in his mailbox. A fisherman will acquire possession of the fish which came into his nets, although at the time he might not be near his nets; when he puts out nets he implicitly expresses his consent to possession.

The nature and the extent of the intention necessary for possession will vary with the circumstances and particularly with the character of the thing the possession of which is in question.

B. **Acquisition of Possession**:

Possession may be acquired by the unilateral act of a person. If a person picks strawberries in the forest or takes a branch of a tree, he acquires possession of the strawberries or the branch. So, a hunter who kills a wild duck acquires possession unilaterally. A thief or a finder of lost property also acquires possession in the same way. However, the normal way of acquiring possession is to obtain it from the former possessor with his consent. This is usually done by delivery of the property (C. C., Art. 890 I).

The delivery of goods is not always possible, or it may be very difficult. In such cases the transfer of possession may be effected by delivery of keys or papers representing the goods (C. C., Arts. 890 and 893). Thus, the delivery of a bill of lading, for example, transfers possession of goods to be carried by a ship. Sometimes the agreement of the parties may suffice to transfer possession, as in

---

[12] In the case of the death of a person, his successors acquire possession of property without such intention (C. C., Art. 539).

the case of the seller and buyer of a ship thousands of miles away from them (Comm. C., Arts. 867, 868). But here too the new possessor must acquire the possibility to exercise physical power over the ship. The same rule will be applied when coal is delivered in front of a house (C. C., Art. 890 II).

C. Land Registry:

A Land Registry *(Tapu Sicili)* has been established for the purpose of evidencing the transfer of possession and ownership of real property as well as rights such as mortgages. Such registry is also essential to the security of ownership in real property in that it permits the establishment of clear title as a matter of record.

Land Registries are kept by the State in accordance with the provisions of the Regulation of Land Registry *(Tapu Sicili Nizamnamesi)*, dated Oct. 8. 1930. There are separate registries for the various districts in the cities, towns and rural areas. There is a page for each piece of land and all legal matters related to such land are stated on this page. The book, however, only shows real rights, e.g. ownership or mortgage, and not personal rights such as leases. Certain principles regulate land registration:

(1) No real right in immovable property may be acquired without registration of such right (C. C., Arts. 633, 910). If land is bought, this fact must be registered in the Land Registry. Otherwise, the former owner will remain the legal owner and may resell the land to a *bona fide* purchaser who will take the title.

(2) In addition to the entry in the register, the parties must conclude an agreement to the effect that the disposition is to come into force. This agreement may be replaced by some other facts, such as a judgement of a court of law, or prescription.

(3) Registration plus good faith is equal to ownership (C. C., Art. 930). If (A) who is not the real owner, sells Blackacre to (B) and he to (C), (C) will acquire ownership if his name is registered in the Land Registry, and if he has acted in good faith, that is, if he did not know that (B) did not have title to the land. If a right has been registered in the Registry in the name of any person, it is presumed that the right exists and belongs to that person. Similarly, if a right registered in the Registry has been cancelled, it is presumed that the right does not exist. These presumptions are rebuttable.

Ch. 8 LAW OF PROPERTY 153

(4) All interested persons may inspect the Land Registry (C. C., Art. 928).

(5) The liability of the State (C. C., Art. 917) : If any damage results because of improper registration the state will be liable.

(6) Only certain real rights enumerated in articles 918 and 919 of the Civil Code such as ownership or hypothec may be registered but not personal rights.

V. EXTENT OF OWNERSHIP

A. Ownership Under and Above the Land :

Ownership of land carries with it exclusive ownership of the ground under the land and the air space above the land to reasonable limits (C. C., Art. 644).

Putting telephone wires over somebody's land requires the consent of the owner, as does laying petroleum or other pipes under or on the surface of a piece of land, and compensation is payable for this. Such consents should be registered in the Land Registry as easements (C. C., Art. 668). For water or gas pipes or for electric wires a statutory exception has been made among neighboring lands. If installing such wires or pipes on other land is impossible or causes undue hardship, then a landowner must give his permission to such installations upon full compensation (C. C., Art. 668). The owner of land is not deemed the owner of underground water.[13]

B. Component Part or Fixture (Mütemmim cüz) :

(1) Because of the complex nature of the subject matter, ownership and other real rights may some times create difficulties. Property is not always as simple as a piece of bread or a knife or a chair. A piece of movable property loses its separate nature when affixed to other movable or immovable property and becomes a component part. This happens in the case of a house made of bricks and stones or a car of wheels, tires, engine and a body. A fixture is defined in the Civil Code as something which forms an essential element, according to local custom, of the main part and which may not be separated without damaging or destroying the main part (Art. 619). It should therefore be determined whether a piece of property has been actually or constructively annexed to the main part, and whether such annexation or addition is intended to be permanent. Thus, blocks of stone placed one on top of another,

---

[13] C. C., Art. 679 as it is modified by the Law No. 28 and 167. See also Mining Law and Petroleum Law (Law No. 6326, dated March 16, 1954).

though without mortar or cement, for the purpose of forming a dry stone wall become a part of the land, although the same stones, if deposited in a builder's yard and, for convenience's sake, stacked one on top of the other in the form of a wall would remain separate chattels. When the materials of a house, such as bricks or boards, or the rails of a fence, are removed, they assume the character of personal property. When stones are removed from the earth and sold, they become personal property and cease to be immovable or real property (C. C., Art. 620).

(2) Rights in land include the component parts. Therefore:

(a) All buildings on land are considered a part of the land and should be registered in the Land Registry together with the land itself. For this reason ownership of an individual apartment or flat apart from land and building, did not exist in Turkey until the enactment of the Law on Flat Ownership.[14] For the same reason, if a person builds a house with his own material on somebody else's land the building will be registered in the name of the landowner.[15]

As an exception to the rule, pipes and electric pylons on somebody else's land may be subject to separate ownership (C. C., Art. 653).

(b) Plants and crops growing on land are owned by the land owner (C. C., Art. 620).

(c) The owner of land has the right to consume water in a stream crossing his property, provided he leaves sufficient water for reasonable use by downstream landowners (C. C., Art. 679).

(3) Component parts follow the main part. If a car is sold, it is sold with its spare wheel. When land is sold, it is sold together with the trees (C. C., Art. 644 II). Component parts of real property, such as fruit or materials from torn down buildings (C. C., Art. 620) may be sold as personal property, if, after their separation from the land, it is intended that they pass to a buyer as personal property (C. O., Art. 184 II).

C. **Accessories** (Teferruat):

Goods which are attached to movable or immovable property are considered accessories, if they become part of the main property in using them properly. Furniture in a hotel, tools in a factory, or

---

[14] Law No. 634, dated July 2, 1965. It became effective on January 2, 1966.
[15] However the landowner must pay certain compensation to the builder. C. C., Art. 648 I. See Arts. 648 and 649 where a person builds a house with somebody else's material on his own land.

a pin attached to a lady's dress are accessories. Accessories may be transferred independently of the main property to which they are attached. However, in the absence of special provision, the transfer of property includes the accessories (C. C., Art. 621).

VI. PARTICIPATION OF SEVERAL PERSONS IN OWNERSHIP

A. Co-ownership (İştirak halinde mülkiyet, el birliği ortaklığı) :

If two or more persons own property as co-owners, no one of them can dispose of his share without the consent of the others, and none of them holds a separate part of the property (C. C., Art. 629). Examples of this type of ownership are the rights of partners in partnership property in the case of an ordinary partnership and the rights of the heirs in the estate of a deceased person. Co-ownership only exists when expressly provided in law.

B. Joint Ownership (Müşterek mülkiyet) :

Joint ownership exists where property belonging to several persons is joined together so as to form a unit in which each person has a share (C. C., Art. 623). In contrast to co-ownership, each joint owner is free to dispose of his share without the consent of the others; it can be inherited; a creditor may levy against it (C. C., Art. 623 III).

Example : A and B each own a haystack, which the wind blows together in such a way that it is impossible to say which hay belongs to A and which to B. However, each person has ownership rights in his portion of the combined hay and may transfer it to others (C. C., Art. 700). Thus A may own 1/3 of the haystack and has the right to sell 1/3.

VII. ACQUISITION OF OWNERSHIP

A. Acquisition of Movable Property :

1. Transfer of Title:

Transfer of ownership *(mülkiyetin nakli)* in respect of movables requires delivery of the property, that is to say the transfer of possession (C. C., Art. 687). Furthermore, there must be an agreement between the present owner and the person to whom ownership is to be transferred if that title is to pass (e.g. sale, gift). There are some exceptions to this rule, as in the case of transfer of ownership in a ship where an agreement alone without delivery is sufficient (Comm. A., Art. 867). Title may also pass by operation of law, as in the case of succession.

2. Original Acquisition:

(a) Personal property which is in its natural state and over which no one yet has taken full and complete control or which is abandoned belongs to the first person reducing such property to his exclusive possession (C. C., Arts. 691 and 692). Examples of this are catching fish or wild animals.

(b) Finding lost property (C. C., Art. 693) or treasure (C. C., Art. 696).

(c) Conversion *(hukuki tağyir)* (C. C., Art. 699): When a person, by using his skill and labor in good faith increases the value of property, and if the value of the labor is higher than the value of the property, he acquires ownership of the property. An example of this is the stone used by a sculpture to make a statue.

(d) Confusion and accession *(karışma ve birleşme)* (C. C., Art. 700): Confusion of fungible property, such as grain, wine, or coal belonging to various owners, results in a joint ownership.

Property permanently added to another larger item of property and forming a minor part of the finished product becomes a part of the larger item (C. C., Art. 700 II). Bricks used in building a house are an example of accession.

(e) Acquisition by way of prescription *(iktisabî müruruzaman)*: A person who, in good faith, keeps possession of property which belongs to somebody else, for five years without interruption and dispute, becomes the owner of such property by way of prescription (C. C., Art. 701).

B. Acquisition of Immovable Property:

Generally, transfer of title to real property is valid only if recorded in the Land Registry either by way of entry or by a cancellation of an existing entry. Such registration is the equivalent of the transfer of possession of personal property by delivery. In order to register property there should generally be an agreement between the parties, which if it is to be valid, is made before the land registration officer.[16]

Another method, acquisition by way of prescription (or adverse possession) is seen frequently in Turkey today. This happens with respect to land not previously registered in the Land Registry. In such cases, if a person occupies land as if he were the real owner for twenty years without interruption and dispute, he may, request

---

[16] *Tapu Sic. Niz.* Art. 26 and C. C., Art. 634. There are several exceptions, Example: C. C., Art. 633, Comm. C., Art. 285 II.

a court to order the registration of the land in his name[17] (C. C., Art. 639).

VIII. SERVITUDES

A. Definition :

A servitude *(irtifak hakkı)* is a real right which is imposed as a burden on a property. A servitude may be personal, that is vested in and tied to a person, or real, that is attached to the ownership of another piece of property.

B. Usufruct :

The most important personal servitude is usufruct *(intifa hakkı)*, or the right of using and enjoying the property of another without impairing the substance. The usufructuary, who is the person having the usufruct, has the right to derive the full economic benefit of the property. He is entitled to the possession, administration, and the profits to be gained from the exploitation of the property (C. C., Art. 727). However, he does not have the power to dispose of the property. The usufruct on a goat, for example, includes taking milk and wool, but the goat may not be sold by the usufructuary *(intifa hakkı sahibi)*. When the object of the usufruct is consumable goods, the usufructuary becomes the owner of the goods and must pay the value of the goods to the person having title to them (C. C., Art. 744).

A usufruct is transferable unless it is limited by its terms to its enjoyment by a particular person [18] (C. C., Art. 730). It will be terminated with the death of such a person (C. C., Art. 721). Property which is subject to a usufruct may not be transferred without the consent of the holder of the usufruct.[19] A transfer of the property by the owner does not, unless the usufruct holder consents, terminate the usufruct and the usufruct may be declared against the new owner.

C. Real Servitude :

A real servitude (or easement, *gayri menkul lehine irtifak hakkı*) is a right belonging to the owner of one piece of land against the owner of another piece of land. It requires two distinct pieces of land, a servient one which is subject to the (servitude or) easement

---

[17] See Oğuzman / Seliçi, 326 ff.
[18] Habitation *(sükna hakkı)*, the right of usage applied to a house may not be assigned (C. C., Art. 748).

and a dominant one to which the right belongs or is appurtenant. An easement cannot be separated from the dominant estate of which it is a part; it passes with a transfer of such estate. The most common form of easement is that of a right of passage over the land of somebody else. Real servitudes may be created by registration in the Land Registry (C. C., Art. 704).

D. Mortgage [20]:

A mortgage *(rehin)* is a credit device of great importance in the field of business. It is created by agreement whereby an interest is created in property as security for the performance of a pecuniary obligation, which is to cease upon the performance of the obligation.

When the transaction relates to personal property, the agreement creates a chattel mortgage (or pledge, *menkul rehni*); when it relates to real property, it is simply called a mortgage (hypothec, *(gayri menkul rehni, ipotek)*. The person whose interest in the property is given as security is called the mortgagor and the person who receives the security is known as the mortgagee.

The mortgagor may sell the property subject to a mortgage to somebody else. In such a case the mortgagee may assert his rights against the new owner. In order to protect mortgagees and not to mislead the *bona fide* buyers of mortgaged real property, mortgages in real property (hyopthec) must be registered in the Land Registry (C. C., Art. 786). A chattel mortgage on the other hand may, as a general rule, be effected by delivery of the mortgaged property to the mortgagee.[21]

SELECTED BIBLIOGRAPHY

Akipek, Jale G.: **Türk Eşya Hukuku**, (Ankara 1972 - 1974).

Ayiter, N.: **Eşya Hukuku** (Ankara 1977).

Oğuzman / Seliçi: **Eşya Hukuku** (İstanbul 1975).

Reisoğlu, Safa: **Türk Eşya Hukuku**, Cilt I, **Giriş, Zilyetlik, Tapu Sicili** (Ankara 1977).

Tekinay, S. Sulhi: **Eşya Hukuku Dersleri**, (İstanbul 1970 - 1974).

Velidedeoğlu, Hıfzı Veldet: **Türk Medeni Hukuku** pp. 627 ff. (İstanbul 1963).

---

[19] Velidedeoğlu, 756.
[20] The term comes from French *mort* (= dead) and *gage* (= pledge).
[21] The mortgage of a commercial enterprise (Law No. 1447, dated July 21, 1971) and mortgage on animals (C. C., Art. 854) are possible without delivery.

CHAPTER 9

LAW OF OBLIGATIONS[1]

Prof. Dr. Tuğrul ANSAY *

Three different kinds of obligations are the general subjects of the Turkish Code of Obligations : (1) A person may be under an obligation because of signing a contract ; (2) he may commit a tortious act and therefore may be under an obligation to pay damages to another person; and (3) finally he may have been unjustly enriched, and, as a result, be under an obligation to pay the losses of another party.

PART 1
CONTRACTS

I. DEFINITION AND CLASSIFICATION

A. Definition :

A contract is a legal transaction which may be defined as an exchange of assents by two or more persons, resulting in an obligation to do or to refrain from doing a particular thing which is enforceable by law. A contract may also be described «as an agreement creating legally enforceable obligations» (C. O., Art. 1). There are many agreements which by this definition, are not contracts and do not create legal relations and against the breaking of which there is no legal sanction.

Examples : (A) and (B) mutually agree that they will meet each other in front of «Ulus Sineması» and go to a coffee house together. This is not a contract. The agreement contemplates social, not legal relations. (A) cannot sue (B) if he does not appear.

(A) and (B) may promise to marry each other. This is called an engagement. Such a promise is not wholly enforceable. If (A) does not want to marry (B) there is no effective sanction[2] (C. C., Art. 83).

(A) promises to sell his icebox for T.L. 5000 and (B) consents to buy it. (A) is under an obligation to transfer the ownership of the icebox and (B) must pay T.L. 5000.

---

* Faculty of Law, University of Ankara.
[1] Code of Obligations, dated Oct. 4, 1926.
[2] But see Chapter 6 on Family Law.

For a contract to be valid and enforceable there should be the following elements:
(1) A valid agreement.
(2) Between parties with capacity to contract.
(3) A legal cause (legal ground, *hukukî sebep*).
(4) A legal subject matter
(5) Based upon real or genuine assent (intention).
(6) Made in the form required by law.

Example of a valid and enforceable contract: In consideration of 450 T.L. which Ahmet Gür agreed to pay to Turhan Yar, Turhan Yar agrees he will deliver to Ahmet Gür a record player.

B. Classification of Contracts:

Contracts may be classified, in terms of the degree of their enforceability, as valid, void or voidable.

Valid contracts are those possessing all the elements mentioned in A above. Such contracts are fully binding and enforceable.

Void (=null) contracts *(batıl akitler)* are those which have no legal effect either because they are against law or morals, because of incapacity, lack of formality or impossibility.

If the owner of a shop agrees to purchase stolen goods from a thief and later refuses to buy the goods, the thief has no recourse at law, because the contract is against morals and void. Because of the public interest, a person does not have to have any special standing to challenge the validity of a void contract, and may do so at any time.[3]

Voidable contracts *(fesih edilebilir akitler)* are those which may be binding and enforceable, but due to the lack of one or more of the elements of a valid contract, may be rejected at the option of one or both of the parties. They are valid until declared void. Contracts made by mistake are generally considered voidable (C. C., Art. 26).

The validity of a voidable contract may only be challenged by an interested party; in the case of mistake, for example, only by the party who is misled by the mistake. The period during which a voidable contract may be voided is usually fixed by law[4] (e. g. C. O., Art. 21, 31, 226).

---

[3] Sometimes a contract may be partly void. Contracts which are against price control legislation are partly void. See below VI B 2.

[4] See below IV A 3.

II. A VALID AGREEMENT
A. In General :

As stated above, a contract requires an exchange of assents, that is expressions of intentions, between at least two parties. There is an agreement when the parties lead each other reasonably to believe that they are of the same mind about a given transaction. This point is reached by an offer on the one side, and an apparent acceptance of the offer on the part of the other.

The best example of offer and acceptance may be seen when two persons bargain. This frequently happens at a store when offers are made by both parties several times before a bargain ends in a contract. Suppose (A) offers a certain radio to (B) for T.L. 800. (B) replies that he will give (A) T.L. 700. (B) has rejected (A)'s offer and made one himself which (A) is free to accept or reject. (A) may say «I can't take that, but I will split the difference and sell to you for T.L. 750». This is (A)'s new offer which (B) may accept or reject. (B) may come back with an offer of T.L. 725 which (A) may accept. At this point, if (A) accepts, there would be a contract.

B. The Offer (İcap) :

An offer is a declaration of intention by one party, known as the offerer *(icapçı)*, whereby he expresses his willingness to enter into a contract.

There are three requisites to a valid offer : (1) It must be made with the intention of creating a legal relation. If the offerer is not serious and only makes a joke, then there is no real offer. (2) The offer must be definite and certain; otherwise it would be impossible for the other party to understand the real intention of the offerer and, therefore, there could be no agreement. (3) The offer must be communicated to the offeree. Generally, the offeree must be known, although there are a few cases where the offeree may not be known. An example would be the case of a reward offered to the public.

C. The Acceptance (Kabul) :

An acceptance is a declaration of intention to agree to the terms of the offer given by the party to whom the offer is made. The making of an offer does not mean that anyone may accept. Only the offeree is entitled to turn the offer into an agreement, and an acceptance by any other party is ineffective. As noted in (B) above, however, an offer may be made to the public. For example, an offer of reward is generally made to the public; therefore any person may accept it.

III. CAPACITY *(Muamele ehliyeti)*:

As it is stated in the chapter on the Law of Persons, our law distinguishes between the ability to be the subject of rights (in German: *(Rechtsfaehigkeit)* and the capacity to enter into legal transactions. All persons, even an unborn child, are subject to rights (C. O., Art. 11). The legal validity of a transaction such as a contract depends, however, on the capacity (in German: *Geschaeftsfaehigkeit)* of the person who enters into the transaction. There can be no real or genuine assent if the person purporting to give the assent lacks capacity. As noted in the chapter on personality, persons may be unable to act for themselves because of natural or legal incapacity. Natural incapacity exists when incapacity is due to some natural cause, as in the case of an idiot, lunatic or an immature child. Legal incapacity is the result of a rule of law, as in the case of the incapacity of a business association in certain circumstances.[5]

IV. GENUINENESS OF ASSENT

Since the basis of a contract is the exchange of assents, it is essential that the assents of the parties be genuine, that is to say that there be a genuine meeting of the minds. Unintentional differences of assent may be due to several causes such as mistake, fraud or duress.

A. Mistake:

Mistake *(hata)* results where the expression is unintentionally inconsistent with the state of mind being expressed. A person may sign a lease contract although he wants to sell, or signs an invoice instead of a receipt; he may order item number 135 from a catalogue instead of 153; the buyer says 500 kg. instead of 50 kg.

There are different kinds of mistakes:

1. *Immaterial Mistake:*

A mistake relating solely to the motives for entering into the contract is not material and may not be the basis for voiding a conract (C. O., Art. 24 II). For example when a person, thinking

---

[5] See Chapter 4 on the Law of Persons and Chapter 5 on Legal Persons.

of a new government decree which he believes will raise prices, makes a contract, this contract is valid even though the decree is not issued and the prices do not go up.

2. *Material Mistakes:*

Only material mistakes can be the basis for voiding a contract. A material mistake may be a:

Mistake as to the identity of subject matter (error in object): If the mistaken party had in mind a subject other than the subject of the contract entered into (C. O., Art. 24/2).

Mistake as to the identity of parties (error in person): If the mistaken party had in mind a person other than the one with whom the contract was made (C. O., Art. 24/2).

Mistake as to the nature of the transaction: If the mistaken party had the intention of entering into a contract other than that to which he expressed his assent (C. O., Art. 24/1).

Mistake as to quantity: If the mistaken party undertakes a substantially greater obligation or accepts a substantially smaller one than the intended (C. O., Art. 24/3) the contract is voidable.

Mistake as to the necessary state of facts of a contract: As stated above, mistake in motives are not considered material and do not invalidate contracts. If the mistake is related to the absence of a necessary state of facts which, according to sound commercial custom, may be considered to be an essential element of the contract, the agreement is voidable (C. O., Art. 24/4). When (A) buys a cow upon the assumption that it is a breeding cow but the cow proves to be barren and valuable only for butchering purposes, there is a material mistake. If, on the other hand, (A) buys a horse on the assumption that it can trot one kilometer in two minutes, whereas it can trot no faster than one kilometer in two and a quarter minutes, the mistake probably is not material.

3. *The Effect of Mistake:*

In the case of material mistake, the contract is voidable by the party who is mistaken, that is to say, misled by the mistake. The contract is valid until declared void, which must be done within one year of the making of the contract; otherwise the contract is deemed ratified [6] (C. O., Art. 31).

---

[6] A mistaken party may not base his claim on a mistake where the allegation of such mistake is contrary to good faith. He is, particularly bound with the contract as understood by him, if the other party agrees with it (C.O., Art. 25).

B. Fraud:

Fraud *(hile)* is an intentional misstatement by which one person obtains or seeks to obtain an unfair advantage over another. Where a party to a contract has been induced to enter into it by the fraud of the other party, the defrauded party is not bound by the contract (C. O., Art. 28) and may declare it void within one year of the making of the contract. Alternatively, the defrauded party may abide by the contract but demand compensation for any damages suffered.

C. Duress:

Duress *(ikrah, korkutma)* may be defined as coercion by threatened injury or restraint which prevents one from exercising his free will.

Where a person is induced to enter into a contract because of duress by the other contracting party, he is not bound by the contract if he notifies the other party within one year of the making of the contract (C. O., Art. 29 and 31).

V. LEGAL CAUSE

The common law term and concept of consideration is unknown to Turkish law. Turkish law, however, requires every contract to have a cause (legal ground, consideration, *hukukî sebep*). The parties must have a purpose when they enter into a contract. For example, in a contract of sale the obligation of the seller is to transfer title to the goods sold, and the buyer's obligation is to pay the price. The cause of the obligation undertaken by the seller, that is to say his purpose in entering the contract, is to secure the buyer's obligation. In a contract of bailment or credit, the cause is to transfer certain goods or a certain amount of money. In a contract in the nature of a gratuity, the cause is to make a donation, or give a gift.

VI. LEGALITY OF THE SUBJECT MATTER

A. Freedom of Contract:

Turkish law recognizes freedom of contract. The parties may choose the type of contract and the subject and terms of a contract at their discretion. There are provisions in the Code of Obligations and Commercial Code on several types of contracts such as sale, tenancy, agency, guaranty etc.. However, the parties may enter into a contract which is not covered by the law. And they may put provisions into their contracts which may be different from statutory provisions. There are limitations on this freedom.

B. Limitation of Freedom of Contract :

1. General Remarks :

Turkey has introduced planning into its economy, and there is also state economic activity. These bring certain limitations to the freedom of contract. For example, trading in some kinds of goods is under state monopoly. Some kinds of contracts are valid only with the state's approval (for example, forming a corporation requires state permission) ; sometimes persons are obliged to enter into contracts (employment agreements between employers and employees are void in so far as they are not consistent with applicable collective bargaining agreements and the void terms are replaced by the provisions of the collective employment contract (C. O., Art. 317).[7]

2. Specific Limitations of the Freedom of Contract :

a) Contracts against law are void :

(1) Altough limited in number, there are some obligatory provisions in the Code of Obligations and Commercial Code which a contract cannot violate. For example, agreements stipulating in advance that interest shall be added to principal and that there shall be compound interest *(mürekkep faiz)* are invalid (C. O., Art. 398); also a party cannot, in advance, waive the effect of the statute of limitations *(müruruzaman, zamanaşımı)*.[8]

(2) The subject matter of a contract may be barred by certain prohibitive provisions. Contracts for black-marketing are, for example, prohibited, to deal in foreign exchange transactions without permission is prohibited. Contracts to sell forbidden goods, such as narcotics, are against the law. Contracts for the sale of goods contravening the price control legislation are considered invalid to the extent that the permitted price is deemed substituted for the prohibited contractual price (Comm. C., Art. 1466 and C. O., Art. 20).

---

[7] See also the Law of Collective Labor Agreements, Strikes and Lockout, Law No. 275, dated July 24, 1963. As amended by the Law No. 503, dated July 16, 1964, Art. 3 and Traffic Law, Law No. 6085, dated May 18, 1953, Art. 51. Compulsory third party automobile insurance contracts.

[8] C. O., Art. 139 I. Also C. O., Art. 99 I, 127, 134 II, 189 III, 196, 223, 224, 332, 343, 484, 496, Comm. C., Art. 6.

(3) Parties sometimes enter into contracts which are indirectly against the law. This is called a fraud against the law *(kanuna karşı hile)* and such a contract will be deemed a direct violation of law. For example, there are some prohibitive provisions in relation to installment sales *(taksitle satışlar)* (C. O., Arts. 22 - 224). The parties, in order to evade these provisions, may enter into a so-called hire - purchase contract. There is a fraud against the law, if the statutory provisions are evaded, with the result that the hire-purchase contract will be void.

b) Contracts contrary to good morals are void : Examples are contracts which have as their purpose the suppression of bidding at auction sales,[9] contracts to bribe a judge, to testify falsely in court. Sometimes contracts in restraint of trade are deemed against good morals.

c) Contracts against individual rights : According to article 23 of the Civil Code, no person can renounce all or part of his capacity to have rights and to enter into legal transactions. No person can alienate his personal liberty, nor impose any restrictions on his own enjoyment thereof which are contrary to law or morality.[10]

Some specific examples of contracts against individual rights are the following : «Where services for life or for a longer period than ten years have been contracted, the servant may, after the expiration of ten years, terminate the contract by giving one month's notice without liability for damages» (C. O., Art. 343). «A condition in restraint of trade is only valid within such appropriate limits of time, place and subject matter as will not unreasonably impede the economic future of the servant» (C. O., Art. 349). Where an ordinary partnership agreement has been entered into for an indefinite period of time or for the lifetime of one of the partners, it may be terminated by any partner by giving six months' notice (C. O., Art. 536).

d) Impossibility *(imkânsızlık)* : If the performance of the subject matter of a contract is impossible prior to the making of the contract, such contract is void.[11] For example, a contract to sell a fine painting of a famous painter, when in fact it is completely

---

[9] See C. O., Art. 266 which entitles any interested party to contest within ten days the validity of an auction sale which is effected by illegal acts or by acts which are against good morals = *müzayedeye fesat karıştırmak*.

[10] See Chapter 4 VIII on the Law of Persons.

[11] For impossibility which occurs after the making of a contract see below VIII C.

burned, or an intact piece of furniture, when in fact that piece is already broken, is void, since the subject matter does not exist at the time of the contract.

VII. FORM OF CONRACT
A. In General:

A contract may either be oral or written. The written form has certain advantages. It clarifies the assents of the parties and if the wording is definite and concise, it may prevent misunderstanding, misrepresentation and fraud. It may more easily be proved in the courts. It also makes it possible for the parties to think over the contents of the contract before they finally enter into it.

B. Effects of the Written Form:

1. Written Form as a Means of Proof:

As a rule, contracts are valid without any special form under Turkish law (C. O., Art. 11 I). This means that contracts are valid even if the terms are expressed in spoken words. This is usually referred to as the principle of «freedom as to form» *(şekil serbestliği)*. However, article 288 of the Code of Civil Procedure states the following: «Legal transactions to establish, transfer, convert, renew, state, satisfy, or release a right must be proved by a written instrument if the same exceeds five hundred liras (500 T.L.) in value».[12] Therefore, the so-called «freedom as to form» is replaced in practice in such cases by the principle of the «necessary written form». In other words, a written form is not required by the law and an oral contract is valid, but its existence may not be proved in case of dispute.

2. Written Form as a Prerequisite of Validity:

The written form is necessary where a statutory rule expressly prescribes it, or where the parties have agreed that a contract or part of it can only be concluded in a written form and its observance is a condition of the validity of the contract (C. O., Art. 11 II. In such cases every alteration of the contract must also be in writing, C. O., Art. 12). The legal effect of this rule is that, if the requirement of form is not fulfilled, then the contract is not valid.

There are different types of written contracts:

a) Simple written form *(alelâde yazılı şekil)*: A contract which must, by law, be in writing must bear the signature of all

---
[12] See Chapter 11, Part 2 on the Law of Procedure.

persons whom it is intended to bind. Therefore in a guaranty where one wishes to enforce a contract against a guarantor *(kefalet akdi)*, the guarantor's obligation must be in writing, must state the amount, and the guarantor must have signed the contract.

b) Official or authentic form *(resmî şekil)* : When a written contract is authenticated by public officers it is called an official form or document. The authentication may not be the same in each case. Sometimes the public certification of a signature is required. Usually certifications by notaries are found sufficient. For example, the signatures on a partnership agreement must be certified by a notary. Contracts related to real property (sale of real property, for example), on the other hand, are only valid if they are made before a Land Registry Officer and authenticated by him.[13] Sometimes a contract must be registered, as in the case of articles of incorporation of a business corporation.

There is a legal presumption that the text of an official document is correct unless the contrary is proved (C. C., Art. 7).

VIII. TERMINATION OF CONTRACTS

The obligations in an agreement may be terminated in several ways:

(1) Normally contracts are discharged by performance of the terms of the agreement. In that event the contract is completely terminated in the sense that both parties are freed from further obligations.

(2) What has been created by agreement may be terminated by agreement. There may be an express or implied provision in the original agreement as to termination, or the parties may make a subsequent agreement or may select other methods such as release *(feragat)* or novation *(tecdit)*.

(3) Impossibility *(İmkânsızlık)* : An obligation is discharged to the extent of its performance becoming impossible by circumstances for which the obliger cannot be made responsible [14] (C. O., Art. 117 I). For example, when there is a promise to sell the grapes to be grown in a specific vineyard, and the grapes are destroyed by blight, the contract is terminated. On the other hand, where there is a contract to sell a certain quantity of grapes, without limitation

---

[13] Land Registration Act *(Tapu K.)*, Law No. 2644, dated, Dec. 22, 1934, Art. 26.
[14] If the performance of the subject matter of a contract is impossible prior to the making of the contract such a contract is void.

or restriction as to a particular vineyard, the promisor is not released when a particular lot of grapes is destroyed by blight.

(4) Statute of Limitations *(Müruruzaman, zaman aşımı)*: The right of action on a contract is barred if no action is brought within a specified time. One of the purposes of the statute of limitations is the suppression of stale claims which are difficult to prove because proper evidence has been lost by the death or removal of witnesses or forgotten through lapse of time. The statutory period of limitations for contract actions is ten years, unless there is a specific statutory provision varying the period.[15]

(5) A contract may be terminated by one of the parties unilaterally if the other party breaches the contract and does not fulfill his obligation properly (C. O., Arts. 96 ff.).

PART 2
TORTS

I. GENERAL

The law gives each individual such freedom of activity as is compatible with the rights granted to others. When one acts beyond the restrictions imposed by law upon individual conduct, the acts become wrongful. If a wrongful act results in an injury to another, the law requires that redress be made in the form of compensation for such injuries. Such a wrongful act is a tort *(haksız fiil)*. In addition to the civil sanctions against wrongful acts, certain wrongful acts may also be punished under the provisions of the Criminal Code.[16]

II. CONDITIONS FOR TORTS

There are several conditions for tortious liability:

(1) Acts against law:

A tort is an act which is against law. By law is understood not only the provisions of the statutes, but also regulations and by-laws.

Omissions may also be considered torts. The landowner who leaves a hole in front of his garden will be liable if somebody falls into that hole because no satisfactory warning is given to the public. A man who buys and sells explosives will be liable if the goods are

---
[15] C. O., Art. 125, Five years: C.O., Art. 126.
[16] See Chapter 10 on Criminal Law.

not kept safely and someone is injured as a result. An omission, however, can be a basis for liability only if there is a duty for a person to act.

In exceptional cases, otherwise wrongful acts may not be considered torts. The acts of government civil servants (government employees) or soldiers are sometimes regulated by special provisions. Legitimate self-defense is another example. A person would not be liable for damages given to the person or property of an attacker because of such self-defense (C. O., Art. 52 III).

(2) Damage:

The second condition of a tort is damage to another person. This may be material or immaterial (moral) damage *(maddî ve manevi zarar)*. A house may be burned, or car damaged. These are material damages. On the other hand a man may become ill and incur hospital expenses because of the death of his only son. In such a case the person who causes the death may be obliged to pay moral damages. Normally the law requires the compensation of material damage; moral damages may be recovered only if specifically provided for in the statute. Thus anyone injured in his person or reputation may, where the injury and negligence are grave, demand moral compensation (C. O., Art. 49, C. C., Art. 24). In case of unfair competition, too, moral damages may be demanded [17] (Comm. C., Art. 58).

(3) Causal relation:

The third condition of liability is the existence of proximate cause. In order to hold a person responsible as a wrongdoer in the eyes of the law there must be causal relation between the act or omission and the injury. There are various tests to determine the proximate cause. If, for example, according to the normal rules of life, a situation such as the one produced by the act or fact would have resulted in the damage that has actually been caused, there is a presumption of causal relation *(uygun illiyet rabıtası)*. The foreseeability of the consequences may also indicate the causal relation.

(4) Negligence:

Finally there must be a ground for liability. Generally this ground is intent to do an act *(kasıt)* or negligence *(kusur, ihmal)*. A person cannot be negligent unless he has ability to make fair judg-

---

[17] Also in case of breach of engagement. See Chapter 6 on Family Law.

ments. Consequently minors lacking such capacity have no tortious liability [18] (C. C., Art. 15). Yet to limit liability to cases where there is intention or negligence may cause some unjust results. Therefore in exceptional cases a man may be liable even without negligence. The owner of a building or other structure is liable for the damage caused by defective design or construction or by deficient upkeep (C. O., Art. 58 I). A master is liable for damages caused by his employees or servants in the course of performing their duties, unless he proves that he exercised all care reasonable in the circumstances to prevent such damage, or that the damage would have occurred notwithstanding the exercise of such care [19] (C. O., Art. 55). This is an example of responsibility for the negligence of others and is called vicarious liability.

The modern trend in Turkey is to make the wrongdoer responsible for his acts, even if he has not acted negligently.

PART 3

UNJUST ENRICHMENT

I. GENERAL

A person who acquires something at the expense of another without any legal ground is bound to return it to him (C. O., Art. 61). Unjust enrichment *(sebepsiz zenginleşme)* is considered as a secondary source of obligations; if a claim can be based on a contract, there will be no cause of action for unjust enrichment.

II. CONDITIONS

The conditions of unjust enrichment are the following: There must be enrichment in the property of a person, measured as the difference between the previous value and the value after the acquisition of the property. Such enrichment may result from services performed on property or acquired possession of a thing.[20] A person may also be enriched by avoiding expenditures, although there may be no increase in his assets. Thus, if (A) ploughs (B)'s land by mistake, (B) is enriched.

---

[18] See Chapter 4 on the Law of Persons. The head of the family may be responsible for a minor's torts under Art. 320 of the C. C.
[19] Other examples of tortious liability without negligence: C. O., Arts. 541, 56, C. C., Arts. 48 II, 656, Comm. C., Arts. 177 II, 256, 321 V.
[20] S. Reisoğlu, *Sebepsiz İktisap Dâvasının Genel Şartları* 77 ff. (Ankara 1961); Tunçomağ, 370 ff.

There must be a decrease in the value of property of the other person, though it need not be equal in either quantity, or quality, to the benefit acquired by the former. There must be sufficient causal relation between the benefit and the decrease.

The enrichment must be without any legal ground. If (A) pays (B) interest of 15 % pursuant to a contract there would be an increase in the property of (B), as against the property of (A). But this enrichment has a legal ground, that is, a valid contract. If, however, there is no legal contract between the parties, as in the case where one of the parties lacks capacity to enter into a valid contract, the incapable party may demand the repayment of an amount he has paid.

The enriched person is obliged to pay the difference in his property before and after the enrichment, unless he has acted in bad faith (C. O., Art. 63).

SELECTED BIBLIOGRAPHY

Feyzioğlu, F. N. : **Borçlar Hukuku, Genel Hükümler,** Cilt : I ve II (Istanbul 1976 - 1977).

İnan, Ali Naim : **Borçlar Hukuku, Genel Hükümler,** Kitap 1 ve 2 (Ankara 1971 - 1973).

Reisoğlu, Safa : **Borçlar Hukuku,** Cilt : 1 (Ankara 1977).

Tunçomağ, Kenan : **Borçlar Hukuku Dersleri,** Cilt : 1, **Genel Hükümler** (İstanbul 1972).

Text :

An English text of the Turkish Code of Obligations may be found in Wettstein and others : **The Swiss Federal Code of Obligations with the Turkish Alterations** (Zürich 1928).

CHAPTER 10

CRIMINAL LAW

Prof. Dr. Feyyaz GÖLCÜKLÜ *

I. INTRODUCTION

A. Purpose :

The essential purpose of law is to impose order on human society. Law does this by sanctions against certain kinds of behavior which violate that order. Where private law provides for damages, restitution between private parties, and the like, criminal law defines violations of the social order - called crimes - and prescribes punishment and rules governing its application. What constitutes a crime and the nature of punishments may vary from country to country, according to moral and cultural values.

B. Theories of Punishment for Crimes :

All human societies have defined crimes and prescribed punishments. Punishment has been justified on various grounds in different ages and places. These grounds have included : (1) expiation - the criminal pays for his crime and squares his account with society; (2) retribution or revenge - punishment satisfies a demand that justice be done; here there has been a movement away from the theory of personal revenge for the victim to that of a retribution for the society as a whole. Rousseau based this idea on the «social contract,» whereby society agrees to perform the function for the individual. Kant believed punishment by the society is a requirement of «absolute justice» ; (3) prevention - removal of the criminal from society to prevent further crime ; (4) deterrence - fear of punishment instills respect for law and deters violation; and (5) reformation and rehabilitation - reformation of the criminal results in his future obedience to the law.

The Classical School, which has had a considerable influence on the development of criminal law in Europe, emphasized retribution and deterrence as the basis for punishment. According to this school of thought, punishment depends upon the moral

---

* University of Ankara, Faculty of Political Sciences.

responsibility or fault of the criminal. It is assumed that men have free will and the capacity to form mature judgments. When these are lacking because of youth, mental illness, or other incapacity, no basis for punishment exists.

The Positivist School, in reaction to some of the perceived shortcomings of the Classical School, viewed crime more as a social than a moral phenomenon. Just as viruses and microbes cause sickness, so crime is caused by social and other environmental conditions; and crime can only be avoided by eliminating these conditions. In the eyes of the Positivist School, the individual does not have free will; his behavior is determined by conditions beyond his control. The only utility of punishment is to protect society from the criminal with strength of the punishment being dependent upon the degree of danger the criminal poses to society. This school of thought attaches importance to the personal welfare of the criminal and has given a new dimension to criminal law.

Different theories and schools have influenced the law, in varying degrees. Today's law is increasingly concerned with reform of the criminal, rather than with retributive punishment.

II. CRIME

A. Definition of Crime and its Elements :

Criminal statutes list acts which are considered crimes, but they do not define crime itself. Criminal lawyers define it according to the school of thought to which they subscribe. From the point of view of «positive law», a crime is any act which is punishable by law.

An act is considered a crime only when certain elements exist. Those which are elements of all crimes are called the «general elements of crime». In addition, there are «specific elements» for certain crimes, such as theft, murder and others. These are the subject matter of the «Special Part» of the Criminal Code, however, and are not dealt with here.

B. General Elements of Crime :

1. The Legal Elements :

Since the crime may be defined as an act punishable by law, the act must first be described as criminal in nature, and then a penalty must be provided for it by a law. This is the «legal element» of a crime.

Turkish law accepts the principle that there can be «no crime and punishment without law» *(Kanunsuz suç ve ceza olmaz)* ; it does this in order to avoid arbitrary accusation and punishment and to protect personal liberty.[1]

Article 33 or the Constitution states that «no person shall be punishable for an act which is not considered an offense under the law in force at the time the act was committed. Punishments and penal measures shall be established only by law». Article 1 of the Turkish Criminal Code states that «no one may be punished for an act which is not expressly defined by law as a crime; no one can be subjected to a punishment not prescribed by law». In Turkish law, therefore, the source of all crimes and punishments is a provision of the written law.[2]

The legislature must define every crime and its penalty as clearly as possible in the statutes, and the judge can apply a law to an act only if it is exactly the same as the one defined in the law. Interpretation by analogy is prohibited in the criminal law. Penal provisions have no retroactive effect, except when they favour the accused[3] (Cr. C., Art. 2).

a) Sources of the Turkish Criminal Code :

During the period of the Ottoman Empire, Islamic Law was the foundation of the criminal law practice in Turkey. Though some statutes existed relating to penal matters, they were limited to incomplete listings of the most serious crimes and their penalties, rather than a complete and systematic penal code. The first Turkish criminal code in a modern sense was the Imperial Penal Code *(Ceza Kanunname-i Hümayunu)*, published in 1858. This was Turkish translation of the French Penal Code of 1810 and it remained in force until 1926.

The bulk of the criminal law may be found in the Turkish Criminal Code, which is based almost entirely on the Italian Criminal Code of 1889, adopted by Turkey in 1926.[4] This Code has been amended many times, and more than half of its articles have been changed.[5] The Code specifies most crimes and contains the general

---

[1] See Chapter 1 on Sources of Turkish Law.
[2] See Chapter 1 on Sources of Turkish Law.
[3] See Chapter 1 on Sources of Turkish Law.
[4] Law No. 765, dated March 1, 1926, as amended. An English translation of the Turkish Criminal Code may be found in the American Series of Foreign Penal Codes, No. 9, *The Turkish Criminal Code* (1965).
[5] The last amendment was made by the Law No. 1490, dated Oct. 3, 1971.

principles of Turkish criminal law which are applicable to all criminal matters, unless another statute specifically provides otherwise (Cr. C., Art. 10). The general principles are in Book One (Arts. 1 - 124); the crimes are specified in Books Two and Three (Arts. 125 - 592). There are two categories of crimes: felonies *(cürümler)* and misdemeanors *(kabahatler)*.

In addition to the Criminal Code, there are many penal statutes which contain specific crimes and regulate special fields of criminal law. Many civil laws also prescribe penalties for certain criminal acts.

b) Scope of the Criminal Code:

The Turkish Criminal Code adopts the principle of territoriality as a general rule, with a few exceptions (Cr. C., Arts., 3 - 8). This means that «whoever commits a crime in Turkey shall be punished in accordance with Turkish law». Under Articles 3 through 8 the systems of individual and universal criminal jurisdiction are accepted, under certain conditions, in order not to let the criminal go unpunished. This means that a crime committed outside of Turkish territory, by Turkish citizens or against them, or by foreigners or against them, will be prosecuted and punished in accordance with Turkish law.

Article 9 contains some provisions concerning extradition. According to this Article, extradition *(suçluların geri verilmesi)* of a Turkish citizen to a foreign State is not allowed, nor is extradition of a foreigner to another State for prosecution for political or related felonies. If a foreign State requests extradition, the Court of General Criminal Jurisdiction *(Asliye Ceza Mahkemesi)* in the area in which the person resides in Turkey, must determine his citizenship and the nature of the felony committed. If this court determines that the requested person is a Turkish citizen or that the crimes are political, military, or related felonies, extradition cannot be granted. Alternatively, the government may accept the request and the local investigating magistrate *(sorgu hakimi)* may issue a warrant of arrest for the person. It should be noted that Article 9 does not exhaust all the problems which may arise in this area; treaties and conventions signed by Turkey contain many complementary provisions concerning extradition.

The criminal law applies to all persons, again with some exceptions. Most notably, the President of the Republic and members of parliament, as well as foreign officials with diplomatic immunities, are not subject to the criminal law.[6]

2. *The Material Element of a Crime:*

With a few exceptions (Cr. C., Arts. 256, 313), criminal thought itself is not punishable nowadays; there must also be a completed criminal act. However, an unsuccessful attempt to commit a felony may itself be a crime. «Anyone who commences the execution of an intended felony by effective means, and, who, due to reasons beyond his control, cannot complete the acts necessary to complete the felony, shall be punished» (Cr. C., Art. 61, incomplete attempt *nakıs teşebbüs)* ; and «anyone who completes all the acts for the execution of the felony he intended to commit, but where, due to reasons beyond his control, the felony does not take place, shall be punished...» (Cr. C., Art. 62, complete attempt = *tam teşebbüs).* Punishment for such attempts is lighter than in the case of completed felonies.

The necessity of proving a criminal act assures greater objectivity in the application of the law and punishment and is a safeguard of personal liberty.

3. *The Moral Element of a Crime (Mens rea):*

a) Criminal capacity *(Ceza ehliyeti):*

The Turkish Criminal Code embodies the Classical School concept of the moral responsibility of the criminal. For a man to be guilty of a crime, he must have both criminal capacity and criminal intent. Thus, Article 46 of the Criminal Code provides that «anyone afflicted with a mental illness which causes a complete loss of consciousness or of freedom of action at the time of commission of the act, shall not be punished». However, during the preparatory investigation the decision to subject such person to custody and medical treatment must be rendered by the Justice of the Peace, during the preliminary investigation, by the investigating judge, and during the final investigation by the competent court. The custody and medical treatment continues until such person is cured, but a defendant accused of a crime entailing heavy imprisonment may not be released prior to one year. The person thus places in custody and subjected to medical treatment shall be released by the competent court upon a hospital board report

---

[6] Const., Arts. 98, 99, 79. The Status of Forces Agreements between Turkey and certain countries, regulate the extent to which foreign military personnel are subject to Turkish laws.

of the institution where the patient was kept, indicating that it is medically understood that the patient has recovered. This report shall include a decision as to whether, in view of considerations of social security, the nature of the disease and the defendant's alleged crime, the person shall be subjected to medical control and an examination; if so, it shall state the time and intervals for periodic examinations. If, during the treatment period, the disease appears to recur, the person shall be placed in custody and subjected to medical treatment by order of the judge or court. (For diminishing responsibilty, see, Cr. C., Art. 47). Article 48 provides that this rule shall be applicable to anyone who, during the commission of a crime, was incapacitated for extraneous reasons. Acts committed while voluntarily under the influence of alcohol or narcotics, are excluded from the provisions of this article.

Criminal capacity also depends upon age. «Whoever has not attained the age of twelve at the time of the commission of an act, shall not be prosecuted and punished» (Cr. C., Art. 53). Between the ages of twelve and eighteen, this capacity may vary according to the mental development and age of the child. According to the Code, children over eleven and under fifteen years of age have criminal responsibility, provided that they have the ability to make fair judgments, but punishments shall be reduced (Cr. C., Art. 54). For children between fifteen and eighteen years of age, it is not necessary for the prosecution to prove judgment ability (Cr. C., Art. 55).

In all these cases, the punishment of juveniles is reduced as specified by related articles. If the offender is under the age of eighteen years at the time he begins serving his sentence, punishment restricting his personal liberty will be served in a reformatory or in a special section of the adult penitentiaries. If the child is below the age of responsibility (11 years old), and if his act constitutes a felony punishable by imprisonment for more than one year, he shall either be placed in the custody of his parent or guardian, or be committed to an institution, under government administration or supervision. Such institutional custody will last until the child reaches eighteen years of age, but is subject to revocation at any time if deemed necessary for the purposes of education and reform.

These are the only provisions in the Turkish Criminal Code regarding juvenile delinquents, and it is clear that they are insufficient to fight the juvenile delinquency problem in Turkey. Such judicial organizations as a juvenile court system with special penal procedures, a probation system, and youth institutions with sufficiently qualified personnel, are entirely lacking at present. Without these, little can be done to protect Turkish society from future habitual offenders.

b) Criminal intent *(Suç kastı)* :

According to Article 45 of the Turkish Criminal Code, absence of criminal intent precludes punishment of felonies. There is an exception for those cases where the law prescribes a punishment for consequences of the perpetrator's acts or omissions (unintentional offenses). For misdemeanors, an offender is responsible for his act or omission in the absence of criminal intent.

In criminal law, criminal intent refers to a willing and conscious desire to commit the action and to expect its consequences.

Mistake of law *(hukukî hata)* does not affect guilt. Ignorance of the law is no defense (Cr. C., Art. 44). But mistake of fact *(fiili hata)* may be relavent. Thus, it is stated in Article 52 that if a person, as a result of a mistake or defect, commits a felony against a person other than he intended, the matters of aggravation arising from the status of the injured party shall not be imputed to the perpetrator. Such cases may be dealt with as if the felony had been committed against the person intended, but the perpetrator shall benefits from any matter of mitigation applicable to the felony. Also the mistake of fact may sometimes negate the criminal intent necessary to commit a crime.

c) Personal liability :

Personal liability is another important principle of modern criminal law. If a person did not commit the act personally, and if the act is not morally imputed to him, he cannot be held responsible for this act and is not, therefore, liable to punishment. In other words, no one can be punished for an act which is not committed by him, but by someone else. Article 33 of The Turkish Constitution states that «criminal liability is personal».

d) Cases of Justification *(Hukuka uygunluk sebepleri)* :

According to Article 49, no punishment shall be imposed if the perpetrator has acted 1) in order to execute the provisions of a statute or on order given by a responsible authority, execution of which is the perpetrator's duty; 2) in immediate necessity to repel an unjust assault against his own or another's person or chastity (legitimate self-defense = *meşru müdafaa*) ; 3) in necessity, if there was no other means of protection, to protect himself or another person against a grave and certain danger not knowingly caused by himself (state of necessity = *zaruret hali*).

In the first case, if the order issued is contrary to law, the punishment for the felony resulting from the violation of the law shall be suffered by the person who has issued the order. Whoever, while performing an act in one of the cases of justification above mentioned surpasses the limits prescribed either by law, by competent authority or by necessity shall be held responsible for it, but the punishment will be lessened at the rate specified by the Article 50.

C. Participation in a Crime :

A participant is one who has taken part in a crime knowingly and willingly either before or during the commission of the act. There are several degrees of participation in a crime . A person who abets another to commit a felony or misdemeanor is deemed a principal and full participant (*aslî iştirak*) (Cr. C., Art. 64) and is subject to the full punishment for the act.

There are also (material or moral) «accessories» (*fer'i iştirak*) to a crime (Cr. C., Art. 65) : Anyone who participates in a crime, by inciting or encouraging another to commit a crime, by promising him aid and assistance after commission cf the act or by giving instruction as to the manner of commission of the crime (moral) ; by procuring the means which will aid the commission of the act, or by facilitating the commission of the crime through rendering aid and assistance before or during the commission of the crime (material) is an accessory. Accessories are subject to lesser punishment than the principals.

According to Turkish law, participation in a previous crime is not generally a ground for aggravation of penalty, except in some specific cases (Cr. C., Arts. 417, 479, 491).

D. Multiplicity of Crimes and Punishments

(Suçların ve Cezaların İçtimaı) :

If a person is convicted of several crimes (multiplicity of crimes) or if the same person, after a judgment, is convicted of another crime committed previously or thereafter (multiplicity of punishments), all punishments shall be united in accordance with the provisions prescribed in Articles 70 and after (Cr. C., Arts. 68, 69). Thus more than one sentence of life imprisonment results in the death penalty; and in the case of at least two heavy imprisonments of not less than twenty-four years each, life imprisonment shall be applied. If a person is sentenced to identical kinds of temporary punishment restricting liberty (or, to fines of the same kind), the total of the punishments shall be applied.

On the limits of the addition of punishments, the Turkish Criminal Code provides as follows: the total of punishments of the same category restricting liberty may not exceed thirty-six years of heavy imprisonment; or twenty-five years of imprisonment; or ten years of light imprisonment. The total of various kind of punishments restricting liberty may not exceed thirty years.

On the other hand, whoever commits a crime in order to be able to commit or conceal another crime, or while perpetrating a crime commits another act punishable by law shall be punished as in the cases of multiplicity of crimes or of punishments if such acts or crimes are not, by provision of law, elements of the principal crime or if they do not constitute aggravating circumstances (Cr. C., Art. 78). And if a person has violated several provisions of law by a single act, he shall be punished under the provision of the article involving the most severe punishment (Cr. C., Art. 79). Violation of a provision of the law several times, in the course of the execution of a decision to commit a crime, though such violations occur at different times, is considered as a single crime; but the punishment to be imposed shall be increased (Cr. C., Art. 80).

III. PUNISHMENT ; PREVENTION OF CRIME
A. General :
1. Nature of Punishment ; Prevention Measures :

The Criminal Code prescribes different punishments for different crimes. Certain «secondary» penalties are in fact measures designed to prevent crime. These include police supervision (Cr. C., Art. 28), confiscation of property (Cr. C., Art. 37), custody and treatment of mentally ill persons (Cr. C., Art. 46), commitment to an institution or placing children who do not have criminal capacity into the custody or their parents (Cr. C., Art. 53), and custody and treatment of drug addicts and alcoholics (Cr. C., Arts. 404, 573).

2. Categories of Crimes :

As earlier stated, the Turkish Criminal Code divides crimes into two main categories : felonies *(cürümler)* and misdemeanors *(kabahatler).* They are distinguished from each other by the severity of punishment. Therefore, in order to say whether an offense is a felony or a misdemeanor, one must look to the punishment to which the offender is subject. Offenses are further grouped, such as felonies against the State, felonies against public decency and family order, offenses of rape etc.

3. *Punishments*:

Punishments for felonies are death (by hanging) *(idam)*, heavy imprisonment *(ağır hapis)*, imprisonment *(hapis)* (up to 20 years), heavy fine *(ağır para cezası)* (up to 25.000 TL.), disqualification from holding public office *(kamu hizmetlerinden yasaklılık)* temporary or for life; and for misdemeanors: light imprisonment *(hafif hapis)* (up to 2 years), light fine *(hafif para cezası)* (up to 10.000 TL.), disqualification from practicing a profession or trade *(muayyen bir meslek veya san'atın icrasının tatili)* (Cr. C., Art. 11). According to Article 14 of the Turkish Constitution «No individual shall be subjected to ill-treatment or torture. No punishment incompatible with human dignity shall be imposed».

Heavy imprisonment for more than five years disqualifies the convicted person from holding public office for life; heavy imprisonment from three to five years disqualifies a person for a period equal to the sentence (Cr. C., Art. 31). Conviction of a crime may have other consequences; civic disqualification (i.e. to vote), deprivation of paternal rights and the legal rights of a husband,[7] payment of damages or restitution of property, payment of court expenses, as well as the secondary penalties referred to in III A 1 above (Cr. C., Art. 32).

The Law of Execution of Punishments[8] modified the manner of implementation of Articles 12 ff. of the Criminal Code. This law divides punishments into three categories: 1) death (by hanging), 2) long or short term punishments restricting personal liberty (more than six months and less than six months), and 3) fines. It has also repealed «banishment» *(sürgün)* as a penalty and has completly modified the prison system and conditional release (an institution similar to parole); it has introduced something along the lines of probation for short term imprisonment (punishments and measures applicable in place of short term imprisonment); and it has made provision for the observation of convicted criminals during long-term imprisonment. The Turkish penal system does

---
[7] See Chapter 6 on Family Law.
[8] Law No 647.

not permit indeterminate sentences, except for drug addicts and alcoholics.

B. Application of Punishment :

Judges are given some discretion in fixing punishment. In some cases they may choose between imprisonment or fine; and they decide whether to impose the minimum or maximum punishment or something in between.

The following factors are to be taken into consideration in determining the punishment : provocation *(tahrik)*, recidivism *(tekerrür)* and discretionary mitigating causes *(takdirî hafifletici sebepler)*. Thus, if a person commits a crime in the heat of anger or under influence of grief caused by an unjust provocation, the punishment prescribed for the crime shall be reduced; this reduction is greater if the provocation is grievous or severe (Cr. C., Art. 51). In terms of Article 81 of the Criminal Code, if a person commits a new crime within ten years of serving a sentence of more than five years, or after such a sentence is set aside, or within five years in case of other punishments, the punishment to be imposed for the new offense shall be increased by not more than one sixth. If the new crime is of the same kind as the previous crime, the punishment shall also be increased. Finally, apart from statutory matters of mitigation, wherever discretionary matters of extenuation in favor of the offender are accepted by the court, heavy imprisonment for thirty years, instead of heavy imprisonment for life, shall be imposed. Other punishments shall be reduced by not more than one sixth. Article 29 of the Criminal Code specifies how these factors are to be applied : «Unless explicity provided by law, punishments can neither be increased, nor decreased, nor changed. Where the law provides for aggravation or mitigation, the court will first determine the punishment for the act without considering grounds for aggravation or mitigation, and then shall increase or decrease the punishment as required by the aggravation or mitigation». If several grounds for aggravation or mitigation concur, increase or decrease shall be made first for the earlier grounds for aggravation or mitigation. Increase or decrease for later grounds shall be applied to the punishment resulting from the increase or decrease made for the earlier grounds. Where some of the grounds require an increase and others require a decrease of punishment, those requiring an increase shall be applied first. In all events, the perpetrator's age, his state of mind, matters of discretional extenuation and recidivism shall be taken into consideration last, in this order. In increasing or decreasing the punishment, the limits prescribed by law for every punishment shall not be exceeded, except where otherwise specifically provided by law.

A public prosecution shall be dismissed, if the perpetrator of an offense punishable only by fine deposits in the concerned office, before the hearing in court, the minimum amount of the fine prescribed for this offense. If this amount is paid before a public prosecution has been initiated, the perpetrator shall not be prosecuted at all.[9]

C. Suspension of Punishment (Cezanın ertelenmesi):

The Turkish criminal law does not provide for probation or parole as such. However, suspension of punishment, conditional release *(şartlı salıverme)* and some measures for short-term prisoners in the Law of Execution of Punishments referred to above and in the Turkish Criminal Code (Art. 89 ff.) can be considered as similar to parole. For crimes with relatively light penalties (fines, imprisonment up to one year, the judge, in certain circumstances (no previous punishment other than a fine; and if the court considering the past conduct and moral attitude of the offender believes that suspension of his punishment will cause him to abstain from committing a crime in the future), may suspend the execution of punishment, and release the offender without any supervision. In this event, the reasons for suspension shall be indicated in the text of the judgment. If, during the period prescribed by the Code, the convicted person does not commit another crime of certain specified degree of seriousness, the conviction will be considered as non-existent. Otherwise both punishments shall be executed separately.

D. Dismissal of Action and Setting Aside of Punishments:

In some cases the penal action and prosecution may be dismissed *(davanın düşmesi)* or the punishment may be set aside *(cezanın düşmesi)* (Cr. C., Arts. 96 - 120). The causes of dismissal and setting aside are: death of the accused or convict, amnesty, pardon, withdrawal of complaint, prescription and payment of fine before hearing.

---

[9] See Cr. C., Art. 119, as amended by the Law No. 1696 (1973) concerning Criminal Procedure, added Articles 5 ff.

The death of the accused shall terminate public prosecutions. The death of a convict will set aside the conviction, including light and heavy fines not yet executed, together with all its consequences (Cr. C., Art. 96).

Amnesty *(genel af)* terminates public prosecutions and sets aside punishments together with all their penal consequences (Cr. C., Art. 97). A pardon *(özel af)*, according to its terms, may set aside, reduce or change the punishment and remove a disqualification. However, a pardon will not ordinarily effect the penal consequences of the conviction nor secondary punishments, unless the contrary is specified in the pardon law (Cr. C., Art. 98).

According to Article 64 of the Constitution, the Grand National Assembly is empowered to grant pardons and amnesties and the President of Republic may commute a sentence or grant a pardon on grounds of chronic illness or old age.[10]

Where a public prosecution depends on a complaint by the aggrieved party, the public prosecution shall be discontinued if such a party waives his suit or complaint. However his waiver will not bar execution of punishment, unless the contrary is provided for by law (Cr. C., Art. 99, exception : Art. 444).

Except as otherwise prescribed by law, public prosecution shall be dismissed upon the lapse of the periods stated in the law (Cr. C., Art. 102). Punishments shall also be set aside with the lapse of the periods indicated in Article 112.[11]

E. Restoration of Rights (Yasak Hakların İadesi) :

Articles 121 and 124 of the Criminal Code provide for the restoration, upon the completion of a sentence, of rights taken away as a result of penal conviction. The decision to restore divested rights is made by the court, upon the request of interested parties. The procedure for such restoration is given in the Turkish Code of Criminal Procedure (Cr. C., Arts. 416 - 420).

---

[10] Cr. C., Art. 97, See also Arts. 68 and 131.
[11] See also Cr. C., Arts. 103 - 109 and 113 - 118.

SELECTED BIBLIOGRAPHY

Dönmezer / Erman : **Nazarî ve Tatbikî Ceza Hukuku,** Cilt : I, II ve III (İstanbul 1974 / 76).

Erem, F. : **Türk Ceza Hukuku,** Cilt : I ve II **Genel Hükümler** (Ankara 1974 / 76).

Erem / Toroslu : **Türk Ceza Hukuku, Özel Hükümler** (Ankara 1975).

Gölcüklü, F. : **Türk Ceza Sistemi** (Ankara 1966).

Text :

The Turkish Criminal Code (With an Introduction by Nevzat Gürelli), American Series of Foreign Penal Codes, No. 9 (London, 1965).

CHAPTER 11

LAW OF PROCEDURE

PART 1

INTRODUCTION *

I. GENERAL

The law of procedure is the field of law which deals with the administration of justice and the procedural aspects of substantive law. When a person has been deprived of any lawful right to his property or to his personal security or of any civil right either by its being denied to, or withheld from him, or has suffered any legal wrong, he may appeal to a court or to arbitrators for a remedy. The law of procedure deals with the means of securing these remedies.

In contrast to substantive law, in the law of procedure rules are formal and strict. This ensures effective administration, without which substantive law would have little value. Therefore, procedural law is practically the basis of the substantive law. If a person cannot, for example, claim his property right in court, it would be as if he had no property right at all.

II. COURT STRUCTURE

Although the rules of civil and criminal procedure are basically similar, civil procedure is distinguished from criminal procedure, in that in civil matters the public interest is not so paramount as in criminal matters. The civil and criminal courts are therefore different and separate.

The courts in Turkey are in fact divided into civil, criminal and administrative courts. These courts are further divided into lower and higher courts.

The lower courts of civil jurisdiction are the Courts of First Instance, Peace Courts (Justice of the Peace) and Commercial Courts. Execution officers *(icra memurları)*, bankruptcy officers

---

* Part 2 of this Chapter was compiled by Dr. T. Ansay, based on a book prepared by Karlen and Arsel (Civil Litigation in Turkey, Ankara 1957). For the 2nd edition Prof. Ansay made considerable changes upon the suggestions of Prof. Dr. B. Kuru, Professor for Civil Procedure, Execution and Bankruptcy, University of Ankara. Prof. Ansay wishes to thank his friend Prof. Kuru for his most valuable criticism and help.

(iflâs memurları, iflâs dairesi) and investigation authorities *(tetkik mercileri)* also act as judges in certain cases with the capacity to settle monetary disputes by means of summary procedures.

The Civil Court of First Instance *(asliye hukuk mahkemesi)* is the basic trial court with general and residual jurisdiction covering everything not specifically assigned to other tribunals. There is one in almost every «ilçe» or sub - province.[1]

Peace Courts *(sulh mahkemeleri)* are established to hear certain cases including those where the amount in controversy does not exceed 5000 TL. (about $ 280), eviction cases, claims of support, and requests for permission to marry.

Some civil matters involving commercial transactions are heard in Commercial Courts[2] *(ticaret mahkemeleri)*. A commercial case may also be commenced in an ordinary civil court, if the defendant does not object, or in the absence of a commercial court in the area (Comm. C., Arts. 4 and 5).

Criminal courts of original jurisdiction are the Peace Courts, Courts of General Criminal Jurisdiction and Aggravated Felony Courts.[3]

The Council of State *(Devlet Şurası, Danıştay)* handles administrative disputes and has jurisdiction over civil disputes involving the government. It is a court both of original jurisdiction and of last resort.[4]

Attempting to draw the jurisdictional line between the Council of State and the ordinary civil courts may cause difficulties. Many disputes involving the government are in fact tried in the ordinary courts. A special court, the Court of Conflicts, solves jurisdictional problems between ordinary civil courts and the Council of State.[5]

Notwithstanding the division among the courts, there is one high court for both civil and criminal matters. This court is called the Court of Cassation or the Supreme Court *(Yargıtay)* and considers the legality of lower court decisions.[6]

In addition to the above courts there are more specialized courts such as military courts, special courts for land registration and

---
[1] See Chapter 3 III B on Administrative Law.
[2] In some large cities three judges are sitting in Commercial Courts.
[3] See Part 3 of this Chapter.
[4] See Chapter 3 V E on Administrative Law.
[5] See Chapter 3 V E on Administrative Law; Karlen / Arsel 20, 21 ; S. Ş. Ansay 23.
[6] See Part 2 V of this Chapter.

courts for labor disputes.[7] The procedural rules applied in these last courts, as well as in the Council of State are basically similar to those of civil cases. Different rules are, however, applied in criminal trials.

III. PERSONS PARTICIPATING IN THE ADMINISTRATION OF JUSTICE

A. Judges :

The position of the judge *(hâkim, yargıç)* is important, especially as there is no jury trial in Turkey. His role is substantially larger than that of a judge in the Anglo - American system. He is actively responsible for the administration of justice. He takes the initiative in finding the law applicable to the facts submitted by the parties. The lawyers have the duty to assist the judge in establishing the facts and determining applicable legal provisions.

When a law school graduate decides to become a judge he applies to the Ministry of Justice in much the same fashion as he would apply for any other job. If accepted, he enters upon a period of apprenticeship, during which he learns the work of a judge under the guidance of senior men. At the end of a two - year period may be appointed by the Supreme Council of Judges [7] *(Yüksek Hâkimler Kurulu)* as a full - fledged judge. There are several degrees of judgeship, each carrying a different salary and different specific job possibilities.[8]

After a person becomes a full - fledged judge the power to decide about his personnel matters rests with the Supreme Council of Judges, a completely independent body composed of judges only (Const., Art. 143). He is eligible for promotion every two years. Promotions are determined by the Supreme Council of Judges on the basis of efficiency reports by superior judges and, for those in the lower ranks, also upon his record of reversals and affirmances by the Court of Cassation of a judge's decisions. The same Council also administers any change of function or place of assignment, the initiation of disciplinary proceedings, and any subsequent disciplinary actions taken against them [9] (Const., Art. 134).

---

[7] Law of Supreme Council of Judges and Prosecutors *(Yüksek Hâkimler Kurulu ve Savcılar Kurulu Kanunu)*, Law No. 45, dated April 22, 1962, as amended. For details see, R. Devereux, *Turkey's Judicial Security Mechanism*, 10 Die Welt des Islams 33 ff. (1965).

[8] Karlen / Arsel 73. Law of Judges *(Hâkimler Kanunu)*, Law No. 2556, dated July 4, 1934, Art. 2.

[9] Kuru 33 ff.

The independence of judges has been safeguarded by articles 132 and the following of the Constitution. Under article 132 «judges shall be independent in the discharge of their duties. They shall pass judgments in accordance with the Consitution, law, justice and their personal convictions».

«No organ, office, agency or individual may give orders or instructions to courts of judges in connection with the discharge of their judicial duty, send them circulars, or make recommendations or suggestions».

«No questions may be raised, debates held, or statements issued in legislative bodies in connection with the discharge of judicial power concerning a case on trial...».

Judges may not be dismissed. Unless they so desire, they may not be retired before they are sixty - five years old. They may not be deprived of their salaries, even if their court or post is abolished.[10] The abolition of a court or the post of a judge, or the alteration of the area of jurisdiction of a court is dependent upon the approval of the Supreme Council of Judges (Const. Art. 144 IV).

B. Court Reporters or Clerks :

In each court there is an office of clerks. The chief reporter (or secretary, *başkâtip*) has important duties. He performs the courts secretarial work, and he also replaces execution and bankruptcy officers *(icra ve iflâs memuru)* in their absence. There may be several clerks *(zabıt kâtipleri)* working for him, especially for sending notices and other court documents. Their most important duty, however, is to keep records during trials.

C. Public Prosecutors :

Public prosecutors *(Savcılar, Müddeiumumiler)* are those persons who are appointed by the Supreme Council of Prosecutors to bring suits mainly on matters where public interest exists, primarily the prosecution of criminal defendants. Prosecution of offenders is not a judicial act, but rather a duty of the executive. Therefore the function of public prosecution is attached to the Ministry of Justice, for administrative purposes. But the personnel matters of the prosecutors are governed by the Supreme Council of Prosecutors [11] (Const. Art. 137).

---

[10] Const., Art. 133. Exceptions are also stated in the Constitution.
[11] See also the Law of Supreme Council of Judges and Prosecutors, Arts., 69 ff

The role of the prosecutor is primarily found in criminal offences; he may, however, in the area of civil matters, demand, for example, the dissolution of a society or marriage.[12]

D. Practing Lawyers :

Practicing lawyers *(Avukatlar)* represent the parties in court and defend the accused in criminal cases. No distinction between solicitors and barristers exists in Turkey. There is a law on Practicing Lawyers [13] which enumerates the conditions for becoming a lawyer. In order to be able to practice in court, lawyers must join local bar associations. There are organized bar associations *(barolar)* in many provinces *(iller)*. Bar associations are empowered to give disciplinary punishments to lawyers.

Parties to a law suit in Turkey do not have to be represented by lawyers.[14]

E. Notary :

A notary *(Noter)* is a person who prepares deeds and other documents such as wills, authenticates them, sends official notices and performs other similar function.[15] To become a notary a person must be a law graduate and appointed by the Ministry of Justice. Notaries are controlled by the same Ministry although they receive no salary, but only a fee for each transaction.

PART 2

CIVIL PROCEDURE [16]

I. COMMENCING AN ACTION

A. General :

The manner in which an action is commenced depends upon the nature of the claim involved. In general, claims may be divided into two categories :

Those where liability for a liquidated sum of money depends upon a written instrument signed by the defendant , or where there

---

[12] Other duties : C. C., Arts. 245, 295. S. Ş. Ansay, 62 ff.; Kuru 168 ff.
[13] *Avukatlık Kanunu*, Law No. 1136, dated March 19, 1969, as amended.
[14] Exception : Code of Civil Procedure, Art. 71. On legal aid *(adli yardım)* see C. C. Pr., Arts. 465 ff. See Part 3 for criminal cases.
[15] Law of Public Notaries *(Noterler Kanunu)*, Law No. 1512 dated Jan. 18, 1972, Arts. 1, 60 ff.
[16] Civil Procedure is regulated by the Code of Civil Procedure (C. C. Pr.), Law No. 1086, dated June 18, 1927 and the Code of Execution and Bankruptcy (C. E. B.) Law No. 2004, dated June 19, 1932, as amended. (The latest amendment is Law No. 538, dated Febr. 18, 1965. Official Gazette *(Resmî Gazete)* No. 11946).

is a court decision directing payment of a determined amount of money. For this class of cases, a summary and extremely streamlined procedure is available.

For the second category of cases, where liability depends on some other issues, lengthy and cumbersome procedure is followed. This is called ordinary procedure.

B. Ordinary Procedure :

1. Jurisdiction:

When the plaintiff proceeds in an ordinary court he must draft a petition and should file it in the appropriate court. The problem of determining which is the appropriate court is essentially a problem of jurisdiction and it has two aspects. First of all the court should be the competent court. Secondly the provisions of the Code of Civil Procedure on venue should be fulfilled.

a) Competence *(görev, vazife)* : The competence of the civil courts must be distinguished from that of other types of courts; there are also distinctions in the suits which may be brought in the several civil courts. A criminal case may not be heard by a civil court. In civil matters, as is mentioned above, claims where the amount in controversy does not exceed 5,000 TL. shall be heard by the Peace Courts (C. C. Pr., Art. 8).

The statutory provisions on the competence of courts are based on reasons of public order. Therefore, parties to a case may not agree to submit it to a different court from those specified as competent by statute, and a judge must refuse to hear a case if he deems that the court is not competent. An objection of lack of competence may be made by the **defendant** at any stage of the proceedings before the judgement.[17]

b) Venue *(yetki, salâhiyet)* : In addition to choosing an appropriate type of court, the plaintiff must also commence his case at a proper place for trial. The general rule in Turkey is that suit must be brought in the place of the defendant's domicile which will be determined according to the Civil Code (C. C. Pr., Art. 9).

There are exceptions, expanding or changing this general rule of venue. A tort action, for example, may be brought where the events giving rise to it took place (C. C. Pr., Art. 21). If the action is based on a contract, it may be brought at the place where the

---

[17] There are some exceptions : S. Ş. Ansay 76/77.

contract is to be performed, or at the place where it was signed if, at the time of suit, either the defendant or his attorney is physically present or resident at that place (C. C. Pr., Art. 10). (3) If the claim involves real reporty, it must be brought where such property is located [18] (C. C. Pr., Art. 13).

Where there is a choice of venue, the plaintiff will make his choice at the time he commences the action. The parties may also agree to the venue before the action is brought [19] (C. C. Pr., Art. 22).

2. Petition of the Case:

To start an action the plaintiff must file a petition of the case *(arzuhal, dilekçe)*. This is a document prepared under the general requirements of the Code, according to the needs of the case.

After some preliminary information such as the names of the parties and the type of action, the petition must state the following (C. C. Pr., Art. 179):

(a) Statement of facts: The plaintiff should state the facts *(dava sebepleri)* on which his claim is based. If the claim is for damages because of a tortious act, then the plaintiff should set out the act committed, the unlawfulness of the act, the damages suffered and the causality between act and damages.[20]

(b) A summary of the legal basis *(hukuki sebep)* or the law relied upon: Theoretically no action may be brought unless it is based upon some provision of an existing code or statute. However, there might be cases which do not fit precisely under any existing provision. Such a problem is solved by reliance upon the famous article 1 of the Civil Code which reads as follows:

«Where no provision is applicable the judge should decide according to existing customary law and in default thereof, according to the rules which he would lay down if he had himself to act as legislator».[21]

It is the duty of the judge to determine the real cause of action.[22] If the plaintiff has mistaken the cause of action (for example, if he bases his claim on agency contract, instead of contract of employ-

---

[18] Karlen / Arsel 23; S. Ş. Ansay 95.
[19] Kuru 123.
[20] S. Ş. Ansay 230.
[21] See Chapter 1, II on Sources of Turkish Law.
[22] «The Judge must, on his own initictive, apply Turkish law» (C. C., Pr., Art. 76).

ment) the judge cannot refuse to hear the case. Rather, he must decide the case according to the provisions on employment contracts.[23]

(c) A statement of claims (the prayer for relief = *talep neticesi*) :

At the end of the petition the plaintiff specifies what remedy he seeks. «The most common by far is a money judgment, usually sought for the collection of a bill or other debt, seldom for personal injuries received as a result of an auto accident or other tort».[24] Dispossession of the defendant from real property for non-payment of rent, restitution of chattel, or ejection of the defendant from immovable property, specific performance of a contract, or an injunction commanding the defendant to do or refrain from doing certain acts are other examples of claims.

(d) An indication of the time allowed the defendant to answer. This must be at least 10 days.[25]

The petition must be filed with the clerk of the court (C. C. Pr., Art. 178). The case is considered commenced when the petition is filed with the clerk and the necessary fees paid. Filing also has other consequences :[26]

The statute of limitations stops to run ; interest begins to run when there is no special agreement as to interest ; it prevents the plaintiff from bringing another action on the same claim, or from expending his contentions or changing their nature without the consent of the defendant ; it also prevents him from discontinuing the action without the consent of the defendant.[27]

---

[23] S. Ş. Ansay 238; Kuru 273; Bilge 319/320.
The Turkish plaintiff, however, is bound by the facts and legal theory stated in his petition. «If he states that a divorce case is based upon adultery (C. C., Art., 120) and fails to prove adultery but proves instead that the offending spouse is living a dissolute life (this is an equally good ground [for divorce] under Art. 131 of the C. C.) [see Chapter 6 on Family Law] a decree of divorce cannot be granted». (Karlen / Arsel 33 and 34). In such a case the plaintiff may amend (reform) his petition and state the correct facts. Without amendment the other party may object to introduction of new facts (Reformation = *Islah*. C. C. Pr., Arts. 83-90). While this can be done only once, it is allowed at any time up to the end of trial, with consequences being : (1) the payment of fees for earlier proceedings (Karlen / Arsel 34) under the unreformed or amended petition ; and (2) the admissibility of new evidence relating to any new issue raised by the reformed petition (S. Ş. Ansay 187; Kuru 609 ff.).
[24] Karlen / Arsel 35.
[25] S. Ş. Ansay 240.
[26] S. Ş. Ansay 216 ff.
[27] C. C. Pr., Art. 185. Kuru 294 ff.

3. *Notice to the Defendant* (Tebligat) [28]

After the plaintiff's petition has been filed, the clerk of the court prepares a summons which, together with a copy of the petition, is sent by the court to the defendant. The usual method of service in Turkey is by registered mail.[29]

4. *Defendant's Response (Petition of reply* = Cevap lâyihası) :

A petition of reply should be submitted within ten days (or other period permitted by law) after service of summons and petition on the defendant.

The petition of reply follows the same general structure as the plaintiff's petition of the case. It contains the following (C. C. Pr., Arts. 115, 116 and 200) :

Legal defenses : The defendant may state the following defenses in his petition of reply (these may not be raised afterwards) : «Lack of venue; another action pending; connection with another pending case, with which the instant case should be consolidated; petition legally not sufficient».[30] These legal defenses must be raised by the defendant at the beginning and may not be made on the court's own initiative. They are waived if not asserted by the defendant.

Lack of jurisdiction (competence) may, however, be raised at any stage of the trial (C. C. Pr., Art. 7).

With respect to legal insufficiency, if the defendant claims that the plaintiff is relying upon an inappropriate statutory provision or legal theory, or, if he disagrees with the interpretation placed by the plaintiff on the particular statutory provision relied on, he states so in his reply.[31]

The defendant may dispute the facts stated by the plaintiff and may assert new facts.

The defendant may include in his petition of reply a counter-claim *(karşılık dava)* if it has some connection with the plaintiff's claim and if it requires no new parties» although what constitutes an adequate connection is not specially defined.[32] The counter - claim is considered as an independent suit.[33] The defendant, therefore, need not assert his counter - claim in his petition of reply. He may, however, submit it in the form of separate petition within the

---

[28] On this matter there exists the Law of Notices *(Tebligat Kanunu)*, Law No. 7201, dated, Febr. 11, 1959.
[29] Art. 1 of the Law of Notices.
[30] Karlen / Arsel 49.
[31] Karlen / Arsel 50.
[32] Kuru 599.
[33] Kuru 606.

time allowed for the petition of reply. He may also bring an independent action.[34]

5. Pre-trial Practice :

Between the pleadings and the trial there is a first hearing at which usually nothing more is done than to fix a date for a subsequent hearing.

«Sometimes neither party appears, either personally or by attorney, at the first hearing. If that happens, the case is held in abeyance until one of the parties goes to the clerk's office and schedules a new hearing. This must be done within six months in order to avoid starting over completely».[35]

«Sometimes only one of the parties is present and the other absent. If it is the defendant who is absent, the judge asks the plaintiff whether he wishes to proceed with the case. If the answer is 'no', the case is put aside to await the scheduling of a hearing by one of the parties. If, on the other hand, the plaintiff wishes to proceed, as is normally the situation, the judge fixes a date for another hearing and instructs the plaintiff to go to the clerk's office within five days and have the clerk issue what might be called a 'default summons' *(gıyap kararının tebliği)* (C. C. Pr., Art. 400). It advises the defendant to come to the next hearing and warns him that if he fails to appear, the court will hear the plaintiff's evidence while the defendant will be foreclosed from offering any. This lays the groundwork for a sort of proceeding by default».[36]

If the plaintiff fails to appear for six months, then upon the demand of the defendant the case will be dismissed (C. C. Pr., Art. 409).

II. EVIDENCE (Delil) :

A. Burden of Proof :

After the exchange of petitions, the facts on which the claim is based must be proved. Since proof may be difficult, each party tries to escape from the burden of proof *(İspat yükü)*. The general rule on the burden of proof is stated in article 6 of the Civil Code : Each party must prove the facts on which he has based his claim, unless the contrary is stated by law. There are some exceptions

---

[34] Karlen / Arsel 54, 55.
[35] Karlen / Arsel 59.
[36] Karlen / Arsel 60 ; S. Ş. Ansay 326 ff.

to the rule. If a fact is admitted by the other party, it is deemed that there is no dispute between the parties, therefore no proof is necessary (C. C. Pr., Art. 236). This is called an admission *(ikrar)*. Facts which are beyond the area of reasonable dispute shall be accepted without proof.

In some specific instances the law states who must prove the facts (C. C., Arts. 28, 185, 193. C. O., Arts. 42, 54, 55, 62, 96). There are also presumptions *(karineler)* which indicate the existence of certain facts.[37]

B. Means of Proof :

There are different types of instruments of proof. Some of them, such as deeds *(senetler)*, are binding on the judges, and others, such as testimony of witnesses are left to the discretion of the judge.

1. Written Instruments or Deeds :

As it is mentioned earlier [38] some transactions are unenforceable in the absence of particular kinds of proof. In some cases the written form is a condition of a valid transaction. For example, a sale of real property is valid only if it is made before a Land Registry Officer and authenticated by him.[39]

The written form is also important from the point of view of civil procedure. Here, the written form is a means of proof, not a condition of the validity of a transaction. An example of this is the rule that debts of more than 500 TL. may only be proved by written documents and not by the testimony of witnesses.[40]

«A 'deed' proves a transaction without any further evidence, whereas a written instrument merely initiates a line of proof, which may include testimony by witnesses, expert evidence, and oaths». A deed «is an instrument which is created for the purpose of being used as legal proof. It need not be accomplished with any particular formality, nor need it be notarized. The test of whether a particular document is a 'deed' or merely a written instrument is whether it is prepared with the formality which a judge later considers appro-

---

[37] C. O., Art. 31. Certain presumptions may be rebutted by contrary proof as stated in articles 3, 194, 241 of the C. C. and 174 III, 218, 254, 263, 472 of the C. O.
[38] See Chapter 9 on the Law of Obligations.
[39] See Ch. 8 VI C on the Law of Property and Ch. 9 VII on the Law of Obligations.
[40] C. C. Pr., Art. 288. However, there are exceptions. For example, a debt of more than 500 TL. can be proved without a written instrument if the transaction is between husband and wife or between close relatives (C. C. Pr., Art. 298).

priate to the nature of a transaction it records».[41] Thus if a document is found to be a deed it may be conclusive even if it is written on a cigarette box, on the condition that it fulfills the statutory requirements (signature, etc.). In some exceptional instances, related to transactions among merchants, specific formality may be required for a deed, such as delivery by registered mail or notarization (Comm. C., Art. 20 III).

2. *Books of Account:*

An exception to the usual rule that written instruments require corroborating evidence is made in the Commercial Code for books of account. According to article 82 of this Code, books of account of merchants shall be admitted as evidence in controversies arising from commercial transactions between merchants. However, if a merchant tries to collect a bill from an ordinary customer, he can not prove his case by his account books.

Among merchants it is also customary to send letter of confirmation *(teyit mektubu).* Such letters, as well as invoices *(faturalar)* are considered legally valid documents of proof in suits against merchants (Comm. C. Art. 23).

3. *Witnesses:*

Witnesses *(şahitler, tanıklar)* are third persons, other than parties to a trial, who give information on the events in issue.

Witnesses testify orally on the basis of their knowledge. They are not allowed to submit written statements or to refer to them except for the limited purpose of refreshing their recollection as to dates or numbers (C. C. Pr., Art. 269).

Questioning of witnesses is done by the judge himself. Lawyers can, however, suggest questions, which the judge is free to accept or reject (C. C. Pr., Arts. 266 - 268).

«A witness should be asked only to relate his personal observations not what he has learned from others».[41a]

The judge has no power to call additional witnesses beyond those requested by the parties, and he cannot limit the number desired by the parties. But no additional witnesses may be demanded by the litigants if the names are not given upon the request of the judge (C. C. Pr., Art. 274).

---

[41] Karlen / Arsel 84.
[41a] Karlen / Arsel 86.

The attendance of witnesses is secured either by private notice from one of the parties or by a court order, which is called subpoena *(celpname)*. The subpoena «is not served personally, but by mail. Its issuance is procured by oral request of counsel in the course of a hearing, based upon a list of witnesses previously submitted. If a witness fails to appear in response to a subpoena, the judge orders his arrest, and he is brought to the next hearing forcibly by the police. He may also be fined» [41b] (C. C. Pr., Art. 253).

A witness is first asked preliminary questions to identify him; if there is any relation between him and either party (C. C. Pr., Art. 260). After that, the judge cautions him about the necessity of telling the truth, and then questions him as to the merits of the case (C. C. Pr., Art. 261).

Immediately after testifying, the record is read to him. He signs the record and where appropriate an oath may be required (C. C. Pr., Art. 262).

There are three kinds of witnesses :

(1) Those who are competent, but who may refuse to testify (C. C. Pr., Arts. 245-246). If they consent to testify, they do so without oath.[42] A party's spouse or fiancée is in this group.

(2) Persons who can be forced to testify, but not under oath (C. C. Pr., Art. 247), such as persons under fifteen years of age.

(3) All other persons (except government employees who have not been given permission by competent higher authority) may be forced to testify under oath (C. C. Pr., Art. 271).

The oath is given after the witness testifies. Prior to his testimony, however, the judge cautions the witness that he will be given an oath and informs him of the penalties for perjury.

If a witness refuses to answer or to take an oath (when it is required), he may be fined (C. C. Pr., Art. 271).

Even when an oath is given it does not mean that the testimony is binding. The judge can disregard testimony as false, so long as it is not a party who is testifying.[43]

4. Oath :

There are two different types of oath according to the persons who require it.

[41b] Karlen / Arsel 87.
[42] Karlen / Arsel 96.
[43] Karlen / Arsel 100 ; S. Ş. Ansay 273, 336.

a) The judge, on his own initiative, if he deems the proof offered by the parties not satisfactory enough, can request either of them to take an oath (C. C. Pr., Art. 337).

If a party refuses to take an oath, the judge has to assume that his testimony would have been adverse to the party. If, however, the party takes an oath, his testimony is treated as conclusive.[44]

b) A party may request his opponent to testify under oath (C. C. Pr., Arts. 344 - 354). He can exercise his right whenever he feels he cannot prove his case by other legal evidence. The judge is supposed to remind a party of his right to tender an oath to his opponent and cases have been reversed by the Court Cassation for the failure of the judge to do so.[45]

The party who is in the position of taking an oath has several possibilities :

If he agrees to take an oath and give evidence, his answers will be conclusive. He can, however, tender back the oath to the party who requested it. In such a case the original party must give testimony and swear to it, or refuse to do so with the possibility of losing the case. His refusal might be treated as a conclusive admission. If he neither takes oath nor tenders it back to the other party, he loses the case. His refusal is treated as a conclusive admission (C. C. Pr., Art. 347).

These alternatives are not open when the oath is tendered by the court on its own initiative.[46]

5. Expert Evidence :

An expert *(bilirkişi, ehli vukuf)* is a person who renders a written report with respect to certain aspects of a case. He is not retained by one of the parties, but by the court; he is not limited as to the sources of his information or as to the nature of the opinion which he can express; he frequently works as one member of a team of several experts (usually consisting of three persons, but sometimes as many as five or seven).[47]

«The parties have no power to subpoena any expert but only the right to suggest to the judge that expert evidence is needed. The judge has wide discretion, for there are no rigid rules as to what matters are properly within the scope of expert evidence. For

---

[44] S. Ş. Ansay 312.
[45] Karlen / Arsel 92-93.
[46] Karlen / Arsel 93-94.
[47] Karlen / Arsel 101.

example, experts have been used to testify as to the fit of a woman's suit and its conformity to the latest fashion». [48] An expert may question a party, but only in the presence of the other party. He may also consult such authorities as he wishes and visit such places as are necessary. At the end of his inquiries he renders his report.

Experts usually do not appear in court except by special request to answer questions related to their written reports (C. C. Pr., Art. 283).

The judge is not bound by an expert's opinion. [49]

C. Depositions :

When the need for taking testimony away from court arises during the course of a trial - if for example a witness is in a hospital - the judge himself takes it or has a substitute judge take it (C. C. Pr., Art. 255).

If a witness is living in another province, then the court issues an order to a judge of the province where the witness can be found and demands the testimony *(istinabe)*.

D. View and Real Evidence :

In some cases it may be necessary to take a view *(keşif)* of the premises involved in litigation. For such a purpose the judge fixes a date, giving the parties an opportunity to attend personally or with their attorneys. At the prearranged time the judge goes to the premises with the court clerk and if necessary with the bailiff. He may, at that time, take testimony on the spot (C. C. Pr., Art. 363 - 366).

III. RENDITION OF JUDGEMENT :

A. Final Decision :

After the receival of all the evidence the parties may submit final petitions arguing why judgment should be rendered in their favor. Then the judge «proceeds to study the record, including all documents filed and summaries of all testimony. This may lead him to call for additional evidence, involving a reopening of the hearings, or to render his final determination».

«The final decision necessarily embodies his conclusion on the evidence, on relevant substantive law, and on the application of

---

[48] Karlen / Arsel 102.
[49] C. C. Pr., Art. 286. S. Ş. Ansay 278; Kuru 470; Karlen / Arsel 103, On official experts see Karlen / Arsel 103, 104.

such law to the facts found. It should be distinguished from the interlocutory decisions previously rendered throughout the course of the hearings. Each time the judge fixes a date for a hearing or takes some other procedural step, his determination is called a 'decision', but these are quite different, both in form and substance, from the final decision».[50]

B. Form of Judgement :

The final decision follows a set form (C. C. Pr., Art. 388), such as the title of the court, the name of the judge, the names, occupations, and addresses of both parties. These are followed by a summary of the contentions of both parties, the legal basis upon which the decision is rendered and the decision proper, granting or denying a remedy. If the remedy is a money judgment, the plaintiff is entitled to recover it from the defendant. If it is not paid voluntarily, it is realized by the execution officer seizing assets belonging to the defendant. If the judgment is something other than payment of money it takes the appropriate form. For example, it states that the defendant should do or refrain from doing a certain act.[51]

In addition to granting a remedy, the judgment also fixes the costs to be paid by the losing party, consisting of filing fees, witness fees and lawyer's fees for the winning party (C. C. Pr., Arts. 413 - 426). Lawyer's fees are fixed in conformity with an official tariff (C. C. Pr., Arts. 421 - 423). They do not represent the actual fees, for such are a matter of private agreement between lawyers and their clients which may be fixed in advance. If the amount is not definite, then the agreement is null and void. In such a case instead of the agreement, the tariff of lawyer's fees would be applied.[52]

After the decision is filed in the office of the clerk, either party may secure a copy *(ilâm)* by paying the necessary fees. With the service of the decision or, in the Peace Courts, its announcement, the time for appeal starts to run (C. C. Pr., Arts. 160, 161, 393, 434, 490).

---

[50] Karlen / Arsel 113.
[51] See below VI.
[52] Court of Cassation, General Assembly on the Unification of Judgments, dated April 7, 1954, No. 12/9, and dated May 23, 1960, No. 11/10. Law on Practicing Lawyers, Art. 163.

C. Effect of Judgement :

A final judgment cannot be retried. The plaintiff cannot sue again on the same claim.[53] This is called the res judicata *(kesin hüküm)* effect of a judgment. Exceptionally, however, the losing party may demand the re-opening of the proceedings (in accordance with article 445 of the Code of Civil Procedure = *İadei muhakeme, yargılamanın iadesi)*. The grounds specified there can be summarized generally as : newly discovered deed or document, perjury, and fraud. A motion to reopen must be made within three months after the discovery of the cause for re-opening.

IV. APPEAL (Temyiz) :

A. General :

There is an appellate court which is called the «Court of Cassation», or sometimes the «Supreme Court» *(Yargıtay, Temyiz Mahkemesi)*.[54] It is divided into twenty four chambers, each of which has four associate Judges and a President. They are aided by sufficient number of reporters.[55] There is also a First President of the entire court.

Nine chambers are penal. Of the remaining fifteen, which are called Civil Chambers, one is concerned with bankruptcy and execution proceedings, one with commercial matters and the remaining with various civil litigations. Each of these, however, has its particular subject matter, one dealing with real property disputes, others with inheritance questions, labor disputes, tenancy contracts and so forth.[56]

An appeal goes from the first instance court to the Chamber of the Court of Cassation which handles the type of subject matter involved. After rendition of the decision either party may ask the court of cassation to reconsider it (C. C. Pr., Art. 440) for a variety of reasons. The competent Chamber may either approve or disapprove the lower court's judgment (C. C. Pr., Art. 423, 429).

If the final decision of the Chamber is to affirm the judgement of the lower court no further review is possible. Only exceptionally a revision *(karar tashihi)* may be demanded.[57] If, the Chamber disapproves the judgment of the lower court, the case is returned

---
[53] Karlen / Arsel 115.
[54] See Chapter 1 IV C on Sources of Turkish Law.
[55] Law of the Court of Cassation, Law No. 1730, dated, May 16, 1973, Art. 37, also see Arts. 35-36.
[56] Karlen / Arsel 123-124.
[57] C. C. Pr., Art. 440; Kuru, 758 ff.

to that court for action (C. C. Pr., Art. 429).

When the trial court insists that the original disposition was correct the case may be sent back to the Court of Cassation, where it is considered by all civil or criminal chambers. The decision of this assembly must be followed by the lower court (C. C. Pr., Art. 429).

If two civil Chambers reach different decisions in cases involving substantially similar facts, or if the same Chamber renders contradictory decisions in different cases involving similar facts, the discrepancy may be resolved, by all civil chambers sitting together [58] (Civil Assembly Decision, *Hukuk Genel Kurulu Kararı*).

«In the event of a conflict between one of the civil chambers and one of the penal chambers in their interpretation of a code or statute (e. g. as to the meaning of the price control act, which may govern either a civil or a criminal case) or in the event that one chamber disagrees with a decision by its own assembly»,[59] the the difference would be resolved by all twenty four Chambers called into special session sitting together.[60]

All final judgments are appealable as a matter of right, except those of the Peace Courts for less than 2.000 TL. In such cases the decision of the trial court is final.

B. Questions Open on Appeal :

The Court of Cassation reviews not only the factual determinations but also legal questions (C. C. Pr., Art. 428 V). Grounds for reversal include «erronous judgement of the principal facts». «This means incorrect fact finding — a matter extraordinarily difficult to review for any appellate court, because of its lack of opportunity to see and hear witnesses and observe their demeanour while testifying».

«A violation of procedure is ground for reversal... if it is so 'excessive' that it requires the judgment to be changed» [61] (C. C. Pr., Art. 428 II).

If the evidence offered by one of the parties is improperly rejected it constitutes ground for reversal (C. C. Pr., Art. 428 IV).

Interlocutory rulings are not appealable, only final decisions are (C. C. Pr., Art. 427).

---

[58] Karlen / Arsel 125/126.
[59] Karlen / Arsel 127.
[60] Code on Organization of Court of Cassation. Art. 8 (General Assembly on the Unification of Judgements, *İçtihadı Birleştirme Kurulu*). Such decisions are published in the Official Gazette and they have binding effect. See, Chapter 1 IV C on Sources of Turkish Law.

C. Procedure :

A party wishing to appeal must file a petition of appeal within fifteen days after service of the judgment for Court of First Instance cases and within eight days after announcement of the judgment for the Peace Court cases (C. C. Pr., Arts. 432 ff.). The members of the Chamber and the rapporteur examine the file. Usually there is no oral argument. Only in those cases where the subject matter exceeds 10.000 TL. an oral argument may be demanded (C. C. Pr., Art. 438).

The decisions of the Court of Cassation are generally very brief. They contain a brief summary of the case and the nature of the judgment rendered below, and the decision of the Court of Cassation with reasons for affirming or reversing. Especially those decisions which might be considered as precedent for similar cases in the future have lengthy discussions and conclusive reasonings.

The decision also regulates the costs. Costs are paid by the respondent in the event of affirmance. In the event of reversal, appeal costs go to the ultimate winner.

V. SUMMARY PROCEDURE

There are special procedures in which parts of the steps to be taken in an ordinary procedure are simplified and shortened. These procedures are applicable only on certain conflicts stated in the law.

1. A c c e l e r a t e d P r o c e d u r e *(Ser'i Yargılama Usulü)* (C. C. Pr., Art. 501 - 506) is, for example, applied to cases concerning perishable goods or to cases against persons having no determinable domicile, who are about to escape. The S i m p l i f i e d P r o - c e d u r e *(Basit Yargılama Usulü)* (C. C. Pr., Art. 507 - 511) is, on the other hand, used in another group of cases such as alimony, parental authority, guardianship etc.[62]

2. A summary procedure is also used in cases of demands for execution, if the claim is not based on a deed. Here the plaintiff files a form with the execution officer *(icra memuru)* giving the names and addresses of himself and of the defendant; a very brief statement of the amount and nature of the claim; and an indication of the relief sought [63] (C. E. B., Art. 58 as amended in 1965). There-

---

[61] Karlen / Arsel 130.
[62] Kuru 947 - 948.
[63] Karlen / Arsel 15.

after a notice (order of payment = *ödeme emri*) is sent by the execution officer to the defendant. The notice requires that within 7 days the defendant pay the debt, or submit a statement of his income and assets, or if he wishes to contest the claim, a denial thereof (C. C. B., Art. 58 as amended in 1965).

«If the defendant does not deny the claim, he is deemed to have admitted it, and appropriate action is taken to realize from his assets an amount sufficient to pay the plaintiff's claim, plus costs and attoreny's fees, just as if judgement had been rendered after a full trial».

«If the defendant fails to submit a statement of his income and assets within the required time, or if he makes a false statement, he is subject to imprisonment»[64] (C. E. B., Arts. 74 and 76).

The defendant may deny the plaintiff's claim, simply by way of a general statement, without revealing precisely the nature of his defenses or the reasons for his position (C. E. B., Arst. 62-65). Thereupon the plaintiff has two choices : He may bring the defendant before an ordinary court ; or he may proceed further before the Investigation Authority *(tetkik mercii)*.

The plaintiff proceeds before the Investigation Authority if he thinks that the claim can be conclusively and summarily proven (C. E. B., Art. 68 as amended in 1965). The only issue open before this Authority is the genuineness of the signature on the document with which the defendant is charged. If the document has been signed at the notary, or if there is in the possession of the plaintiff an acknowledged signature by the defendant which can be compared with the one in dispute, the matter can be concluded summarily (C. E. B., Art. 68 a). Otherwise the claim should be proven in the ordinary way at a normal civil court [65] *(borçtan kurtulma davası)*.

VI. EXECUTION AND GARNISHMENT PROCEDURE :

1. If the remedy granted is an award of money, the successful party applies to the execution officer. This officer thereupon sends a notice to the defendant requiring him to pay his debt within 7 days and to submit a statement of his income and assets.

Depending upon the wishes of the plaintiff and the condition of the defendant's assets, execution may take the following forms : «If the plaintiff asks for a seizure of the defendant's assets and

---
[64] Ibid.
[65] Karlen / Arsel 16.

pays the proper fees to the execution officer, that officer seizes enough of the defendant's property to satisfy the claim, taking care, however, to omit personal clothing and the tools of the debtor's trade (if any), which are exempt from execution... Then the execution officer devises a schedule for the defendant to pay the debt in installments. Customarily there are four equal monthly installments, the first of which is due immediately. The parties may, however, agree in writing upon some other pattern».[66]

The creditors may also secure payment from third persons owing money to the defendant. This is possible through the garnishment procedure (C. E. B., Arts. 355, 356). In such a case creditors, in order of their priority in entering judgment, may secure at least one-fourth of the income of the defendant from his employer (C. E. B., Art. 83).

If the defendant transfers property fraudulently to his wife or other persons with the intention of avoiding payment of his just debts, such transfers may also be set aside (C. E. B., Art. 339, 340 and 355 as amended in 1965).

The plaintiff may ask that the defendant, if he is a merchant, be declared bankrupt, and that all his assets be collected and distributed proportionally among his creditors (C. E. B., Arts. 37, 177, 154 ff.). The debtor may also demand his own bankruptcy (*iflâs*).

2. If a judgement is for the recovery of immovable property, the defendant is ordered by the execution officer to leave. If he does not comply with this order, he and his movable property may physically and forcibly be removed from the premises by the execution officer (C. E. B., Arts. 26 ff.).

3. «If the judgment is in the nature of a negative injunction, commanding the defendant to refrain from doing an act, disobedience is punished criminally in Turkey. The party's failure to obey is made a crime by statute, and he is subject to punishment in a separate criminal action»[67] (C. E. B., Art. 30 as amended in 1965).

4. If the judgement orders the defendant to perform an affirmative act, then upon his failure, the execution officer accomplishes it by force and with the same effect as if the defendant himself had complied with the judgment. «For example, if an order required the defendant to return a child to the plaintiff, or a chattel, and

---

[67] Karlen / Arsel 118.
[68] Karlen / Arsel 119.

he failed to do so, the execution officer would take direct forcible steps to accomplish the command of the judgment».[68]

PART 3

CRIMINAL PROCEDURE

Prof. Dr. Feyyaz GÖLCÜKLÜ [*]

I. SUBJECT OF CRIMINAL PROCEDURE

In general, criminal procedure is, as the term suggests, concerned with the enforcement of criminal law. It deals with such matters as the identification and the collection of evidence of crime, the apprehension and indictment of criminals, and finally the procedure of criminal trials and selected proceedings. Although criminal procedure is concerned with form, it is in fact closely related to the substantive law.

In Turkey the protection of «fundamental rights» during criminal proceedings, is a branch of the law of criminal procedure. There are instances, during trials, where «personal freedoms» (Const. Art. 14), such as privacy and freedom of communication (Const., Arts. 15-17), guaranteed by the Constitution, must be limited in the public interest. Criminal procedure seeks to avoid the arbitrary limitation of these personal rights and to base these limitations on consistent legal principles.

Violation of the criminal law can be considered a great deal more serious for the individual than violation of the civil law, and application of the criminal law cannot usually be left to the initiative of individuals as in civil law. Criminal prosecution is a function of the State. The application of criminal law must satisfy the requirements of due process prescribed by the Code of Criminal Procedure (as well as the principles of the Constitution).

Punishment of the criminal is not the sole purpose of the law of criminal procedure (and criminal law). It also aims at rehabilitation of criminals to reclaim them for normal society.

---

[66] Karlen / Arsel 116.
[*] Faculty of Political Sciences, University of Ankara.

II. SYSTEMS OF CRIMINAL PROCEDURE

There are three basic systems of criminal procedure.

A. Accusatorial System :

The accusatorial system was generally followed in ancient Greece and Rome. It arose from the primitive concept of crime as a conflict between two individuals, with the judge acting as an umpire. In this type of procedure one party accused the other. The judge had no power to initiate his own investigation, but rather had to be satisfied with the evidence brought forth by the parties. The testimony of the accused could not be used against him, nor could he be coerced into a confession. He could however make statements in his own defense. Although the right of accusation was initially granted only to the victim of the alleged crime and his relatives, this later became the right of public accusation and was extanded to every citizen.

In the accusatorial system, the trial was oral, open and was conducted in the presence of the parties.

B. Inquisatorial System :

This procedure derived from the *extra-ordinem* procedure applied to slaves and later to certain crimes (public offenses) under Roman Law. In such cases, the crime was considered a menace to the public and investigation of the crime was made not by an individual, but by a representative of the public (public prosecutor = *savcı, müddeiumumi*). In addition, the judge could take the initiative and bring a criminal to trial. In this system, the judge plays an active role; he himself does the questioning and collects the evidence; the role of the defense is kept to a minimum.

In this system the trial was based on written report and was conducted in secrecy and in the absence of the parties.

C. Mixed System :

Turkey follows a procedure which is a mixture of the inquisatorial, with its emphasis on effective investigation, and the accusatorial system, with its respect for the defendant's personal rights and freedoms. The public prosecutor brings the case before the court; and, with some exceptions, neither the judge, victim, nor any private person can bring the case to law. The public prosecutor is required to prove the case, although the judge can initiate his own investigation to determine the facts.

In this system, a criminal proceeding has three stages; the preparatory investigation, the preliminary investigation, and the final trial, all of which are described below. In the first two stages, the investigation is based on a written report and is conducted in secrecy in the absence of the accused. The third stage, the trial, takes place in open court, testimony is taken and the accused can confront the prosecution and witnesses.

III. THE STRUCTURE OF THE JUDICIAL SYSTEM

A. General Principles:

In Turkey, civil and criminal cases, except in large cities, are heard in the same courts and by the same judges. This is due to reasons of economy and is criticised today, along with the belief that all branches of the law can not be known by one set of judges. Intermediate appeal courts and courts with more than one judge are favored by many jurists, as providing additional safeguards for the defendant in criminal trials; the latter, however, are not widespread in Turkey, while the former do not exist. Courts with benches of judges do exist to try felony cases.

B. Sources of Turkish Criminal Procedure Law:

The Turkish Code of Criminal Procedure of April 20, 1929, (Law No. 1412), still in force today, is a translation of the German Code of Criminal Procedure of 1877, adopted with some changes. This Code has been amended many times, most significantly by the Laws of June 16, 1936; June 7, 1937; June 28, 1938; January 30, 1942; and last by March 5, 1973. A separate Law of June 3, 1936 (Law No. 3005) introduced a special procedure for flagrant offenses *(meşhut suçlar)*.

C. Judges and Courts:

Objectivity and independence are very important concepts in every trial. In fact, judicial decisions achieve their special significance because they are rendered by an independent judiciary.

The Turkish Constitution and procedural laws contain many provisions for securing the i n d e p e n d e n c e and i m p a r t i a l i t y of the judges and the courts. Independence from the executive branch of government was secured mainly through the adoption of the principle of separation of powers, which is stated in the Constitution, and is enforced by special statutes concerning the judiciary. Judges may not be dismissed. Unless they so desire, they may not be retired before the age of their sixty-fifth year.

A judge who has a personal interest in a case, or is related to a defendant, or if he is involved in the same suit for some reasons such as Public Prosecutor or when circumstances raise doubts concerning his impartiality, he must disqualify himself or his disqualification may be requested by the parties, in order to assure an objective and impartial trial (C. Cr. Pr., Art. 21-28). To further ensure objectivity and public confidence in the judicial function, open trials and reasoned decisions are also required (Const., Art. 135). Trial by jury or by lay assessor court, which can be found in some other countries and which would be useful for securing the above-mentioned independence, are not accepted in the Turkish judicial organization.

Independence within the judiciary is secured through the absence of a hierarchic relation between judges and courts and the acceptance of the principles of separation of the offices of prosecution (public prosecutor), investigation (investigating judge), and trial (court).

The immunity of judges against parties litigant for their decisions is adopted as a general principle; thus their independence before the parties is secured. There are some exceptions to this general rule, but they are very few and narrowly defined (C. Cr. Pr., Arts. 573 - 576).

D. Criminal Courts :

Turkish criminal courts are of two types : general and special courts. Justice of the Peace Courts *(Sulh Ceza Mahkemeleri)*, Courts of General Criminal Jurisdiction *(Asliye Ceza Mahkemeleri)* and Aggravated Felony Courts *(Ağır Ceza Mahkemeleri)* are the general courts (Introductory law to the Turkish Criminal Code, *Mer'iyet Kanunu*, Arts. 25 ff.). Justice of the Peace Courts and Courts of General Criminal Jurisdiction have one judge, and generally speaking, they are both located in the county capitals *(ilçe)*. Aggravated Felony Courts are composed of three judges one of which being the Chief Justice. They are located in the provincial capitals *(il)*. Above these courts is the Court of Cassation *(Yargıtay)*. This is the court of last instance for reviewing the decisions and verdicts rendered by the above-mentioned courts. The Court of Cassation reviews only questions of law, and secures, by its final decisions, the unity of jurisdiction and uniformity in legal interpretation of laws throughout the country. In exceptional cases, it has original and final jurisdiction in those specific cases defined by law (trials of some high ranking civil servants such as governors or ambassadors, etc.).[1]

As the name indicates, general courts try every kind of criminal case, except those expressly reserved by law to courts of special jurisdiction. Among these, we may note the Military Courts, Constitutional Court (functioning as a High Court, *Yüce Divan*) in order to try the President of the Republic, the members of the Council of Ministers and others (Const., Art. 147), Traffic Courts, Courts of Press (courts on offenses committed by means of press) etc. Juvenile Courts are still contemplated, but have not yet been established. Generaly speaking, Military Courts are entitled to try the military personnel for military offenses, for offenses committed by them against military personnel, or in military areas, or in connection with military services and duties. They also try non-military persons in exceptional cases prescribed by special laws (see Const., Art. 138). Decisions and verdicts rendered by military courts are reviewed, in the last instance, by the Military Court of Cassation (Const., Art. 141).

IV. JURISDICTION : «NATURAL» JUDGE AND COURT

Under Turkish law, an offender is guaranteed the right to be tried by the «legal» (natural) judge *(kanunî yahut tabiî hakim)*. This guarantee means that the jurisdiction of courts and judges must be determined by law before the crime which is to be tried was committed. According to Article 136 of the Constitution, the establishment of the courts, their jurisdiction, function, and procedures must be defined by law. The guarantee of a natural judge and courts is in keeping with this provision of the Constitution, and Article 32 of the Constitution, in fact, provides that no one can be brought before any court other than the natural one, «no one can be brought before an agency other than the court to which he is legally submitted». The main purpose of this principle is to bar the establishment of exceptional courts that is to say, courts with powers other than those existing prior to the commission of a crime. Article 32 of the Constitution further provides that no exceptional court shall be established which will result in depriving a defendant of his right to be brought before his natural judge.

---

[1] See Part 2 IV of this Chapter.

Generally, the jurisdiction of a court means the extent of the court's judicial power. Jurisdiction may be defined by subject matter, locality or person. Jurisdiction by subject matter *(görev=vazife)* is based on the nature (or gravity) of the offense. Thus the subject matter of the jurisdiction of the Peace Court generally covers misdemeanors and other cases of lesser importance, which are listed in great detail in the Introductory Law to the Turkish Criminal Code (Art. 29). The Aggravated Felony Courts try crimes punishable by a minimum of five years imprisonment, penal servitude, or death (C. C. Pr., Art. 421). All offenses outside these two groups are subject to the jurisdiction of the Court of General Criminal Jurisdiction.

There are exceptions, however, such as the disposal by a court of higher jurisdiction, under certain circumstances, of a case over which a court of lower jurisdiction has original jurisdiction (C. Cr. Pr., Arts. 2, 4 and 262) : the joinder of cases for connected offenses in any court with power to try either of them, that is, in the court of highest jurisdiction between them (C. Cr.,Pr., Art. 12).

Jurisdiction by locality (or venue = *yetki, salâhiyet*) means the limitation of the geographic area over which a particular court has jurisdiction. The court with venue is the court of the place where the offense has been committed. If this is unknown, the court of the place where the accused is seized has venue. If he is not seized, the court of his place of domicile, and if he is not domiciled in Turkey, the court of the place where he last resided in Turkey, has venue. If under the foregoing rules, it is still impossible to determine the proper court, then the court which took the first initiative in the criminal proceeding shall have venue (C. Cr. Pr., Arts. 8 - 9).

In cases of criminal attempts, or continuing or successive offenses, the place where the last act was committed shall be the place of the trial. The court having venue over offenses committed in foreign countries which should be prosecuted in Turkey according to articles 4 through 8 of the Criminal Code is determined according to the above - mentioned rules (C. Cr. Pr., Art. 10). If an offense is committed on a vessel or aircraft bearing the Turkish flag on the high seas, in the air, in a foreign port, in foreign territorial waters, or if the crime is committed by means of such a vessel or aircraft, the court of the port of first arrival of the vessel or aircraft in Turkey, after the commission of the offense, or the court of the place of registry of the vessel or aircraft, shall have venue (C. C. Pr.,

Art. 11). There are also some exceptions to the rules of venue: the transfer of a case to another court of equal rank, by the common court of higher jurisdiction, when for legal or factual reasons a judge or a court having venue is unable to perform his or its judicial duties, or if the investigation (or trial) cannot be conducted without prejudice to the public safety at the place where the action is pending. Transfer for reasons of public security is requested by the Minister of Justice.

Jurisdiction by person depends upon the status of the wrongdoer. The jurisdiction of the Military Courts are examples of this kind of jurisdiction.

The rules of jurisdiction are dictated by public policy, and their application is therefore obligatory. The parties (that is to say, the prosecutor and defendant) cannot agree to vary them. A conflict of jurisdiction between courts is generally resolved by the common court of higher jurisdiction.[2]

V. PARTIES TO CRIMINAL PROCEEDINGS

A. Public Prosecutor [3]:

Offenses are, in the great majority of cases, prosecuted in the name of the people by public prosecutors *(savcı)* who are virtually representatives of the executive branch of the Government within the judiciary (Const., Art. 137).

There is a public prosecutor with deputies at every Court of General Criminal Jurisdiction. The function of public prosecutor in an Aggravated Felony Court is performed by the public prosecutor assigned to the Court of General Criminal Jurisdiction of the locality in which the Aggravated Felony Court is situated.

There is no public prosecutor in a Peace Court. This means that a public prosecutor is not present at the trial, but proceedings in these courts are also initiated by accusation of the public prosecutor of the Court of General Criminal Jurisdiction. The function of the Chief Prosecutor of the Republic *(Cumhuriyet Başsavcısı)* in the Court of Cassation is not accusation, but presentation of the State's views during review of decisions of the High Court.

According to the Turkish Code of Criminal Procedure, the preliminary and final investigation (trial) may commence only after a public prosecution is initiated (C. Cr. Pr., Art. 147). The duty of

---

[2] See C. Cr. Pr., Arts. 13-14 and Introductory Law, Art. 3.
[3] See also Part 1, II C of this Chapter.

initiating public prosecution rests with the public prosecutor (C. Cr. Pr., Art. 148). As soon as he is informed of the occurrence of an offense, the public prosecutor should make the investigation necessary to decide whether public prosecution should be initiated. He investigates evidence both against the accused and in his favor, and helps to preserve proof which otherwise might be lost (C. Cr. Pr., Art. 153).

If, at the end of his investigation, the public prosecutor decides not to prosecute, he will inform the accused if he has testified, or if a warrant of arrest has been issued against him (C. Cr. Pr., Art. 163, 164). No one may be convicted under an indictment in which he is not named, nor may he be convicted of a crime not specified in the indictment (C. Cr. Pr., Art. 150). The public prosecutor, as a party in criminal proceedings, cannot be challenged by the defense for disqualification as a judge may be challenged under Turkish criminal procedure.

In the case of some lesser offenses specified by law, where the injury is deemed more private than public, the injured party may himself institute criminal proceedings by filing a private complaint without participation of the public prosecutor (personal action = şahsî dava; C. Cr. Pr., Art. 344). In these exceptional cases, the private party enjoys all the rights given to the public prosecutor by law. Furthermore, the person injured by an offense may intervene in any public prosecution, and he becomes a party to the action by virtue of his intervention (Müdahele yolu ile dava, C. Cr. Pr., Art. 365).

B. The Defendant :

The defendant or accused (davalı, sanık, maznun) is a person brought before the court who is charged with an offense punishable by law. As noted before, the law of criminal procedure is intended not only to secure effective prosecution of offenses, but also to secure to the accused an effective defense. The law is designed to protect innocent citizens. The principal provisions giving this protection are the following :

According to article 31 of the Constitution, «Every individual is entitled to litigate and defend his case as plaintiff or defendant before judicial authorities by availing himself of all legitimate methods and procedures.»

Under the Code of Criminal Procedure, the prosecutor, in his preparatory investigation, should collect not only the evidence against the accused, but also the evidence for his defense, either at the request of the defendant, or, in the absence of such request, on his own initiative (C. C. Pr., Arts. 153, 159).

During the next stage of the criminal proceedings, the preliminary investigation (discussed further below), the accused is examined at least once by the examining magistrate (C. Cr. Pr., Art. 185). Prior to this examination, the magistrate must inform the accused of the offense or offenses of which he is accused. At this examination, the accused may offer evidence in his defense (C. Cr. Pr., Art. 135). The examining magistrate must communicate to the accused his decision to commence the preliminary investigation (C. Cr. Pr., Art. 185), and, if necessary, hear the accused in person before deciding to commence the preliminary investigation (C. Cr. Pr., Art. 173).

Article 33 of the Turkish Constitution provides that «no person shall be coerced into making statements or into giving testimony liable to incriminate himself or his legally defined next of kin.»

The accused or his counsel has the right to be present at inspections or other discovery proceedings *(keşif ve muayene)* connected with the preliminary investigation and at the examination of witnesses or experts who are not expected to be present at the trial, and they must receive notice of such discovery proceedings and examination (C. Cr., Pr. Art. 186).

The accused may ask the examining magistrate to permit experts who the accused wants to call at the trial to participate in the proceedings of the preliminary investigation (C. Cr. Pr., Art. 188).

If, at the conclusion of the preliminary investigation, an indictment (accusation = *iddianame)* is issued, the indictment will be communicated to the accused, and he will be asked, if he desires more evidence to be collected for his defense (C. Cr. Pr., Arts. 194 - 195). The indictment must clearly define the offense or offenses with which the accused is charged, give the legal elements of the offense, and show the evidence supporting it (C. Cr. Pr., Art. 193).

Before the trial or final investigation *(son soruşturma* or *duruşma)* may be commenced, a summons must be served on the accused (C. Cr. Pr., Art. 208) which again spells out the legal definition and elements of the offense, the provisions of law governing the crime, and the court before which the accused will be brought (C. Cr. Pr., Art. 200). In cases where a preliminary investigation is not necessary, the prosecutor's indictment takes the place of the summons.

At least one week must pass between the serving of the summons and the beginning of the trial (C. Cr. Pr., Art. 210). At the time the summons is served, the accused is given the opportunity to make any further statement concerning his defense (C. C. Pr., Arts. 209, 221, 237). In like manner, if the presiding judge of the court does not accept the defendent's demand to call his witnesses and experts, the defendant has the right to bring them before the court without any further notice (C. Cr. Pr., Art. 213). If the presiding judge or prosecutor calls for any witnesses on his own initiative, their identity must be made known to the accused (C. Cr. Pr., Art. 215).

The accused has the right to obtain the advice and assistance of one or more defense counselors. The rights and duties of counsel are defined in the Law (C. Cr. Pr., Arts. 136 ff., 220, 227).

However, the participation of counsel in the preparatory and preliminary investigation is very limited, as these investigations are secret and generally conducted without the presence of the accused, except as previously noted. The principal task of the defense counsel begins at the conclusion of the preliminary investigation when the complete file of the case is made available to the defense (C. Cr. Pr., Art. 143).

Other rights of the defendant include the right of the defense to examine the records of the trial (C. Cr. Pr., Art. 181) the requirement that any decision may only be made after the parties are heard, the right to reject the judge or experts on certain grounds (C. C. Pr., Arts. 21 ff., Art. 67), and the possibility of amendment of judicial decisions.

The Turkish Constitution provides detailed provisions for personal liberty of the accused during criminal proceedings. In general, the immunities and freedoms enjoyed by the individual shall not be restricted except in cases explicitly prescribed by law and on the proper decision of a judge duly passed (Const., Art. 14). Both the Constitution and the Code of Criminal Procedure give the basic conditions under which the accused may be arrested and confined. According to the Constitution (Art. 30), persons about whom there exists a strong suspicion connecting them with a particular crime can be detained *(tutuklama)* by a decision of the judge for purposes of preventing escape, or alteration of evidence, or in other cases specified by law. Preliminary detention of the accused *(yakalama)* is resorted to only *in flagrento delicto (suçüstü)* or in cases where delay is likely to thwart justice. The conditions for such detainment are specified by law. Individuals detained or held in custody shall be notified immediately in writing of the reasons for their detention as well as of the charges against them. Persons detained or held in custody should be sent to the nearest court and brought before a judge within 48 hours or, for collective offenses expressly determined by law, within 15 days of their arrival. After the lapse of this time, such person cannot be detained without a decision of a judge. All damages suffered by persons subjected to treatment other than that specified above are to be compensated for by the State according to law.

Arrest is never obligatory, rather, it is left to the discretion of the judge. During the preparatory investigation, warrants of arrest *(tutuklama müzekkeresi)* are issued by the Justice of the Peace *(sulh hakimi)*; during the preliminary investigation by the examining magistrate *(sorgu hakimi)*, in charge; and during the trial by the court. Although arrest is in theory without time limit, the person arrested can object to the warrant of arrest at every stage of proceeding, and the judge issuing the warrant may cancel it at any time on his own initiative. Furthermore the decision of arrest shall be examined periodically by the judge who made it. Such an examination must be made within thirty days from the day of the arrest. If the judge, upon examination decides not to release the accused, he will at that time set another date for further review of the necessity for detention. Subsequent examinations are made at intervals of not less than three weeks nor more than two months, but, upon the accused's request, they may be held at more frequent intervals.

Release on bail is possible at every stage of the investigation.

Arrest for a misdemeanor is exceptional and limited by very strict and well defined restrictions.[4]

VI. EVIDENCE ; BURDEN OF PROOF

The accused is favored in criminal proceedings by the presumption of innocence. The burden of proof rests on the public prosecutor or the private complainant, and the defendant is con-

---

[1] For further provisions see, C. Cr. Pr., Arts. 104 ff., Arts. 127 ff.

sidered innocent until his guilt is established by final judgment. When the court is not satisfied by the evidence of the prosecution or a reasonable doubt exists, the court must give a judgment of acquittal.

The law of evidence is based on the system of the so-called «intimate conviction» *(vicdanî kanaat)* of the trier of fact. The judge weighs the probative value of all evidence submitted during the preparatory and preliminary phases, and during the trial, taking into account the credibility of the witnesses and other evidence to the best of his ability and in good conscience (C. Cr. Pr., Art. 254). The law prescribes the forms of proof admissable to establish the guilt of the accused, i.e. confession, testimony of witnesses, writings and records of officials, evidence gained through discovery, judicial notice, searches and seizures (C. Cr. Pr., Art. 86), and the opinion of experts. The law stipulates in detail the conditions governing the admissibility of each of these means of proof in order to prevent abuses and to ensure that they contribute to the establishment of the truth.[5]

VII. COMMENCMENT AND CONDUCT OF PROCEEDINGS
A. Preparatory Investigation :

The public prosecutor, upon being informed of the occurence of an alleged offense, makes a preparatory investigation *(hazırlık soruşturması)* in order to ascertain the identity of the offender and to decide whether it is necessary to institute a public prosecution. If he concludes that a public action is necessary, he institutes a case either by an indictment *(iddianame)* or by a written demand *(talepname)* to the examining magistrate to commence a preliminary invertigation (C. Cr. Pr., Arts. 163, 192). If a public action is unnecessary he decides not to prosecute. The Minister of Justice may, by order, direct the prosecutor to initiate a public prosecution (C. Cr. Pr., Art. 148).

The public prosecutor may, for the purpose of his inquiry, demand any information from any public employee. He is authorized to make his investigations either directly or through police officers. The police are obliged to execute orders of the prosecutor concerning legal procedures (C. Cr. Pr., Art. 154).

In cases where a private complaint is submitted to the public prosecutor and the prosecutor finds no reason for prosecution or

---
[5] For details see, C. Cr. Pr., Arts. 45 ff.

decides not to prosecute after a preparatory investigation, he informs the petitioner of his decision. If the petitioner is, at the same time, the aggrieved party, he may, within fifteen days after notice, object to the Chief Justice of the nearest court which hears aggravated felony cases. If the court is convinced that the petition is well founded and rightful, it orders a public prosecution; the prosecutor in charge of the case executes this decision. Otherwise, the court refuses the petition, and after such action a public prosecution may be opened only upon production of newly discovered evidence (C. Cr. Pr., Arts. 164 ff).

In a few cases determined by law, the initiation of a public prosecution is subject to a permission or a decision or a private suit (a private complaint).

A public prosecution shall be dismissed when, the perpetrator of an offense punishable only by a fine deposits the minimum amount of the fine prescribed for the specific offense in the appropriate office before the court hearing. If this amount is paid by the offender before a public prosecution has been initiated and in ten days time from the date of commission of the offense, the perpetrator shall not be prosecuted at all.[6]

B. Preliminary Investigation :

The preliminary investigation *(ilk soruşturma)* is opened and conducted by the investigating judge (C. Cr. Pr., Art. 177) *(sorgu hakimi)*, in order to clarify a complicated case. It involves the gathering and preserving of evidence sufficient to decide whether there should be an opening of a final investigation (trial) or a dismissal of the case (C. C. Pr., Art. 183).

A preliminary investigation may be opened only upon a written demand *(talepname)* of the public prosecutor (C. Cr. Pr., Art. 163) for serious and complicated cases, but it is not permitted for cases that will be tried by a Justice of the Peace Court (C. Cr. Pr., Arts. 171, 172). Such a demand may be refused by the investigating judge on the ground that the court lacks jurisdiction, that the public prosecution is not valid, that preliminary investigation is not necessary for the type of crime charged, or that the charged offense is not punishable by the law (C. Cr. Pr., Arts. 173 and 176). Each investigation is recorded (C. Cr. Pr., Art. 181).

---

[6] See Law No. 1696, amending the C. Cr. Pr., added Arts. 5 ff.

As soon the investigating judge is convinced that the purpose of the preliminary investigation has been accomplished, he turns the documents over to the public prosecutor so that he may present his case. Within seven days, the prosecutor must turn over the investigation documents and his petition to the investigating judge. For the commencement of a trial the petition must be in the form of an accusation clearly indicating the charges. A copy of the accusation initiating the trial is forwarded to the accused by the investigating judge, and the accused is asked to state within three days whether or not he wishes to have more evidence obtained, or if he has any objection to the commencement of the trial. Finally the investigating judge decides whether to order a trial, temporarily suspend the case, or dismiss the charges (C. Cr. Pr., Arts. 190 ff.).

The preliminary investigation, as well as the preparatory investigation, is secret, in written form, and performed without the presence of the parties. For the preliminary investigation, however, there are some exceptions to the rule concerning the absence of the accused during the investigation (See, C. Cr. Pr., Arts. 186-188). The public prosecutor may examine any relevant documents at any time during the investigation (C. Cr. Pr., Art. 189).

C. Final Investigation :

The final investigation (or trial, *son soruşturma*) begins when the decision to commence the trial on the indictment (in all cases where a preliminary investigation has taken place) or on the accusation (in all other cases) is sent to the court which will try the case. The final investigation has two stages : the preparation for trial *(duruşma hazırlığı)* and the trial itself *(duruşma)* (C. Cr. Pr., Arts. 206 ff.). Its object is to examine all evidence before the court, and reach a judgment with respect to the guilt of the accused.

After the preparation for trial has been concluded, the trial commences on the date previously set for trial, at a designated court room, and after the formation of the court in accordance with law and in the presence of the parties. The trial cannot proceed if the defendant does not appear in court (C. Cr. Pr., Art. 223). The trial begins with a roll-call of the witnesses and experts. Thereafter, the identity of the accused is registered. This is followed by the reading of the trial order (the indictment) or the accusation, followed by the questioning of the accused, in the absence of the witnesses (C.

Cr. Pr., Art. 236). This is followed by the introduction of evidence. Evidence is submitted to the court in the manner prescribed by statute and then contested. After the defendant has heard any witness, expert or accomplice, and after the reading of any document, he is asked whether he wants to challenge the evidence presented (C. Cr. Pr., Art. 250). Upon completion of the introduction and adjudication of the evidence, statements may then be made by the complaining witnesses, the Public Prosecutor, other interested parties, and finally, the accused. The public prosecutor may reply to the accused, and the accused and his counsel may reply to the prosecutor. The accused has the right to make the last reply (C. Cr. Pr., Art. 251). The trial ends with the judgment, consisting of two parts: the judgment proper *(hüküm)* (or decision); and the justification of the judgment *(gerekçe)* (C. Cr. Pr., Art. 260 ff.).

The court weighs the evidence submitted in accordance with its assessment of the investigation and the trial (C. Cr. Pr., Art. 254).

Final investigation is open to the public. The court may decide, however, for the protection of public morals and security, to hold partly or completely closed sessions (C. Cr. Pr., Arts. 373-375). The trials of children under fifteen years of age must be conducted in closed sessions.

All phases of final investigation are conducted in the presence of the defendant (C. Cr. Pr., Art. 240). The Turkish Code of Criminal Procedure has adopted the trial in absentia as an exception only in cases where light sentences are involved; that is where the offense is punishable by fine, light imprisonment, confiscation, or any combination thereof. A trial may even proceed if the defendant does not appear in court. On his own motion, a defendant may be excused from attending trial, and send a defense counsel in cases where his presence is not necessary (C. Cr. Pr., Art. 225-226). Trial may also be instituted against an absentee defendant when the offense involves a fine, confiscation, or both (C. Cr. Pr., Arts. 269 ff.).

The final investigation is oral. During the trial all procedural transactions are concluded orally: the accused, witnesses and experts are examined by the court. Records are read aloud, with the court having direct access to all the evidence (C. Cr. Pr., Arts. 238, 242, 244, 249).

The trial is held without interruption in the presence of the judges who will take part in formulating the judgment. In cases of necessity, however, the trial may be adjourned or suspended (C. Cr. Pr., Arts. 219 ff.).

During both the preliminary investigation and the trial, the investigating judge and the court have authority to introduce evidence; they need not satisfy themselves solely with evidence introduced by the parties.

VIII. LEGAL REVIEW :

Legal review *(kanun yolu)* provides the opportunity to examine decisions of the judges or judgments of the courts. Its purpose is to ensure the proper application of the law. Review is of two kinds : those calling for action by a higher court (ordinary legal review) and those calling for action by the trial court itself (extraordinary legal review). Exception *(itiraz)* and appeal (to the Court of Cassation *(temyiz)*, belong to the first group, while a new trial in favor of the accused *(sanık lehine muhakemenin yenilenmesi)*, reversal by a written order *(yazılı emir ile bozma)*, correction of the decision (revision, *karar düzeltmesi, tashihi karar*) and the Chief Public Prosecutor's protest of a decision given by one of the Criminal Chambers of the Court of Cassation belong to the second group (C. Cr. Pr., Arts. 297 ff.).

The right to appeal judicial decisions is open to the public prosecutor, the accused, the defense counsel, the legal representative, and a husband. An appeal by the public prosecutor may result in a judgment's being changed in favor of the accused (C. Cr. Pr., Arts. 289 ff.).

Except as otherwise prescribed by law, exceptions may be taken against the decisions of judges (when they are not part of the trial proceedings), but not against court decisions. The authorities which review exceptions are given in article 299; generally speaking it is the higher judge. The submission of a petition of exceptions does not postpone the execution of a decision against which the exception was taken ; however, the reviewing authority may order such a postponement. Decisions on exceptions are final.[7]

Judgments rendered by criminal courts may be appealed to the Court of Cassation on the grounds of legal error. The non-

---

[7] C. Cr. Pr., Arts. 297 ff. For procedure regarding urgent exceptions, see, Art. 364.

application or erroneous application of a legal rule is a violation of law, and article 308 states certain circumstances which are considered as absolute violations of law. The appeal must be made within a week after the pronouncement of the judgment by a petition to the court which rendered the judgment (C. Cr. Pr., Art. 310). The appellate petition filed within a week prevents the judgment from becoming final (C. Cr. Pr., Art. 312). The Court of Cassation reverses the judgment on points of law that the lower court incorrectly decided. In exceptional situations and in the circumstances given by article 322, the court will decide a case on its merits. Otherwise, the court forwards the file to the originating court or to another nearby court of parallel jurisdiction for review of its own decision and a new judgment. The courts have the right to insist on their first judgment after their judgment is reversed by the Court of Cassation, but they are obliged thereafter to abide by decisions given by the General Assembly of Criminal Chambers of the Court of Cassation (C. Cr. Pr., Art. 326).

Under the circumstance prescribed in article 327, the accused may be granted a new trial following conviction, and under article 330, a new trial of an acquitted defendant may be held under certain circumstances.

When the Minister of Justice is informed of violations of law in the judgments rendered by courts, which become final without review by the Court of Cassation, he orders the Chief Public Prosecutor's Office, in writing, to appeal to the Court of Cassation for the reversal of this decision or judgment (C. Cr. Pr., Art. 343).

The Chief Public Prosecutor may protest a decision of one of the Criminal Chambers of the Court of Cassation at the General Board of the Court within thirty days after the court decree has been submitted to him (C. Cr. Pr., Art. 322).

The correction procedure against the decision of Criminal Chambers or General Assembly of Criminal Chambers is possible only in case of omissions of consideration during appellate review of points specified in an appellate petition, in an appellate brief or in a notification, which directly affected the essence of the judgment. The right to request a correction of decision lies with the Chief Prosecutor (C. Cr. Pr., Art. 322).

IX. SPECIAL PROCEDURES

The procedure summarized above is the general procedure which is applicable to all cases except as otherwise provided by law. In addition, in the Turkish Code of Criminal Procedure there are some special trial rules. Trial of absentees (C. Cr. Pr., Arts 269. ff.), penal decrees by Justices of the Peace (punishment without trial, *sulh hakiminin ceza kararnamesi*) (C. Cr. Pr., Arts. 386 ff.), procedure of confiscation (C. Cr. Pr., Art. 392), and summary procedure for flagrant offenses should be pointed out under this title. The military courts also use a special procedure, and special procedural rules are applied in the preliminary investigation of offenses committed by civil servants in the performance of their functions.

SELECTED BIBLIOGRAPHY

Ansay, S. Ş.: **Hukuk Yargılama Usulleri** (Ankara 1960).
Ansay, S. Ş.: **Hukuk İcra ve İflâs Usulleri** (Ankara 1960).
Bilge, N.: **Medeni Yargılama Hukuku** (Ankara 1967).
Erem, F.: **Ceza Usulü Hukuku** (Ankara 1973).
Kunter, N.: **Ceza Muhakemesi Hukuku** (İstanbul 1974).
Kuru, B.: **Hukuk Muhakemeleri Usulü** (Ankara 1974, 3. baskı).
Kuru, B.: **İcra ve İflâs Hukuku** (Ankara 1975).
Postacıoğlu, İ.: **Medeni Usul Hukuku Dersleri** (İstanbul 1975).
Postacıoğlu, İ.: **İcra Hukuku Esasları** (İstanbul 1973).
Karlen, D. and İ. Arsel: **Civil Litigation in Turkey** (Ankara 1957).

Texts:

Turkish Code of Civil Procedure, in Karlen and Arsel pp. 157 ff. (Ankara 1957).

The Turkish Code of Criminal Procedure, With an introduction by Feyyaz Gölcüklü, The American Series of Foreign Penal Codes, No. 5 (Sweet and Maxwell 1962).

SELECTED BIBLIOGRAPHY OF BOOKS AND ARTICLES IN ENGLISH ON TURKISH LAW *

1. GENERAL

A. *Dictionaries:*

English - Turkish Law Dictionary (Prepared by : **M. Ovacık**) Ankara 1964, VIII, 355 p.

English - Turkish Administrative Sciences Dictionary, Ankara 1964, XXIV, 352 p.

Turkish - English Law Dictionary (Prepared by : **M. Ovacık**) Ankara 1969, VIII, 292 p.

B. *Treaties:*

Ökçün, A. Gündüz: A Guide to Turkish Treaties (1920-1964). Ankara 1966, 248 pp.

C. *General:*

Davran / Kubalı : Turkey (in : International Encyclopedia of Comparative Law, Dec. 1973).

D. *Law Reforms and Reception of Foreign Codes:*

Ayiter, Ferit : The interpretation of a national system of laws received from abroad, 6 Annales de la Faculté de Droit d'Istanbul, 41-43 (1956)

Belgesay, M. R. : Social, economic and technical difficulties experienced as a result of the reception of foreign law, 9 International Social Science Bulletin, 49-51 (1957).

Fındıkoğlu, Z. F. : A Turkish sociologist's view (Reception of foreign laws in Turkey), 9 International Social Science Bulletin, 13-25 (1957).

Fındıkoğlu, Z. F. : Special aspects of the Turkish reception of law, 6 Annales de la Faculté de Droit d'Istanbul, 155-165 (1956).

Hamson, C. J. : Introduction (Reception of foreign law in Turkey), 9 International Social Science Bulletin, 7-12 (1957).

Hudson, M. O. : Law reform in Turkey, 13 American Bar Association Journal, 5-8 (1927).

Kubalı, H. N. : Modernization and secularization as determining factors in reception in Turkey, 9 International Social Science Bulletin, 65-69 (1957).

Lipstein, Kurt : The reception of western law in Turkey, 6 Annales de la Faculté de Droit d'Istanbul, 11-23 (1956).

Lipstein, Kurt : Conclusions (Reception of foreign law in Turkey), 9 International Social Science Bulletin, 70-81 (1957).

---

* Prepared by Dr. Nurkut İnan and A. Kumrulu, assistants at the Faculty of Law, University of Ankara.

Starr / Pool : The Impact of a legal revolution in rural Turkey 8 Law and Soc. Rev. 533-560 (1974).
Timur, Hıfzı : The place of Islamic law in Turkish law reform, 6 Annales de la Faculté de Droit d'Istanbul, 75-80 (1956).
Timur, Hıfzı : Views on the transition in Turkey from Islamic law to a western set-up, 6 Annales de la Faculté de Droit d'Istanbul, 81-88 (1956).
Wigmore, J. H. : The new regime of law in the Turkish Republic, 21 Illinois Law Review, 83-87 (1926/27).

E. Legal History:

Altuğ, Y. : Legal rules concerning land tenure in the Ottoman Empire, 18 Annales de la Fac. de Droit d'Istanbul, pp. 153-169 (1968).
Onar, S. S. : The Majalla. Law in the Middle East. Vol : I. pp. 292-308.
The Medjelle or Ottoman civil law. Translated by **W. E. Grigsby** London 1895, 433 p.

F. Education:

Cheatham, F. E. : Legal Education in Turkey, 2 J. of Legal Education, 21-25 (1949).
Redden, Kenneth : Legal education in Turkey. A comparative study. Istanbul 1957, 152 p.
Özsunay, E. : Participation of students in university and faculty administration in Turkey, 17 Amr. J. Comp. L. 378 ff. (1969).

2. CONSTITUTIONAL LAW

A. Texts:

The Turkish Constitution. New York 1949, 19 p.
Constitution of the Turkish Republic (text), 16 Middle East Journal, 15-38 (1962).
Constitution of the Turkish Republic. Translated by **S. Balkan** ; **A. E. Uysal** ; **K. Karpat**. Ankara 1961.
Blaustein / Flanz (Eds.) : Constitutions of the World, Turkey (By **Flanz and Arsel**, 1976) Oceana, New York.
Aybay, R. : Some contemporary constitutional problems in Turkey, British Society for Middle Eastern Studies Bulletin, Vol. 4, Nr. 1, pp. 21-27 (1977).

B. General Principles and History:

Arsel, İlhan : Constitutional development of Turkey since the Republic, 18 Ankara Üniversitesi Hukuk Fakültesi Dergisi, 37-54 (1961).
Balta, T. B. ; **Kubalı, H. N.** : The concept of the rule of law in Turkey, 9 Annales de la Faculté de Droit d'Istanbul, 297-309 (1959).
Başgil, A. F. : A summary of constitutional developments in Turkey and on the historical and political sources of the present constitution, 10 Annales de la Faculté de Droit d'Istanbul, 74-84 (1960).

Dönmezer, S. : Evaluation of legislation regulating and limiting the freedom of press, 16 Annales de la Fac. de Droit d'Istanbul 151-177 (1966, Nos. 23-25).

Earle, E. M. : New constitution of Turkey, 40 Political Science Quarterly, 73-100 (1925).

Giritli, İ. : Some aspects of the new Turkish Constitution, 16 Middle East Journal, 1-17 (1962).

Giritli, İ. : The structure and characteristics of the Turkish Constitution, 10 Annales de la Faculté de Droit d'Istanbul, 257-265 (1960).

Kapanî, M. : An outline of the new Turkish Constitution. Parliamentary Affairs No. 1 1962.

Tunaya, T. Z. : Ideologic character of the 1924 Constitution, 10 Annales de la Faculté de Droit d'Istanbul, 99-135 (1960).

Tunaya, Tarık Z. : The establishment of the government of the Turkish Grand National Assembly and its political character, 19 Annales de la Faculté de Droit d'Istanbul, 47-76 (1963).

C. *Governmental Organization* :

Dalmis, Dogan : Turkish Government organization manual. Ankara 1959, 187 p.

Gorvine, Albert : An outline of Turkish provincial and local government, Ankara 1956, 27 p.

Gorvine, Albert ; Barber, Laurence Jr. : Organization and functions of Turkish ministries. Ankara 1957, 212 p.

Organization and functions of the central government of Turkey. (Public Administration Institute for Turkey and the Middle East) Ankara 1965.

Turkish government organization manual (Public Administration Institute for Turkey and the Middle East) Ankara 1966.

Versan, V. : Central and local government in Turkey, 10 Annales de la Faculté de Droit d'Istanbul, 266-278 (1960).

3. ADMINISTRATIVE LAW

A. *General* :

Ansay, T. : Public Private Enterprises in Mixed Economies, Turkey 137 - 191 (Ed. **Friedmann**), London 1974.

Balta, T. B. : Reports on Turkish administrative law and institutions, 6 Annales de la Faculté de Droit d'Istanbul, 186-204 (1956).

Balta, T. B. : Turkish administrative law and institutions, 9 International Social Science Bulletin, 37-48 (1957).

Dodd, C. H. : Politics and Government in Turkey, Manchester : University Press 1969.

Güran, S. : The problem of jurisdiction according to the decisions of the Court of Conflicts rendered in 1965-69 in cases related to recover damages caused by the vehicles of the Ministry of National Defence, 3 Mukayeseli Hukuk Araştırmaları Der. 473-477 (1969, No. 5).

Soysal, M. : Local Government in Turkey, Ankara 1967, VIII, 65 p.
Diblan, Carlson Servine : The liability of the government for service faults in Turkey, 24 International Review of Administrative Sciences, 152-164 (1958).
Onar, S. S. : The analysis and the criticsm of the causes of appearance of the the public corporations in Turkey and the legal and administrative structure of those corporations, 20 International Review of Administrative Sciences, 23-66 (1954).
Presthuis, R. V. ; **Sevda Erem** : Statistical analysis in comparative administration : The Turkish Conseil d'Etat. Ithaca 1953, 55 p.
Presthuis, A. V. ; **Sevda Erem** : The Turkish Conseil d'Etat. Ankara 1955, 42 p.

B. Public Administration and Civil Service :

Caldwell, L. K. : Toward the comparative study of public administration. Bloomington 1957 (Turkey, pp. 117-144).
Gorvine, Albert ; **Arif Payaslıoğlu** : The administrative career service in Turkish provincial government, 23 International Review of Administrative Sciences, 467-474 (1957).
Matthews, A. T. J. : Emergent Turkish administrators. Ankara 1955, 76 p.
Mıhçıoğlu, C. : The civil service in Turkey, Siyasal Bilgiler Fakültesi Dergisi, 89 ff. (1964).

C. Mining and Petroleum Laws :

Redden, Kenneth ; **John Huston** : The Mining Law of Turkey. Istanbul 1956, 227 p.
Redden, Kenneth ; **John Huston** : The Petroleum Law of Turkey. Istanbul 1956, 322 p.
Sarre, D. A. G. ; **Ayhan Ünler** : Modern oil laws, The J. of Business Law pp. 161 - 186 (1960).

4. PRIVATE LAW

A. Texts :

The Swiss Federal Code of Obligations with Turkish alterations. Translated and edited by **G. Wettstein** and others, Zurich 1928.

B. General Notions and History :

Arık, Fikret : The principal differences between Swiss (and Turkish) practice in interpreting the Civil Code, 6 Annales de la Faculté de Droit d'Istanbul, 144-149 (1956).
İzveren, Adil : The reception of the Swiss Civil Code in Turkey and the fundamental problems arising in the practice of Turkish courts, 6 Annales de la Faculté de Droit d'Istanbul, 171-174 (1956).
Saymen, F. H. : Notes on Turkish court decisions, 84 Journal de Droit International, 1037-1061 (1957).
Ülken, H. Z. : The new Civil Code and the traditional customary law (Turkey), 9 International Social Science Bulletin, 60-65 (1957).

C. Law of Persons:

Associations Act (Tr.: **Akgüner**) 22 Annales de la Faculte de Droit d'Istanbul 217-247 (1972, No. 38).

Frumkin, Justice: The legal position of women in Turkey under the old and new regime and in Egypt. 10 J. of Comp. Legislation, 196-202 (1928).

D. Family Law:

Amkan, F.: Comparative study of the Norwegian and Turkish family laws, 51 Women's Law Journal, 14 (1965).

Feroze, M.R.: Family laws of the Turkish Republic, I Islamic Studies (1962).

Redden, Kenneth; Esener, Turhan; Seymen, Neriman: Legal devices to promote marriage stability in Turkey, 8-9 Revue International de Droit Compare, 674-682 (1957).

Timur, Hıfzı: Civil marriage in Turkey: Difficulties, causes and remedies, 9 International Social Science Bulletin, 34-36 (1957).

E. Law of Property:

Aybay, A.: A suvey of the «Gecekondu» Act, 1966, from the standpoint of effective land use, 23 Annales de la Fac. de Droit d'Istanbul, 203-207 (1975, No. 39).

Doğanay, Ü.: Categories of land and the main principles governing them from the point of view of ownership, 23 Annales de la Fac. de Droit d'Istanbul, 85-91 (1975, No. 39).

F. Private International Law:

Law on Turkish Nationality (Text translated by **Gündüz Ökçün**). The Turkish Yearbook of International Relations, 177-193 (1964).

G. Commercial Law:

The Banks Association of Turkey, The Law of Banks with the Statute of the Banks Association of Turkey, Ankara 1965.

Commercial Code (of 1957). Books 1 and 2 (Commercial undertakings and commercial companies) translated by Türk Argüs Ajansı, Istanbul 1957, 96 p. «Mimeo».

Commercial Laws of Turkey. Florida 1962, (Foreign Tax Law Association (Loose leaf).

Patent and trademark regulations (text). 57 Patent and Trade Mark Review 311-320, 343-344, 361-363.

Turkish Copyright Law, translated by **Yusuf Mardin** Ankara, 49 p. (USIS).

An Encyclopedia of World Unfair Competition Law. (Ed. Pinner) Brussels 1965 (Articles on Turkey by **Yaşar Karayalçın**).

Ansay, T.: American Trade-Marks in Turkey, 13 Amr. J. Comp. L. 93-96 (1964).

Ansay, T.: The Commercial Laws of Turkey (in Digest of Commercial Laws of the World, ed. **G. Kohlik**) New York 1967 (Loose-leaf).

Ansay, T.: The control of formation of corporations in Turkey, 2 Banking and Commercial L. J. 73-82 (1963) (Ankara).
Ansay, T.: Turkey : New Commercial Code (New legislation) 6 Amr. J. of Comp. L. 106-108 (1957).
Ansay, T.: Two examples on similarity of trade marks (Turkey). The Journal of Business Law, p. 189 (1966).
Brown, J. L.: Patent and trademark protection in Turkey. Washington 1930, 8 p.
Budek, Mieczyslaw: Turkish commercial aviation, 23 Journal of Air Law and Commerce, 379-478 (1956).
Marşan, M. K.: The Air Carrier Liability Under Turkish Law (Istanbul Technical University Press, 1965).

H. Foreign Investment :

Foreign Investment Encouragment Law (text). Washington 1954, 5 p.
Altuğ, Y.: Turkish legal system of foreign investment, 17 Annales de la Fac. de Droit d'Istanbul, 68-88 (1967, Nos. 26-28).
Anderson, Ervin O. ; Versan, Vakur ; Özgür, Feridun: Joint international business ventures in Turkey, 1959, 71 p.
Ansay, T.: Legal aspects of foreign investment, Turkey (ed. **Friedmann**) pp. 543-561, Boston 1959.
Cenani, Rasim: Foreign capital investments in Turkey. Revised edition. Istanbul 1958, 87 p.
Golbert, A. S.: Legal incentives and realities of private foreign investment in Turkey, 15 Amr. J. Comp. L. 351 ff. (1967).
Investment in Turkey. Washington 1956, 186 p. (U. S. Department of Commerce).

5. LABOR LAW

International Labor Office. Studies and reports No. 25 : Labor problems in Turkey, Montreal 1950.
Aksoy : A brief enxplanation of Turkish labor legislation and social security system (1961).
Oğuzman, K. : The collective bargaining agreement, strike, lock-out and arbitration system in Turkey, 22 Annales de la Fac. de Droit d'Istanbul, 147-169 (1972, No. 38).
Tuna : Trade unions in Turkey, 90 Int'l. Lab. Rev., 413-431 (1964).
U. S. Bureau of Labor and Statistics. Labor Law and Practice in Turkey, Washington, D. C. 1963).
Weight, Oscar : The new Turkish Labor Code, 35 International Labor Review, 753-774 (1937).

6. CRIMINAL LAW

The Turkish Criminal Code. American series of foreign criminal codes, No. 9, London 1965, 190 p. (With an introduction by **Nevzat Gürelli**).
Şener, H. : Comparison of the Turkish and American military systems of nonjudicial punishment, 27 Military L. Rev., p. 111 (1965).

Şensoy, Naci : The reception of foreign codes of criminal law and criminal procedure in Turkey, 6 Annales de la Faculté de Droit d'Istanbul, 182-185 (1956).
Case on the constitutionality of Articles, 141 and 142 of the Penal Code, (Tr. : **Yarsuvat, D.**) 18 Annales de la Fac. de Droit d'Istanbul, 579-606 (1968, Nos. 29-32).
The prevention and treatment of juvenile delinquency in Turkey, 1 Annales de la Faculté de Droit d'Istanbul, 1-42 (1951).

7. LAW OF PROCEDURE

The Turkish Code of Criminal Procedure. Translated by **Yılmaz Altuğ** (With an introduction by **Feyyaz Gölcüklü**) London 1962, 158 p.
The Turkish Code of Civil Procedure (In : **Karlen / Arsel**, Civil Litigation in Turkey, Ankara 1957).
The Law which amended certain articles of the Code of Civil Procedure, numbered 1086, 22 Annales de la Fac. de Droit d'Istanbul 207-215 (1972, No. 38).
Ansay, Tuğrul : Commercial arbitration in Turkey, 12 Arbitration Journal New Series, 31-37 (1957).
Devereux, R. : Turkey's judicial security mechanism, 10 Die Welt des Islams, 33 ff. (1965).
Karlen, Delmar ; Arsel, İlhan : Civil litigation in Turkey. Ankara 1957, 279 p.
Sanders, Pieter (rapporteur general) : International commercial arbitration (Turkey by **N.S. Yelmen,** Paris 1956).
Uluç, R. : The Commercial arbitration of the International Chamber of Commerce and enforcement of its awards in Turkey and United States. 18 Annales de la Fac. de Droit d'Istanbul, 106-136 (1968, Nos. 29-32).
Yarsuvat, D. : Urbanization and administration of justice in Turkey, 22 Annales de la Fac. de Droit d'Istanbul, 393-414 (1972, No. 38).

TURKISH - ENGLISH GLOSSARY
OF LEGAL TERMS

(Figures in parantheses indicate page numbers in the book)

Adi şirket — Ordinary partnership (102)
Adi umumî heyet — Ordinary general assembly (111)
Adlî yardım — Legal aid (191, fn. 14)
Ağır ceza — Aggravated felonies (224)
Ağır ceza mahkemeleri — Aggravated felony courts (211)
Ağır hapis — Heavy imprisonment (182)
Ağır para cezası — Heavy fine (182)
Akit — Contract (161)
Alelâde yazılı şekil — Simple written form (167)
Amme davası — Public prosecution
Amme hizmetlerinden memnuiyet — Disqualification from holding public offices (182)
Amme idaresi — Public administration
Anayasa — Constitution (6)
Anayasa Mahkemesi — The Constitutional Court (48)
Anonim şirket — Stock company, corporation (110)
Arzuhal — Petition of the case (193)
Askerî Yargıtay — The Military Court of Cassation (18, 47)
Aslî iştirak — Full participation (180)
Asliye ceza mahkemeleri — Courts of general criminal jurisdiction (176, 211)
Asliye hukuk mahkemesi — Civil court of first instance (188)
Avukat — Practicing lawyer (191)
Ayrılık — Judicial separation (123)
Azalık — Membership (107)
Babalığa hüküm — Court decision on paternity (126)
Bakanlar Kurulu — The Council of Ministers (43)
Bakanlık — Ministry (62)
Baro — Bar association (191)
Basit yargılama usulü — Simplified procedure (205)
Başkâtip — Chief reporter (190)
Batıl akit — Void, null contract (160)

Belediye — Municipality (63)
Belediye başkanı — President of the municipality, mayor (65)
Bilirkişi — Expert, expert witness (200)
Borçlar hukuku — Law of obligations (161)
Borçtan kurtulma davası — (206)
Boşanma — Divorce (121)
Bucak — District (61)
Bucak müdürü — The head of a district (62)
Büyük Millet Meclisi — Grand National Assembly (25, 36)
Celpname — Subpoena (199)
Cemiyetler — Societies (102)
Cevap lâyihası — Petition of reply (195)
Ceza davasının düşmesi — Dismissal of penal action and/or prosecution (184)

Ceza Yargılama Usulü Kanunu — Code of Criminal Procedure (208)
Ceza yargılama usulü — Criminal procedure (208)
Cezanın ertelenmesi — Suspension of punishment (184)
Cumhurbaşkanı — The President of the Republic (38)
Cumhuriyet Senatosu — Senate of the Republic (37)
Cürüm — Felony (176, 181)
Danıştay — Council of State (17, 188)
Dava sebebi — Cause of action (193)
Davalı — The defendant (215)
Delil — Evidence (196)
Denetçi — Controller, comptroller (113)
Dernek — Society (88, 101, 102)
Devlet Şurası — Council of State (19, 188)
Devletin kamu malları — Public possessions of the state (72)
Devletin özel malları — Private possessions of the State (72)
Dilekçe — Petition of the case (193)
Divanı Muhasebat — Court of Accounts (19)
Dokunulmazlık — Freedom from arrest (38)
Ehlivukuf — Expert witnes (205)
Ehliyet — Capacity (88, 177)
El birliği ortaklığı — Co-ownership (155)
El yazısı ile vasiyetname — Holographic will (137)
Eşya — Property (147)
Evlat edinme — Adoption (126)
Evlenme — Marriage (117)

Evlendirme memuru — Marriage officer
Fatura — Invoice (198)
Feragat — Release (168)
Feri iştirak — Being an accesory to a crime (180)
Fesih edilebilir akitler — Voidable contracts (160)
Fiil ehliyeti — Capacity to act (88)
Füru — Descendant (133)
Gaiplerin muhakemesi — Trial of absentees
Gaiplik kararı — (86)
Gayri menkul lehine irtifak hakkı — Real servitude, easement (157)
Gayrimenkul mal — Immovable property, real property (148)
Gayrimenkul rehni — Mortgage, hypothec (159)
Genel af — Amnesty (185)
Genel kurul — General assembly (105, 111)
Gensoru — Interpellation, motion of censure (40, 75)
Gerekçe — Judicial optinion, reasons for the judgement (222), legislative intention
Gıyap kararının tebliği — Default summons (196)
Görev — Competence (192, 213)
Hacir — Interdiction
Hafif hapis — Light imprisonment (182)
Hafif para cezası — Light fine (182)
Hâkim — Judge (189)
Haklardan istifade ehliyeti — Capacity to be subject of rights (87)
Haksız fiil ehliyeti — Capacity to be liable for torts (88)
Haksız fiil — Tort (169)
Hamile yazılı hisse senedi — Bearer certificate (112)
Hapis — Imprisonment (182)
Hata — Mistake (162)
Hazırlık tahkikatı veya soruşturması — Preparatory investigation (219)
Hile — Fraud (164)
Hizmet kusuru — Service fault (83)
Hukuk devleti — State of law (34, 56)
Hukuk Genel Kurulu Kararı — Civil Assembly Decision (204)
Hukuk yargılama usulü — Civil procedure (191)
Hukukî sebep — Legal cause, legal ground, consideration (160, 193)
Hukukî tağyir — Conversion (156)
Hükmî şahıs — Legal person (99 n. 1)
Hükmî şahsiyet — Legal personality (99 n. 1)

Hüküm — Decision, sentence, judgement (222)
Hükümet tasarrufu — Acts of policy, acts of state (35, 74)
Islah — Reformation (194, fn. 23)
İçtüzük — Standing orders (38)
Iadei Muhakeme — Re-opening of the proceedings (203)
İcap — Offer (161)
İcapçı — Offerer (161)
İcazet — Ratification of a prior transaction (91)
İcra memuru — Execution officer (187, 190)
İçtihadı Birleştirme Kurulu — General Assembly on the Unification of Judgments (17, 90, 108, fn. 17)
İdam — Death (by hanging), execution (182)
İdare hukuku — Administrative law (53)
İdare meclisi — Board of directors (106, 112)
İdarî işlem — Administrative act (83)
İdarî vesayet — Tutelage (59, 68)
İddianame — Indictment, accusation (216, 219)
İflâs memuru — Bankruptcy officer (188)
İhmal — Negligence (170)
İhtiyar heyeti — Village elders (118)
İhtiyarî hacir — Voluntary interdiction (128)
İkâmetgâh — Domicile (92)
İkrah — Duress (164)
İkrar — Admission (197)
İktisabî mürüruzaman — Acquisition by prescription (156)
İktisadî devlet teşekkülleri — State economic enterprises (69, 102)
İl — Province, administrative department (28, 61, 191)
İlâm — Copy of a legal decision (202)
İlçe — Sub-province (61, 211)
İlk tahkikat — Preliminary investigation (220)
İlliyet rabıtası — Causal relation (170)
İmkânsızlık — Impossibility (146, 171)
İmtizaçsızlık — Incompatibility (122)
İntifa hakkı — Usufruct (147, 157)
İntifa hakkı sahibi — Usufructuary (157)
İpotek — Mortgage (158)
İptal davası — Action for annulment (49, 82)
İrtifak hakkı — Servitude (147, 157)
İspat yükü — Burden of proof (196)
İştirak nafakası — Allowance of participation (124)

İlk soruşturma — Preliminary investigation (219)
İstinabe — Deposition of a witness (201)
İştirak halinde mülkiyet — Co-ownership (155)
İtiraz — Exception (223)
İyi niyet — Good faith, *bona fides* (158)
Kabahat — Misdemeanor (176, 181)
Kabul — Acceptance (161)
Kamu malları — Public possession (72)
Kamulaştırma — Expropriation (34)
Kanun — Code, statute, act (7)
Kanun sözcüsü — Speaker of law in the Council of State (80)
Kanun yolu — Legal review (223)
Kanuna karşı hile — Fraud against the law (166)
Kanunî müşavir — Statutory advisor (129)
Kanunî teminat sistemi — The system of legal guarantee (81)
Kanunların makable şümulü — Retroactivity of laws (13)
Kanunsuz suç ve ceza olmaz — No crime and punishment without law (175)
Kanunu bilmemek mazeret sayılmaz — Ignorance of law is no excuse (6)
Kanun kudretinde kararnameler — Law amending ordinances, statutory decrees (8, 49)
Kararnameler — Ordinances, decrees, emergency orders (8)
Karar düzeltmesi — Remedy of correction (223)
Karışma ve birleşme — Confusion and accession (156)
Karineler — Presumptions (197)
Kasıt — Intent (170)
Kaymakam — Sub-governer (62)
Kayyım — Curator (128)
Kayyımlık — Curatorship (129)
Kaza — Sub-province (61)
Kefâlet akdi — Guaranty contract (168)
Kesin hüküm — Effect of a judgement, *res judicata* (203)
Keşif ve muayene — Inspections, discovery proceedings (201, 216)
Kişiliğin korunması — Protection of personality (94)
Kollektif şirket — General partnership (108)
Komandit şirket — Limited partnership (108)
Kooperatif şirket — Cooperative association (109)
Korkutma — Duress (164)

Kullanma ehliyeti — Capacity to act (88)
Kurucu Meclis — Constituent Assembly (28)
Kusur — Negligence, fault (170)
Küllî tevarüs — Universal succession (141)
Limited şirket — Limited liability company, partnership with limited liability (108)
Maddî zarar — Material damage (96, 170)
Mahalleler — Quarters of a town (66)
Mahallî idare — Local administration
Mahdut ehliyet — Limited capacity (91)
Mahfuz hisse — Reserved portion (139)
Mahkûmun lehine yargılamanın iadesi — New trial in favor of the accused (223)
Mal ayrılığı — Separation of property (121)
Mal birliği — Joint property (121)
Mal ortaklığı — Common property (121)
Manevî zarar — Immaterial or moral damage (96, 173)
Mansup mirasçılar — Universal legatees, appointed legatees (138)
Maznun — The defendant, accused (215)
Meclis araştırması — Parliamentary investigation (40)
Meclis soruşturması — Parliamentary inquiry (40)
Memur — Public personnel, civil servant (70)
Memnu hakların iadesi — Restoration of rights (185)
Menfaat ihlali — Infringement of interest
Menkul mal — Movable property, personal property (148)
Menkul rehni — Pledge, chattel mortgage (158)
Merkezî idare — The central administration (59)
Meşhut suçlar — Flagrant offenses (210)
Meşru müdafaa — Legitimate self - defense (96, 180)
Meşruten tahliye — Conditional release (184)
Milletlerarası andlaşma — International treaty (7)
Millet Meclisi — National Assembly (27)
Miras hukuku — Law of succession, inheritance (131)
Miras mukavelesi — Agreement of inheritance (139)
Mirasın intikali — Transfer of estate (141)
Mirasın reddi — Disclaimer of inheritance (144)
Mirasın taksimi — Partition and distribution of the estate (144)
Mirastan iskat — Debartment from inheritance (141)
Mirastan mahrumiyet — Loss of inheritance rights (141)
Muamele ehliyeti — Legal capacity to act (88, 162)

Muayyen bir meslek ve sanatın icrasının tatili — Disqualification from practising a profession or trade (182)
Muhtar — Head official of the village, village headman (66)
Murakıp — Controller, comptroller (112)
Muris — Deceased (132)
Murtabıt dava — Connected case
Musaleh — Particular (specific) legatee (138)
Muvafakat — Approval (91)
Muvakkat yakalama — Temporary custody (222)
Müdahale yolu ile dâva — Action by virtue of intervention (215)
Müddeiumumi — Public prosecutor (190, 209, 214)
Müddeaaleyh — The defendant (219)
Müessisler heyeti — Board of founders of a foundation (113)
Mülkiyet — Ownership (148)
Mülkiyet nakli — Transfer of ownership (155)
Mümeyyiz — One who is able to make mature or fair judgements (88)
Mürekkep faiz — Compound interest (165)
Mürüruzaman — Statute of limitations (165, 169)
Müsadere usulü — Condemnation procedures (225)
Müsteşar — Advisor, top assistant of a minister (61)
Müşavere heyeti — Board of consultants (113)
Müşterek mülkiyet — Joint ownership (155)
Mütemmim cüz — Component part or fixture (153)
Müteveffa — Deceased (132)
Mütevelli heyeti — Board of directors of a foundation (113)
Nakıs teşebbüs — Incomplete attempt (177)
Nama yazılı hisse senedi — Registered share certificate (111)
Nesebi sahih olmayan çocuk — Illegitimate child (125)
Nesebin tashihi — Correction of affinity
Nişanlanma — Engagement (116)
Nizamname — Regulation (8)
Noter — Notary (19)
Nüfus memuru — Census officer (86, 125)
Orta malı — Res in common use
Ödeme emri — Order of payment
Örf ve adet hukuku — Customary law (1)
Özel af — Pardon (185)
Rehin — Mortgage (147, 158)
Resmî Gazete — Official Gazette

Resmî şekil — Official form, authentic form (17)
Resmî tasfiye — Official form, authentic form (17)
Resmî tasfiye — Official liquidation (144)
Resmî vasiyetname — Authentic, official will (136)
Reşit — Major, of age (88)
Rüşt — Majority (89)
Sahih olmayan nesep — Illegitimate affinity (125)
Salâhiyet — Venue, jurisdiction by locality (192, 213)
Savcı — Public prosecutor (190, 209, 213, 214)
Sanık — Accused (215)
Sayıştay — The Court of Accounts (76)
Sebepsiz zenginleşme — Unjust enrichment (171)
Senet — Written instrument, deed (197)
Sermayesi paylara bölünmüş komandit şirket — Limited partnership in which the capital is divided into shares (108)
Seri yargılama usulü — Accelerated procedure (205)
Sıkı yönetim — Martial law (74)
Son tahkikat — Final investigation, trial (216)
Sorgu hakimi — Investigating magistrate (176, 218)
Soru — Question (75)
Sosyal hukuk devleti — Social State (33, 54)
Suça iştirak — Participation in a crime (180)
Suçlarda içtima — Multiplicity of crimes (180)
Suçluların geri verilmesi — Extradition (176)
Sulh ceza mahkemesi — Peace court of criminal jurisdiction (211)
Sulh mahkemesi — Peace court (188)
Sükna hakkı — Habitation (158 n. 18)
Sürgün — Banishment (182)
Şahit — Witness (198)
Şahsî dava — Personal action (215)
Şartlı salıverme — Conditional release (184)
Şart ve mükellefiyet — Condition or charge (138)
Şekil serbestliği — Freedom as to form (167)
Şifahi vasiyetname — Oral will (137)
Tabiî hâkim — Natural judge (212)
Tâbiiyet — Nationality (93)
Tahrik — Provocation (183)
Takdirî hafifletici sebepler — Discretionary mitigating causes (183)
Taksitle satışlar — Installment sales (166)
Talep neticesi — The prayer for relief, a statement of claims (194)

Talimatname — Regulation (9)
Tam ehliyet — Full capacity
Tam ehliyetsizlik — Full incapacity (90)
Tam teşebbüs — Complete attempt (77)
Tam yargı davası — Full remedy action (82)
Tanık — Witness (198)
Tanıma — Recognition (125)
Tapu Kanunu — Land Registration Act (171)
Tapu sicili — Land registry (152)
Tashihi karar veya karar düzeltme — Remedy of correction, correction of the decision (223)
Tebligat — Notice to the defendant, service of summons (195)
Tecavüzün men'i davası — Action for the prohibition of the attack, injunction (95)
Tecdit — Novation (168)
Tedbir ve iştirak nafakası — Maintenance (133)
Teferruat — Accessories (154)
Tehiri icra — Suspension of the administrative act by the court
Tekerrür — Recidivism (183)
Telsik — Naturalization (94)
Temyiz — Appeal, action of cassation (203, 223)
Temyiz kudreti — Capacity to make fair judgements (89)
Temyiz Mahkemesi — Court of Cassation, Supreme Court (17, 188, 203, 211)
Terekenin resmen idaresi — Official administration of the estate (143)
Terk — Desertion (122)
Tesis — Foundation (101, 113)
Tetkik Mercii — Investigation Authority (188, 206)
Teyit mektubu — Letter of confirmation (198)
Ticaret mahkemeleri — Commercial courts (188)
Ticaret şirketleri — Business associations (101, 108)
Tutuklama müzekkeresi — Warrant of arrest (218)
Tüzel kişi — Legal person (99 n. 1)
Tüzel kişilik — Legal personality (99 n. 1)
Tüzük — Regulation (8, 60)
Umumî heyet — General assembly (111)
Uyrukluk — Nationality (93)
Uyuşmazlık Mahkemesi — Court of Conflicts (75)
Üyelik — Membership (107)

Vakıf — Foundation (101, 112)
Vali — Governor (62)
Vasi — Guardian (128)
Vasiyeti tenfiz memuru — Executor (of the estate) (138)
Vasiyetname — Will (135)
Vasiyetnameden rücu — Revocation of wills (137)
Vatan hainliği — High treason (43)
Vazife — Competence (192, 213)
Velayet — Parental authority (126)
Usûl — Ascendant (132)
Tutuklama müzekkeresi — Warrant of arrest (218)
Tutuklama — Detention (217)
Veraset ilâmı — Certificate of inheritance (142)
Vesayet — Guardianship (91, 127)
Vergi İtiraz Komisyonu — Committee of Cassation for Taxes (81)
Vilâyet (İl) — Province, administrative department (31, 61)
Yakalama — Detention (217)
Yargıç — Judge (189)
Yargılamanın iadesi — Re-opening of the proceedings (203)
Yargıtay — Court of Cassation, Supreme Court (17, 188, 203, 211)
Yasak hakların iadesi — Restoration of rights (185)
Yazılı emir ile bozma — Reversal by a written order of the Ministry of Justice (223)
Yetki — Venue, jurisdiction by locality authority, power (57, 192, 213)
Yetki genişliği — De-concentration of the authority (62)
Yoksulluk nafakası — Maintenance, alimony (24)
Yönetim kurulu — Board of directors (112)
Yönetmelik — By-laws, instructions (9, 67)
Yüce Divan — High Court, High Tribunal (212)
Yüksek Denetleme Kurulu — High Control Board (76)
Yüksek Hakimler Kurulu — Supreme Council of Judges (46, 189)
Yürütmenin durdurulması — Suspension of on administrative act by the court (83)
Zabıt kâtipleri — Court clerks (190)
Zaman aşımı — Statute of limitations (169)
Zaruret hali — State of necessity (180)
Zilyetlik — Possession (150)
Zilyetlik iradesi — Intent of possession (151)
Zina — Adultery (122)

ALPHABETICAL INDEX

ABUSE OF CONFIDENCE, 30
ACCELERATED PROCEDURE, 205
ACCEPTANCE, 161
ACCESSORIES, 154
ACCESSORIES (Criminal law), 180
ACCUSATION, 216
ACCUSATORIAL SYSTEM, 209
ACCUSED, 215
ACKNOWLEDGMENT, 125
ACTE DE GOUVERNMENT, 74
ACTION BY VIRTUE OF INTERVENTION, 215
ACTION FOR ANNULMENT, 82
ACTION FOR THE PROHIBITION OF THE ATTACK, 95
ACTS AGAINST LAW, 169
ADMINISTRATIVE ACTS, 34, 82
ADMINISTRATIVE CONTROL, 76
ADMINISTRATIVE COURT SYSTEM, 79
AMDINISTRATIVE CURATORSHIP, 128
ADMINISTRATIVE LAW, 52
ADMINISTRATIVE ORGANIZATION, 59
ADMINISTRATOR, 142
ADMISSION, 197
ADOPTED CHILD, 126, 134
ADOPTION, 118, 126
ADOPTIVE PARENT, 126
ADULTERY, 122
ADVERSE POSSESSION, 157
AFFINITY
    Correction of, 125
AGE, 90
AGENDA, 106
AGGRAVATED FELONIES, 214
AGGRAVATED FELONY COURTS, 211
AGGRAVATION, 183
ALIMONY, 124

ALLOWANCE OF PARTICIPATION, 124
AMNESTY, 119, 185
ANALOGY, 12
ANGLO - AMERICAN LEGAL SYSTEM, 16
APPEAL, 204, 223
APPOINTED LEGATEES, 138
APPOINTMENT OF EXECUTOR, 138
APPROVAL, 91
ARGUMENT A CONTRARIO, 12
ARREST, 218
    Condition of, 218
    Warrant of, 218
ARTICLES OF INCORPORATION, 111
ASSOCIATION, 99
ASSOCIATION OF PERSONS, 101
ATATÜRK, 6, 7, 25
ATTEMPT, 177
ATTEMPTS TO KILL THE DECEDENT, 141
AUCTION SALE, 169
AUTONOMOUS PUBLIC AGENCIES, 67
BAD FAITH ,175
BANISHMENT, 182
BANKRUPTCY 188, 190, 207
BAR ASSOCIATIONS, 68, 191
BEARER SHARE CERTIFICATES, 111
    Transfer of, 111
BENEFICIARIES, 138
BILL OF LADING, 151
BIRTH REGISTRY, 86
BOARD OF DIRECTORS, 106, 112
BONA FIDE BUYER, 158
BONA FIDE PURCHASER, 152
BOOKS OF ACCOUNT, 198
BOOKS OF AUTHORITY, 19
BREACH OF ENGAGEMENT, 170
BREACH OF FIDELITY, 122

BUDGET LAWS, 7, 42
BURDEN OF PROOF, 196, 216
BUSINESS ASSOCIATIONS, 101, 108
   Classification of, 108
   Where capital is important, 110
   Where persons are important, 109
BY-LAWS, 8, 9, 105
CAPACITY, 87, 162, 178
   Full, 88
   Limited, 91
   To act, 88
   To be liable for torts, 88, 91
   To engage, 116
   To make fair judgements, 89
CASE LAW, 3
CAUSAL RELATION, 170, 175
CAUSE OF ACTION, 193
CENTRAL ADMINISTRATION, 57 ff.
CENTRAL DEPARTMENTS, 58
CERTIFICATE OF INHERITANCE, 143
CENSUS OFFICER, 87
CHALLENGING THE CONSTITUTIONALITY OF LAWS, 49
CHAMBERS OF COMMERCE AND INDUSTRY 5
CHARGE OR CONDITION, 138
CHATTELS, 154
CHATTEL MORTGAGE, 158
CHIEF PUBLIC PROSECUTOR, 212, 224
CHIEF REPORTER, 190
CIVIL CODE, 7
CIVIL COURT OF FIRST INSTANCE, 188
CIVIL DEATH, 87
CIVIL DISQUALIFICATION, 182
CIVIL MARRIAGE CEREMONY, 118
CIVIL PROCEDURE, 19
CIVIL SERVANTS, 70
CITY PLANNING, 149
CLASSICAL SCHOOL, 173
CODE OF CIVIL PROCEDURE, 193
CODE OF CRIMINAL PROCEDURE, 10, 210
CODE OF EXECUTION AND BANKRUPTCY, 10, 207
CODE OF OBLIGATIONS, 161

CODICIL, 137
COMITAS GENTIUM, 5
COMMERCIAL COURTS, 188
COMMERCIAL CUSTOM, 5
COMMERCIAL ENTERPRISE, 93, 103
COMMERCIAL REGISTRY, 109
   Regulation of, 8 n. 11
COMMERCIAL USAGE, 5 n. 5
COMMITTEE OF CASSATION FOR TAXES, 81
COMMITTEE OF TAX APPEALS, 81
COMMON PROPERTY, 121
COMMON PURPOSE, 99
COMMUNITY OF HEIRS, 142
COMPETENCE, 192
COMPONENT PART, 153, 154
COMPOUND INTEREST, 165
COMPTROLLERS, 113
CONCILIATION, 129
CONDITION OR CHARGE, 138
CONDITIONAL RELEASE, 182
CONFESSION, 219
CONFISCATION OF PROPERTY, 183, 225
CONFUSION AND ACCESSION, 156
CONFUSION OF FUNGIBLE PROPERTY, 156
CONSANGUINITY, 118
CONSIDERATION, 167
CONSTITUENT ASSEMBLY, 28
CONSTITUTION OF THE FIRST REPUBLIC, 25 ff.
CONSTITUTION, preamble of, 30
CONSTITUTION 6
CONSTITUTIONAL COURT, 7, 48
CONSTITUTIONAL LAW, 23 ff.
CONSTITUTIONALITY OF THE PROVISIONS OF LAW, 48
CONTRACTS, 159
   Against individual rights, 166
   Of bailment, 167
   Essential elements of, 166
   For black-marketing, 165
   Forms of, 167
   Freedom of, 165
   In restraint of trade, 98
   Limitation of freedom of, 165

Of sale, 165
Termination of, 168
Unilateral termination, 169
Void, 160
Voidable 160
CONTROL OF PUBLIC ADMINISTRATION, 74
CONTROL OVER EXECUTIVE, 40
CONTROLLERS, 113
CONVERSION, 156
COOPERATIVE ASSOCIATIONS, 109
CO-OWNERSHIP, 142, 155
CORPORATIONS, 67, 99, 110,
Annual report, 112
Annulment of resolutions, 112
Approval by the Ministry of Commerce, 111
Balance sheet, 112
Board of directors, 112
Formation of, 111
General assembly, 111
Minimum capital of, 111
Scope of business, 112

CORPUS JURIS CIVILIS, 13
CORRECTION OF THE DECISION, 225
COUNCIL OF MINISTERS, 43, 59
Responsibility of, 44
Temporary, 46
COUNCIL OF STATE, 17, 18, 51, 79, 190, 216
General Assembly of, 18
Chief prosecutor of, 18
General Assembly of Judicial Chambers, 18, 80
Judicial Chambers, 80
President of, 18 80
Speaker of Law, 80
COUNTER CLAIM, 195
COURT CLERKS, 190
COURT DECISIONS, 15
COURT OF ACCOUNTS, 19, 75, 81
COURT OF CASSATION, 17, 203, 224
Assembly of Civil Chambers, 17
Assembly of Criminal Chambers, 17
General Assembly of All Chambers of, 17
General Assembly Decision on the Unification of Judgements, 108
COURT OF CONFLICTS, 188
COURT OF FIRST INSTANCE, 188
COURT OF GENERAL CRIMINAL JURISDICTION, 211
COURT STRUCTURE, 187, 211
CRIME, 174
Elements of, 174
Material element of 177
Multiplicity of, 180
CRIME AND DISHONORABLE LIFE, 122
CRIMINAL CAPACITY, 177
CRIMINAL CODE, 7, 10, 175
CRIMINAL INTENT, 179
CRIMINAL LAW, 173
Sources of, 175
CRIMINAL PROCEDURE, 208
CURATOR, 128
CURATORSHIP, 128
CUSTOMARY LAW, 1 ff.
DAMAGE, 170
DEATH, 182
DEATH DUTIES, 131
DECEASED, 131
DECEDENT, 132
DECLARATION OF BANKRUPTCY, 207
DECLARATION OF HUMAN RIGHTS, 13
DECONCENTRATION OF THE AUTHORITY, 61
DECREES, 9
DEED, 197
DEFAULT SUMMONS, 196
DEFENDANT, 215
DEFRAUDED PARTY, 166
DELIVERY OF GOODS, 152
DELIVERY OF KEYS OR PAPERS REPRESENTING THE GOODS, 152
DELIVERY OF THE PROPERTY, 151
DEMOCRATIC STATE 30
DEPOSITIONS, 201
DESCENDANTS, 132, 139
DESERTION, 122

DETENTION 218
DETERRENCE, 173
DEVISEES, 138
DIPLOMATIC IMMUNITIES, 176
DISCIPLINARY PENALTIES, 71
DISCLAIMER OF INHERITENCE, 144
DISCOVERY PROCEEDINGS, 216, 219
DISMISSAL OF PENAL ACTIONS AND PROSECUTIONS, 184
DISQUALIFICATION FROM HOLDING PUBLIC OFFICE, 182
DISQUALIFICATION FROM PRACTISING A TRADE, 182
DISTRIBUTION OF DIVIDENDS, 112
DISTRICTS, 61
DIVORCE, 12
  Grounds for, 122
DOCTRINE, 19
DOMICILE, 92
  By operation of law, 92
  Of choice, 92
DOMINANT ESTATE, 158
DONATION, 128
DURESS, 164
DUTY TO SUPPORT, 120

EASEMENTS, 153, 157
EDICT OF REORGANIZATION OF 1839, 10, 23
ELECTIONS, 31
ELECTION OF THE MEMBERS OF THE HOUSES, 37
ELECTORATE, 37
ELECTRICITY, 148
EMERGENCY POWERS, 73
EMINENT DOMAIN, 149
ENFORCEMENT OF STATUTES, 14
ENGAGEMENT, 116, 170
  Agreement, 116
  Breach of, 116
  Duties resulting from, 116
  Reciprocal return of gifts, 116
  Rights resulting from, 116
  Unilateral breach, 116
ENRICHMENT, 175
ENTRY INTO GOVERNMENT SERVICE, 70

ERROR in *negotio*, 165
  In object, 164
  In person, 165
ESTATE 143, 165
  Debts of, 143
  Distribution of, 144
  Distribution by the court, 144
  Distribution by the heirs, 144
  Official administration of, 143
  Official liquidation, 144
  Partition of, 142, 144
  Partition of agricultural lands, 145
  Protection of, 143
  Transfer of, 141
EVIDENCE, 196, 218
  Gained through discovery, 219
EX POST FACTO LAWS, 13
EXAMINING MAGISTRATE, 216, 218
EXCEPTION, 223
EXECUTION, 206
EXECUTION OFFICERS, 187, 205
EXECUTIVE, 40, 42
EXECUTOR, 138, 142
EXPERT, 200
EXPERT'S REPORT, 200
EXPROPRIATION, 34
EXTRADITION, 176

FAILURE IN FULFILLING STATUTORY DUTY TO THE DECEDENT, 141
FAMILY, 115
  Head of, 120
  Law, 115
FELONIES, 176, 181
FICTION THEORY, 100
FIDELITY, 119
FINAL INVESTIGATION, 216, 221
FINAL TRIAL, 216
FIXTURE, 153
FOREIGN EXCHANGE TRANSACTIONS, 168
FORM, 167
  Authentic, 168
  Freedom as to, 167
  Official, 168
  Written, 167

FOUNDATIONS, 101, 112, 128
    Board of consultants, 114
    Board of directors, 113
    Board of founders, 114
    Changes in the organization, 114
    Control of, 114
    Family, 114
    Formation of, 113
    Obligatory organ of, 114
    Purpose of, 113
    Religious, 114
    State supervision on, 114
FOUNDERS, 99
FRAUD, 30, 164
FRAUD AGAINST THE LAW, 166
FREEDOM OF SPEECH, 38
FREEDOM FROM ARREST, 38
FLAT OWNERSHIP, 154
FULL REMEDY ACTION, 83
GARNISHMENT PROCEDURE, 206
GAS, 148
GENERAL ASSEMELY, 105, 111
GENERAL ASSEMBLY ON THE UNIFICATION OF JUDGEMENT, 17, 18
GENERAL PARTNERSHIP, 108, 109
    Administration of, 109
    Capacity of, 109
    Dissolution of, 110
    Written partnership agreement, 109
GENERAL USAGE, 5 n. 5
GESCHAEFTSFAEHIGKEIT, 88, 162
GOOD MORALS, 168
GOVERNOR, 61
GRAND NATIONAL ASSEMBLY, 36
    The structure of, 36
GRAVE ASSAULTS AND INSULTS, 122
GUARANTY, 128
GUARANTY CONTRACT, 129
GUARDIAN, 128
    Powers of, 128
GUARDIANSHIP, 91, 128
HABITATION, 158
HABITUAL DRUNKENNESS, 91
HANDLUNGSFAEHIGKEIT, 87
HEAD OF A DISTRICT, 6
HEIR, 142

HIRE - PURCHASE CONTRACT, 168
HUMILIATING CRIME, 123
HYPOTHEC, 158
IGNORANCE OF LAW IS NO EXCUSE, 6
IGNORANTIA LEGIS NEMINEM EXCUSAT, 6
ILLEGITIMATE CHILD, 126 134
IMMATERIAL DAMAGE, 97, 117, 170
IMMOVABLE PROPERTY, 148
    Acquisition of, 157
IMPEACHMENT, 41
IMPOSSIBILITY, 166, 168
IMPRISONMENT, 91, 128, 182
IMPROPER REGISTRATION, 153
    Liability of the State for, 153
IN FLAGRANTE DELICTO, 218
INCAPACITY, 90, 117
INCOMPATIBILITY, 122
INCORPORATORS, 111
INDEPENDENT AND PERMANENT RIGHTS, 148
INDICTMENT, 216, 218, 221
INHERITENCE, 139
    Agreement of, 139
    Debartment from, 141
    Disclaimer of, 144
    Loss of rights, 141
    Parents, 140
    Sisters and brothers, 140
    Spouse, 134, 140
INQUISATORIAL SYSTEM, 209
INSPECTIONS, 216
INSTALLMENT SALES, 166
INTENT, 151, 170, 179
INTERDICTION, 128
INTERIM ALLOWANCE, 123
INTERNATIONAL TREATIES, 7
INTERPELLATION, 40
INTERPRETATION, 11
    Grammatical, 11
    Historical, 12
    Logical, 11
    Methods of, 11
    Teleological, 12
INTERVENTION, 215
INTESTATE, 133

INTESTATE SUCCESSION, 131
INTESTATE SUCCESSOR, 141
INTIMATE CONVICTION, 219
INVESTIGATION AUTHORITY, 188, 206
INVOICES, 198
JOINT OWNER, 155
JOINT OWNERSHIP, 155
JOINT PROPERTY, 121
JUDGES, 189
    Independence, 190, 210
    Investigating, 220
JUDGEMENT
    Reasons for, 222
    Justification of, 222
    Rendition of, 222
JUDICIAL CONTROL OF RULE MAKING POWER, 77
JUDICIAL REVIEW, 35, 77
JUDICIAL POWER, 46
JUDICIAL SEPARATION, 124
JUDICIARY, 46
JURISDICTION, 213
JUVENILE COURTS, 212
LABOR UNIONS, 103
LAND LAW, 82
LAND REGISTRATION ACT, 171
LAND REGISTRATION OFFICER, 157, 171
LAND REGISTRY, 148, 151 ff. 156, 158
LAND REGISTRY REGULATION, 8, 152
LAW OF COLLECTIVE LABOR AGREEMENTS, STRIKES AND LOCKOUT, 168
LAW OF THE COUNCIL OF STATE, 8, 18
LAW OF LABOR UNIONS, 103
LAW OF OBLIGATIONS, 159
LAW OF PERSONS, 85
LAW OF POLITICAL PARTIES, 103, 107
LAW OF PROCEDURE, 17, 187
LAW OF PROPERTY, 147
LAW OF SOCIETIES, 103
LAW OF SUCCESSION, 131

LAW RELATIG TO THE PROTECTION OF THE VALUE OF THE TURKISH CURRENCY, 9, 10
LAWYERS FEES, 202
LEGAL AID, 191
LEGAL CAUSE, 164
LEGAL DOCTRINE, 3
LEGAL ELEMENT, 175
LEGAL GROUND, 164, 167, 175, 193
LEGAL PERSON, 88, 99
LEGAL PERSONALITY, 99
LEGAL REVIEW, 223
LEGALLY RECOGNIZED CHILD, 94
LEGATEES, 138, 141
LEGISLATION, 5
LEGISLATIVE POWER, 6
LEGISLATIVE PROCESS, 39 ff.
LEGISLATURE, 36 ff.
LEGITIMACY, 125
LEGITIMATE SELF - DEFENCE, 97, 180
LEGITIMATION, 126
LEGITIMIZING A CHILD, 125
LETTER OF CONFIRMATION, 198
LIFE - TIME MEMBERS OF THE SENATE, 37
LIGHT IMPRISONMENT, 182
LIMITATION OF FREEDOM, 97 ff.
LIMITED LIABILITY, 110
LIMITED LIABILITY COMPANY, 100
LIMITED PARTNERSHIP, 108, 110
LIMITED PARTNERSHIP IN WHICH THE CAPITAL IS DIVIDED INTO SHARES, 108
LIQUIDATOR, 144
LOCAL ADMINISTRATION, 61, 66
LOCAL USAGE, 5 n. 5
LOST PROPERTY, 151, 156
LUNATICS, 127
MAINTENANCE, 124
MAJORITY, 90
MARITAL DUTIES, 119
MARRIAGE, 117
    Age, 118
    Capacity, 117
    Celebration of, 118
    Officer, 87

MARTIAL LAW, 73
MATERIAL DAMAGE, 96, 116, 170
MATRIMONIAL PROPERTY
   SYSTEMS, 120
MAYOR, 64
MECELLE, 2
MENS REA, 177
MENTAL CAPACITY, 118
MENTAL DEFECTIVES, 127
MENTAL INFIRMITY, 122
MENTAL SICKNESS, 89, 123
MENTAL WEAKNESS, 89
MERCHANTS, 93, 108
   Legal person, 108
   Real person, 108
MERIT SYSTEM, 70
MILITARY CHIEF PUBLIC
   PROSECUTOR, 19
MILITARY COURTS, 214
MILITARY COURT OF CASSATION,
   19
MILITARY ADMINISTRATIVE
   COURT 18, 81
MINES, 148
MINING LAW, 148, 153
MINISTERS, 44, 60
MINISTRIES, 60
MINORITY, 89, 128, 178
MINORITY SHARE - HOLDERS, 112
MISDEMEANORS, 176, 181
MISTAKE, 162
   Effect of, 163
   Immaterial, 162
   Of fact, 179
   Of law, 179
   Material, 163
MITIGATION, 183
MORAL DAMAGE, 97, 170
MORAL COMPENSATION, 118
MORTGAGE, 147, 152, 158
MORTGAGED PROPERTY
   Delivery of, 158
MORTGAGEE, 147, 158
MORTGAGOR, 158
MOVABLE PROPERTY, 148
   Acquisition of 156
MUNICIPALITY, 62

NAME
   Family, 93
   First, 93
   Infringment of, 96
   Right to choose, 93
NATIONAL ASSEMBLY, 37 ff.
NATIONAL STATE, 30
NATIONAL UNITY COMMITTEE,
   27 ff.
NATIONALITY, 93
   Acquisition of, 94
   By birth, 93
NATIONALITY ACT. 94
NATURAL COURT, 212
NATURAL JUDGE, 36, 212
NATURALIZATION, 94
NEGLIGENCE, 170
NEGOTIABE INSTRUMENTS, 129
NEIGHBORHOOD RIGHTS, 149
NEW TRIAL IN FAVOR OF THE
   ACCUSED, 224
«NO CRIME AND PUNISHMENT
   WITHOUT LAW», 175
NON - RETROACTIVITY
   Of laws, 13, 36
NON - PROFIT SHARING
   PURPOSE, 103
NOTARY, 191
NOTICE TO THE DEFENDANT, 195
NOVATION, 168
NULLUM CRIMEN NULLA POENA
   SINE LEGE, 4, 175
OATH, 199, 205
OBLIGATION OF ASSISTANCE, 120
OBLIGATION OF COHABITATION,
   120, 124
OCCUPATION, 157
OFFER, 161
   Made to the public, 161
   Of reward, 161
OFFEREE, 161
OFFERER, 161
OFFICIAL GAZETTE, 7, 14, 14 n. 23,
   17 n. 29, 108 n. 17
OFFICIAL INVENTORY, 144
OFFICIAL LIQUIDATION, 143, 144

OPINIO JURIS, 3
OPINIO NECESSITATIS, 3
ORAL FORM, 222
ORDER OF PAYMENT, 206
ORDINANCES, 9, 49
ORDINARY ADMINISTRATION OF PROPERTY, 129
ORDINARY PARTNERSHIP, 102, 155
   Administration of, 102
   Liability of partners, 102
   Purpose of, 102
   Rights on the partnership property, 102
ORDINARY PROCEDURE, 192
ORGANIC THEORY, 101
ORIGINAL ACQUISITION, 156
OTTOMAN CONSTITUTION OF 1876, 9, 23
OWNERSHIP, 147, 148, 150
   Above the land, 153
   Absolute nature of, 149
   Acquisition of, 156
   Meaning of, 148
   Negative subject matter of, 149
   Positive subject matter of, 148
   Transfer of, 155
   Under the land, 153

PARDON, 185
PARENTEL AUTHORITY, 127
   Abuse of, 127
   Termination of, 127
PARENTELS, 131
PARENTS, 125
PARLIAMENT
   Internal regulations, 38
   Personal status of the members, 38
   Terms of members, 37
PARLIAMENTARY DEBATE, 6
PARLIAMENTARY INQUIRIES, 40
PARLIAMENTARY INVESTIGATION, 40
PARLIAMENTARY PRIVILEGES, 38
PARTICIPATION IN A CRIME, 180
PARTICULAR (SPECIFIC) LEGATEES 138
PARTITION OF ESTATE, See ESTATE

PARTNESHIP PROPERTY, 155
PARTNERSHIP WITH LIMITED LIABILITY, 109
PARTIES, 31
PASSAGE OF WIRES OR WATERPIPES, 149
PATERNITY SUIT, 126
PEACE COURTS, 188
PEACE COURTS OF CRIMINAL JURISDICTION, 211
PENAL DECREES BY PEACE COURTS, 225
PERFORMANCE, 171
PERSONAL ACTION, 215
PERSONAL LIABILITY, 179
PERSONAL PROPERTY, 148, 154
PERSONAL REVENGE, 173
PERSONAL RIGHTS, 147
PERSONAL SERVITUDE, 157
PERSONALITY
   Beginning of, 85
   End of, 85
   Protection of, 94
   Theories of, 100
   Protection of, against others, 95
PERSONS, 85
PETITION OF APPEAL, 205
PETITION OF THE CASE, 193
PETITION OF REPLY, 195
PETROLEUM LAW, 153
PHYSICAL CONTROL ON PROPERTY, 150
PLEDGE, 158
PLOT AGAINST LIFE, 122
POLICE STATE, 55
POLITICAL PARTIES, 103
POLYGAMY, 4, 118
POSSESSION, 150
   Acquisition of, 151
   Elements of, 150
   Transfer of, 150
   Restitution of, 150
POSITIVIST SCHOOL, 174
PRACTICING LAWYERS, 191
PRECEDENTS, 16

253

PRELIMINARY INVESTIGATION, 220
PREPARATORY INVESTIGATION, 219
PRESCRIPTION, 152, 156
PRESIDENT OF THE REPUBLIC, 42
    Election of, 42
    Functions, 42
    Veto power, 443
PRESUMPTIONS, 197
PRESUMPTION OF INNOCENCE, 218
PREVENTION, 172
PRICE CONTROL LEGISLATION, 162
PRIME MINISTER, 44, 58
    Selection of, 44
PRINCIPLE OF TERRITORIALITY, 176
PRIVATE LEGAL PERSONS, 102
PRIVATE POSSESSIONS OF THE STATE, 72
PROBATION, 182
PRODIGALS, 127
PRODIGALITY, 128
PROPERTY, 147, 148
    Compensation for injury to, 150
PROVINCES, 60
PROVINCIAL ADMINISTRATION, 60
PROVACTION, 183
PUBLIC ADMINISTRATION, 59 ff.
PUBLIC FUNCTIONARIES, 70
PUBLIC ENTERPRISE, 67
PUBLIC LEGAL PERSONS, 67, 101
PUBLIC PERSONNEL, 69
    Legal status of, 69
    Tort liability of, 70
PUBLIC POSSESSIONS, 72
PUBLIC PROSECUTION, 214
PUBLIC PROSECUTOR, 190, 214
PUBLIC WELFARE, 35, 149
PUNISHMENT, 181
    Application of, 183
    Suspension of, 184
    Theories of, 172
QUESTION, 40
QUORUM, 106
RATIFICATION OF A PRIOR TRANSACTION, 91
REAL EVIDENCE, 201

REAL PROPERTY, 148, 154, 168
REAL RIGHTS, 147
REAL SERVITUDE, 158
REALIST THEORY, 101
RECHTSFAEHIGKEIT, 87, 162
RECIDIVISM, 183
RECOGNITION, 126
RECOGNIZED CHILD, 126
REDRESS, 172
REDUCTION OF DISPOSITIONS, 141
REFORMATION, 194
REGISTERED SHARE CERTIFICATES, 111
    Transfer of, 111
REGISTRY OF MARRIAGE, 86
REGISTRY OF PERSONAL STATUS, 86
REGULATION, 8, 60
REGULATION OF LAND REGISTRY, 148, 152
REHABILITATION, 172
RELEASE, 168
RELEASE UPON DEPOSITING BAIL, 218
RELIGIOUS CUSTOM, 4
RE-OEPNING OF THE PROCEEDINGS, 203
REPEAL OF STATUTES, 14
REPRESENTATIVE CURATORSHIP, 129
RESERVED PORTION, 131, 139
RESTORATION OF RIGHTS, 185
RESTRICTED REAL RIGHTS, 147
RETRIBUTION, 173
RETROACTIVE EFFECT OF PENAL PROVISIONS, 175
RETROACTIVITY OF LAWS, 13
REVERSAL BY A WRITTEN ORDER OF THE MINISTRY OF JUSTICE, 224
REVISION, 203
RIGHTS *IN PERSONAM*, 147
RIGHTS *IN REM*, 129, 1447
RIGHT OF CORRECTION, 127
RIGHT OF PASSAGE, 149
RIGHT TO PETITION, 76
ROMAN LAW, 20, 52

RULE OF LAW, 34, 55
SANCTION, 3
SEARCHES, 219
SECULARISM, 32, 56
SEIZURE, 73, 219
SENATE OF THE REPUBLIC, 37 ff.
   Senators, 37
   Senators appointed by the President of the Republic, 37
   Lifetime senators, 37
SEPARATION OF PROPERTY, 121
SERVIENT ESTATE, 158
SERVITUDES, 147, 157
SHARE CERTIFICATES, 111
   Par-value of, 110
   Transfer of, 111
SHAREHOLDERS, 110, 111
SHIP, 148
SIMPLE WRITTEN FORM, 170
SIMPLIFIED PROCEDURE, 205
SOCIAL STATE, 33, 53
SOCIETIES, 88, 101, 103
   Acquisition of legal personality, 107
   Against law and morals, 103
   Agenda of the meeting, 106
   Annual dues, 105
   Board of controllers, 105
   Board of directors, 105, 107
   By-laws, 104, 105
   Capacity of, 104
   Control, 107
   Formation of, 104
   General assembly, 105, 106
   Meetings, 106
   Membership, 107, 108
   Organs, 105
   Purpose of, 103, 104
   Resolutions, 106, 107
SOURCES OF TURKISH LAW, 1
SPECIAL AUDITOR, 112
SPENDTHRIFTS, 127
STATE ECONOMIC ENTERPRISES, 68, 76
STATE MONOPOLY, 167
STATE OF LAW, 55
STATE PERSONNEL LAW, 71
STATEMENT OF CLAIM, 194

STATEMENT OF FACTS, 193
STATUTE, 7
STATUTE CONCERNING THE APPLICATION OF THE CIVIL CODE, 13, 15
STATUTE CONCERNING THE APPLICATION OF THE TURKISH COMMERCIAL CODE, 13
STATUTE OF LIMITATIONS, 165, 169
STATUTORY ADVISOR, 129
STATUTORY DECREE 8, 49
STATUTORY REPRESENTATIVES, 91
   Transactions without the consent of, 91
STATUTORY SHARE, 140
STATUTORY SUCCESSORS, 141
STOCK COMPANIES, 109
SUB-GOVERNOR, 62
SUBJECTS OF RIGHTS, 87
SUBPOENA, 199
SUB-PROVINCE, 61
SUCCESSION
   Universal succession, 141
   Intestate succession, 131
   Testate succession, 135
SUMMARY PROCEDURE, 205
   For flagrant offenses, 225
SUMMONS, 193, 217
SUPREME COURT, 188
SUPREME COUNCIL OF JUDGES, 46, 189
SURVIVING SPOUSE, 134
SUSPENSION OF PUNISHMENT, 184

TAX COURTS, 81
TESTATE SUCCESSION, 131, 135
TESTATOR, 136, 136 n. 10
TESTATRIX, 136 n. 10
TESTIMONY OF WITNESSES, 201, 219
THEORY OF COLLECTIVE PROPERTY, 100
THRIFTLESSNESS, 91
   Title, 55
TORTIOUS ACT, 169
TORTIOUS LIABILITY, 91, 170
TORTIOUS LIABILITY WITHOUT NEGLIGENCE, 171

TORTS, 169
TOWN QUARTERS, 65
TRADE NAME, 93
TRANSFER OF TITLE, 156, 157
TREASURE, 156
TREATIES, 7
TRIAL, 221
TRIAL OF ABSENTEES, 225
TUTELAGE, 58, 67, 75
ULTRA-VIRES, 112
UNBORN CHILD, 85
UNDERSECRETARY, 60
UNIVERSAL LEGATEES, 138, 142
UNIVERSAL SUCCESSION, 142, 143
UNJUST ENRICHMENT, 159, 171
UNLIMITED LIABILITY, 110
USUFRUCT, 132, 135, 157
USUFRUCTUARY, 157
VACANT SUCCESSION, 129
VALID AGREEMENT, 163
VENUE, 192, 213

VIEW, 201
VILLAGE ADMINISTRATION, 64
VILLAGE HEADMAN, 65
VILLAGE ELDERS, 65, 118
VOTE OF CONFIDENCE, 41, 44
VOTE OF NON-CONFIDENCE, 41
WARRANT, 215, 218
WILL, 135, 140, 141
    Capacity to make a, 136
    Holographic, 137
    Form of, 136
    Official, 136
    Authentic, 136
    Oral, 137
    Revocation of, 137
WITNESSES, 198
WORKER, 70
WRITTEN FORM, 167
WRITTEN INSTRUMENTS
ZONING LAWS, 149